COGNITIVE THERAPY OF
BORDERLINE PERSONALITY DISORDER

COGNITIVE THERAPY OF BORDERLINE PERSONALITY DISORDER

MARY ANNE LAYDEN
University of Pennsylvania School of Medicine
CORY F. NEWMAN
University of Pennsylvania School of Medicine
ARTHUR FREEMAN
Cooper Hospital University Medical Center, Camden, New Jersey
SUSAN BYERS MORSE
Vista Del Mar Hospital, Ventura, California

Foreword by Aaron T. Beck, M.D.

Allyn and Bacon
Boston   London   Toronto   Sydney   Tokyo   Singapore

Copyright © 1993 by Allyn and Bacon
A Division of Simon & Schuster, Inc.
160 Gould Street
Needham Heights, Massachusetts 02194

Library of Congress Cataloging-in-Publication Data

Cognitive therapy of borderline personality disorder / Mary Anne
   Layden ... [et al.] : Foreword by Aaron T. Beck.
       p.   cm.
   Includes bibliographical references and index.
   ISBN 0-205-14807-7
   1. Borderline personality disorder--Treatment. 2. Cognitive
therapy. 3. Borderline personality disorder--Treatment--Case
studies. 4. Cognitive therapy--Case studies. I. Layden, Mary
Anne.
RC569.5.B67C63 1993   93-16298
616.85'852'0651—dc20   CIP

Printed in the United States of America
10 9 8 7 6 5   97 96 95

To our patients

About the Authors

Mary Anne Layden is Senior Consultant at the Center for Cognitive Therapy at the University of Pennsylvania and Instructor in Psychology at Beaver College. In 1989 and 1990 she served as a specialist in psychology at several hospitals and at the Institute of Psychiatry in London, England, lecturing by invitation at a number of hospitals during her stay there. Dr. Layden has also presented workshops in this country and at the European Association of Behavior Therapy Congress in Oslo, Norway. She holds a Ph.D. in psychology from the University of Wisconsin.

Cory F. Newman is Clinical Director of the Center for Cognitive Therapy at the University of Pennsylvania. He is active in all facets of the Center's functions, specializing in "difficult" cases and serving as a clinical supervisor for postdoctoral psychologists, psychiatric residents, graduate practicum students, and visiting scholars. Dr. Newman also is Assistant Professor of Psychology in Psychiatry at the University of Pennsylvania School of Medicine. He has lectured at local, national, and international conference workshops and is the author of numerous papers, articles, and abstracts as well as co-author, with Aaron T. Beck and associates, of two other books on cognitive therapy. He earned his Ph.D. in clinical psychology from the State University of New York at Stony Brook.

Arthur Freeman is a member of the Department of Psychiatry at Cooper Hospital University Medical Center, and Professor of Clinical Psychiatry at the University of Medicine and Dentistry of New Jersey–Robert Wood Johnson Medical School at Camden. He is also Clinical Associate Professor of Psychology in Psychiatry and Senior Consultant at the Center for Cognitive Therapy at the University of Pennsylvania. He has published a number of books on cognitive therapy and has lectured internationally, presenting workshops in fifteen countries over the past ten years. Dr. Freeman has also served as Visiting Professor in the Department of Psychiatry of the University of Gothenburg in Sweden. He holds a doctorate from Columbia University.

Susan Byers Morse is the coordinator of the Cognitive Therapy Program at CPC Vista Del Mar Psychiatric Hospital, Ventura, California. For three years she was Assistant Clinical Director at the Center for Cognitive Therapy at the University of Pennsylvania, after completing a postdoctoral fellowship there. In addition to research and clinical work, Dr. Byers has presented seminars throughout the United States and Europe. She holds a Ph.D. in clinical psychology from the California School of Professional Psychology.

Contents

Foreword

Cognitive therapy has undergone significant developments since the publication in 1979 of *Cognitive Therapy of Depression*. From the early work of treating unipolar depression, the model has been advanced and applied to the treatment of nearly all of the commonly seen clinical syndromes, including generalized anxiety, phobias, panic disorder and agoraphobia, eating disorders, substance abuse disorders, bipolar disorder, and the full range of personality disorders. Furthermore, cognitive therapy has been successfully applied to children, adolescents, and geriatric populations and has been used to treat couples, families, groups, and inpatients as well.

When performed by highly skilled clinicians, cognitive therapy *appears* to be an almost effortless process. The dialogue between therapist and patient seems to flow naturally, as if directing itself, toward new ways of thinking and acting and toward improved patient affect. This apparent simplicity is deceptive. In reality, positive results require considerable sophistication in the application of the model. Novice cognitive therapists frequently remark that what may seem uncomplicated in observation is a challenge in practice. The advanced cognitive therapist synthesizes a number of high-level skills at once—offering help in a low-key way, yet also providing a strong presence; focusing on problems in the here and now, yet understanding these concerns in the context of the patient's complex personal history; accurately judging where the patient needs to go, but achieving this through guided discovery and the teaching of skills rather than through didactic persuasion; and maintaining a spirit of optimism and professionalism while remaining empathic with the patients's hopelessness about therapy and even hostility toward the therapist. These skills, though formidable, are the very qualities that are required of the cognitive therapist, especially in the treatment of personality disorders.

The previous volume by our group, *Cognitive Therapy of Personality Disorders*, sought to explicate the cognitive model and treatment of personality disorders. We described the cognitive profiles of the various diagnostic categories of personality disorders found in the *Diagnostic and Statistical Manual of Mental Disorders*, third edition, revised (DSM-III-R). One of the personality disorders, the borderline personality, has proved to be among the most challenging of all disorders to treat effectively. Although many authors have been successful in describing this phenomenon, few have provided convincing paradigms for treatment that are clear, structured, testable, and teachable. Although our earlier volume *does* provide the reader with a clear understanding of the treatment of the full range of personality disorders, we recognized that the borderline diagnosis requires much more space and attention than we were able to give it in that text. It has been clear that a comprehensive description of the cognitive therapy of borderline personality disorder needs a text unto itself.

Cognitive Therapy of Borderline Personality Disorder fulfills this need admirably. Each of the authors is a past or present senior staff therapist and supervisor at the Center for Cognitive Therapy. Each is a gifted clinician and educator, and their volume reflects this. I am very grateful for this new and exciting addition to the literature on cognitive therapy.

The authors provide the best of both worlds—an extensive, comprehensive review of all the important facets of cognitive treatment with this population, all within the confines of a manageable, easy-to-read practitioner's guidebook. This text enables the reader to comprehend the common beliefs that fuel the emotional fires in this troubled population, and presents helpful guidelines for conceptualizing individual differences among borderline patients as well.

The chapters on developmental issues and case formulation demonstrate the integrative nature of cognitive therapy and highlight the elegance of the thinking process behind the cognitive therapist's conceptualization of each patient's case. The chapters that make up the "Clinical Applications" section of the book are impressive in their breadth and depth. The authors cover the major components of cognitive treatment with the borderline patient—standard cognitive therapy skills, advanced schema-focused methods, use of the therapeutic relationship, crisis management, limit setting, adjunctive medication issues (which psychiatrists and non-psychiatric therapists alike will find extremely up to date and informative), and the management of problematic countertransference reactions—and they do so with clarity, conciseness, wit, and a tangible warmth and understanding for their patients.

I am especially intrigued by their conceptual division of the borderline population into three spectrum subtypes. Given that so many patients diagnosed with the borderline disorder are diagnosed with additional personality disorders as well, the presentation of these subtypes represents a potentially important conceptual advancement in understanding and treating the borderline population as a whole.

Finally, the five cases that the authors present serve as almost perfect illustrations of all that *Cognitive Therapy of Borderline Personality Disorder* strives to communicate. These cases are comprehensive, instructive, engrossing, and refreshingly realistic. It is clear that the authors are as caring and respectful of their patients as they are skilled in applying the sophisticated methods of advanced cognitive therapy.

In sum, this book makes an important new contribution to the literatures on cognitive therapy and borderline personality disorder. It effectively educates the reader in the important facets of cognitive therapy with the borderline population, provides highly stimulating and instructive case studies, and above all is a pleasure to read.

Aaron T. Beck

Preface

The origin of this book traces back to the late 1980s at the Center for Cognitive Therapy in Philadelphia. At this time, we were expanding our postdoctoral training curriculum to include seminars and advanced supervision in the treatment of "difficult, long-term cases." Our post-doctoral Fellows had explained that although they were very happy with the comprehensive instruction and clinical practice opportunities that they were receiving in the cognitive therapy of anxiety disorders and depression, they also wanted additional guidance in the management of personality disorders.

We, too, had noticed in our work as therapists and supervisors that the population of patients at the Center for Cognitive Therapy was becoming more diverse, including a greater proportion of personality-disordered patients in general and borderline personality–disordered patients in particular. Under the direction of Aaron T. Beck, the Center had built a reputation as one of the finest teaching, research, and outpatient therapy facilities. As a result, an increasing number of patients who had been deemed treatment failures in other settings were being referred to us. Clearly, our standard methods and short-term model of cognitive therapy needed some adjustment in order to meet the special needs of the personality disorder cases.

At this same time, Aaron T. Beck, Arthur Freeman, and a host of distinguished cognitive therapy associates were busy at work on the volume that was to become the Beck, Freeman, & Associates (1990) *Cognitive Therapy of Personality Disorders*. As this book began to take shape, its proposed contents were discussed at our regular weekly seminars. Our Fellows were pleased to receive this additional, state-of-the-art training, but once again they suggested that more emphasis be placed on the borderline population in particular. It was decided that the regular seminars on cognitive therapy of personality disorders would continue but that an additional meeting would be held each week in order to delve more deeply into the conceptualization and treatment of borderline personality disorder. Later, this meeting came to be known as "schema seminar," in reference to the therapeutic focus on "schemas," the core beliefs that are so important to address in the treatment of this population.

During "schema seminar," the authors of this volume engaged our Fellows (and other interested clinical associates) in discussions of the literature, theory, new techniques, innovations in case formulation, and group supervision of actual ongoing borderline personality disorder cases at the Center. These meetings provided the impetus for the formulation, testing, and refinement of principles that would become the basis for *Cognitive Therapy of the Borderline Personality Disorder.*

The testing grounds for our clinical findings were in professional workshops as well as actual therapy sessions. With regard to the former, the four of us have presented numerous lectures and training workshops on the local, national, and international levels on the topic of cognitive therapy for borderline personality disorder. Our audiences have tended to comprise (1) clinicians who enthusiastically embraced the cognitive model and expressed excitement at the prospect of applying a structured and well-defined treatment to a most vexing population, and (2) therapists who skeptically claimed that "one cannot do cognitive therapy" with borderline patients. We would agree that one cannot treat a borderline patient as if he or she were someone suffering from an acute unipolar depression. However, cognitive therapy is not a dogmatic, nomothetic approach. Its spirit of empiricism and its flexibility to meet the specific needs of each individual patient make it eminently suitable to application with a wide range of disorders, including those diagnostic categories that were once thought to be the sole province of traditional psychotherapies.

In our own clinical work, we have maintained the basic core of cognitive therapy as presented by Beck, Rush, Shaw, and Emery (1979), while adding the innovations of conceptualization and treatment that will appear in the succeeding chapters of this volume. The results have been very encouraging indeed. Although we cannot make the claim that we have "cured" all of our borderline patients, we have witnessed greater progress in more patients than either clinical lore or the standard psychotherapy literature would lead us to believe could be expected with the borderline patient. As a result of this preliminary level of success, we have collectively increased the number of borderline patients in our caseloads and have begun to specialize in the supervision of such cases as well. We hope that this book will stimulate others to apply cognitive therapy to the borderline population with similar positive results, providing for therapists an increased sense of direction, hopefulness, and sympathy in working with patients who all too often have been looked upon with pessimism and dread.

Although they are too numerous to mention one by one, we would like to thank all the clinical Fellows at the Center for Cognitive Therapy who have helped to stimulate our thinking on this subject, and whose enthusiasm helped propel us to take on this important task. We would like to thank the following valued colleagues who reviewed and commented on preliminary drafts of this book, much to its benefit: Cathy Crandell, Judy Saltzberg, Sharon Silverman, and Hal Urschel. Thanks are also due to Tina Inforzato for her invaluable help in the painstaking task of typing a number of sections of this book. Finally, our acknowledgments would scarely be complete without paying homage to Aaron T. Beck, whose pioneering work has made this book possible, and from whom we have been so fortunate to learn.

COGNITIVE THERAPY OF
BORDERLINE PERSONALITY DISORDER

PART ONE

Description and Theoretical Aspects

Chapter 1

Cognitive Therapy of Borderline Personality Disorder: Introduction

Cognitive therapy, a widely used, efficacious treatment for unipolar depression (e.g., Beck, Rush, Shaw, & Emery, 1979) and anxiety disorders (e.g., Beck, Emery, & Greenberg, 1985), also has been applied successfully to the treatment of personality disorders (Beck, Freeman, & Associates, 1990; Young, 1990). The Beck et al. (1990) and Young (1990) volumes review the cognitive approaches to the treatment of the entire range of personality disorders. Of these disorders, the syndrome known as the borderline personality disorder (BPD) may be the most complex and therefore warrants special attention in its own right. This book reflects the developments that cognitive therapy has undergone in the past decade, both conceptually and technically, in order to deal effectively with patients who present with BPD.

In one sense, the cognitive therapy of BPD progresses in a manner similar to the cognitive therapy of depression and anxiety disorders. The therapist helps patients to identify their biased thinking patterns and to test and modify the meanings of those thoughts and perceptions. The chief goal is to enable patients to evaluate themselves and their problems more objectively, as well as to gain the confidence and know-how to address their life problems constructively and hopefully.

With BPD patients, however, the path toward achieving these goals often can seem a dark and circuitous one indeed. In addition to the requisite of accurately understanding the patients' complex array of problems, therapists must also demonstrate ingenuity in developing techniques that address or circumvent the patients' reluctance to change, as well as great perseverance and ego-strength in weathering the crises that inevitably occur during treatment. Because of the chronic nature of the BPD patients' problems, their frequent referral through family pressure or judicial remand, and their apparent reluctance to change, they often are the most difficult and trying patients in a clinician's caseload. Typically, they require more work within a session, cause greater drain on the therapist's energy, demand more time outside of the session because of emergencies, and evoke more powerful countertransference reactions than do any other patients. Even so, we have found that cognitive therapy offers the kind of structure, support, and learning experiences that are extremely helpful to this population. Similarly, cognitive therapy assists the therapists themselves by providing a framework that makes their work with BPD patients manageable and promising, and as a model for self-help when professional stress levels are high.

IDENTIFYING THE BORDERLINE PATIENT

The borderline patient usually seeks therapy with an agenda that consists of issues *other* than personality problems. These typically include a variety of acute psychological disorders that are described on Axis I of the *Diagnostic and Statistical Manual of Mental Disorders,* 3rd edition (revised) (DSM-III-R; American Psychiatric Association [APA], 1987), such as depression, generalized anxiety, panic, eating disorders, bipolar affective disorder, and others. Consistent with some of these Axis I disorders, BPD patients may present with suicidal ideation or intentions. In addition, BPD patients frequently enter treatment with vague complaints of emotional malaise that are difficult to operationalize (e.g., "I feel detached from the world and empty inside"). The upshot is that most BPD patients initially do not conceptualize their psychological difficulties as being tied to stable, maladaptive personality characteristics (which make up the Axis II diagnoses of the DSM-III-R).

For most BPD patients, there is a feedback loop between the Axis I and the Axis II problems. For example, a patient whose Axis I major depression is based largely on chronic loneliness may have alienated others with unreasonable demands for almost symbiotic nurturance, a characteristic of Axis II disorders such as BPD and dependent personality disorder (DPD). The resultant loneliness and depression may prime such a patient to scare away new potential significant others with a desperate escalation of interpersonal neediness. This result, in turn, feeds back into the patient's loneliness and Axis I depression, and the vicious cycle continues.

Nevertheless, the BPD patients often view the difficulties they encounter in dealing with other people and/or with tasks as being independent of their own behavior. They are characteristically mystified about how they came to be the way they are, how they contribute in any way to their problems, how they affect the lives of other people, and how to change. Some see themselves as victims of an unfair system, of cruel others, or simply of bad luck. Other BPD patients are more aware of the self-defeating nature of their personality problems (e.g., impulsivity, self-mutilation, overdependency, excessive avoidance) but are at a loss as to how to change. Still others seem to cycle between an internal and external attribution style, on the one hand blaming themselves for being "bad" and on the other hand railing against all who are "causing" their misery.

In most cases the borderline pathology may be so obvious that it can be diagnosed rather early in treatment (Casey, Tryer, & Platt, 1985). In some instances, however, the clinician may begin to work on the Axis I referral problems, unaware of the chronicity, pervasiveness, and severity of the patient's personality problems until weeks into the therapy when a crisis occurs (Koenigsberg, Kaplan, Gilmore, & Cooper, 1985). For example, a patient named "Joan" entered therapy ostensibly to deal with marital dissatisfaction. During the first three sessions, she seemed to be a thoughtful, composed, and self-asssured patient. In session 4, she noted how her husband's similarity to her father annoyed her, and she wondered if this phenomenon was causing her to judge her husband in an unduly harsh fashion. The therapist suggested the homework assignment of evaluating the similarities and differences between her husband and father so that she could gain a more objective perspective on the matter. Later that night, she telephoned the therapist in a drunken, suicidal state. The assignment had induced her to think in depth about her father, which triggered memories of his sexually abusing her during her childhood. These memories sparked rage, self-hatred, and suicidal feelings, whereupon she drank a six-pack of beer and called the therapist to cry for help. After weathering the acute crisis, Joan admitted that she had been having numerous impulsive extramarital affairs and that she both mistrusted and loved men to extremes. It had not occurred to her before this time that her painful memories and feelings (and her destructive behaviors) might be placing her at risk not only for divorce but for a wide range of significant life problems. Joan met criteria for BPD.

A common identifying element in most BPD patients is a marked fear of change and a related tendency to live limited and restricted lives. This is typified by patients who believe it is impossible to extricate themselves from unsatisfactory work situations, destructive relationships, or other deleterious life conditions. They underestimate their capacities for taking active steps to improve the quality of their lives, and similarly underestimate the harmful effects of their locking into rigid, predictable patterns of thinking, feeling, and acting. BPD patients who staunchly maintain familiar (though maladaptive) patterns may feel safe, but they pay a heavy price in reduced opportunities and diminished potential in life. When they leave their safety zone, they face the unknown and become vulnerable, thus evoking a high level of anxiety, which BPD patients characteristically find intolerable and try to avoid at all costs. An example of this self-defeating pattern is found in the patient who wants to be loved but who fears rejection so badly that he provokes a breakup with the woman he is dating rather than risk waiting for her to abandon him. His automatic assumption that he will be left alone causes him to avoid taking the potentially worthy gamble of working to nurture the relationship.

Therapy with BPD patients increases their anxiety because they are asked to change, therefore to become more vulnerable. We argue that such anxiety is a necessary part of treatment, although we would add that the therapist must be prepared to help the BPD patient to cope with the consequences and to understand the long-range benefits. As Beck et al. (1985) similarly note in their treatment of agoraphobia,

> It is crucial that the patient experience anxiety in order to ensure that the primitive cognitive levels have been activated (since these levels are directly connected to the affects). The repeated, direct, on-the-spot recognition that the danger signals do not lead to catastrophe . . . enhance(s) the responsivity of the primitive level to more realistic inputs from above. (p. 129)

As therapists help patients to step outside their safety zones, they must also teach them the skills to manage anxiety, lest the patients immediately revert to old maladaptive patterns (see Beck et al., 1985, for a comprehensive review of antianxiety techniques).

The borderline disorder can be diagnosed clinically using both formal and heuristic markers. Formally, DSM-III-R defines BPD as "A pervasive pattern of instability of mood, interpersonal relationships, and self-image, beginning by early adulthood and present in a variety of contexts, as indicated by at least five of the following"

1. A pattern of unstable and intense interpersonal relationships characterized by alternating between extremes of overidealization and devaluation
2. Impulsiveness in at least two areas that are potentially self-damaging, such as spending, sex, substance abuse, shoplifting, reckless driving, or binge eating (do not include suicidal or self-mutilating behavior covered in criterion 5)
3. Affective instability: marked shifts from baseline mood to depression, irritability, or anxiety, usually lasting a few hours and only rarely more than a few days
4. Inappropriate, intense anger or lack of control of anger—for example, frequent displays of temper, constant anger, recurrent physical fights
5. Recurrent suicidal threats, gestures, or behaviors, or self-mutilating behavior
6. Marked by consistent identity disturbance manifested by uncertainty about at least two of the following: self-image, sexual orientation, long-term goals or career choice, type of friends desired, preferred values
7. Chronic feelings of emptiness or boredom
8. Frantic efforts to avoid real or imagined abandonment (do not include suicidal or self-mutilating behavior covered in criterion 5)[a]

In addition to the DSM-III-R criteria, there are a number of heuristic signs that may point to the possibility of BPD. While no single indicator is the sine qua non of BPD, the presence of any one of them can serve as a red flag indicating the need for further exploration (Beck et al., 1990; Freeman & Leaf, 1989). These include the following :

---

[a]Reprinted with permission from the *Diagnostic and Statistical Manual of Mental Disorders,* third edition (revised), copyright © 1987 by the American Psychiatric Association, Washington, DC, p. 347.

1. The patient states, "I've *always* been this way. This is who I am."
2. The patient demonstrates ongoing noncompliance with the therapeutic regimen (especially indicative of BPD when the patient is uncooperative in a hostile manner).
3. Therapeutic progress seems to come to a sudden halt for no apparent reason.
4. The patients seem entirely unaware of the negative effects of their behavior on others.
5. The patients' personality problems appear to be acceptable and natural for them. Motivation for change is low.
6. The therapist has very powerful, potentially antitherapeutic reactions to the patient. This feeds into the BPD patient's propensity for mistrusting the therapist.
7. The patient misses many therapy sessions, arrives late for many sessions, and sometimes leaves abruptly during sessions.
8. The patient exhibits an extreme all-or-none thinking style.
9. The patients have difficulty moderating or modulating their emotional reactions, especially outbursts of anger.
10. The patient frequently does things that cause some sort of self-harm.

Many of these symptoms may be indicative of personality disorders other than BPD. Taken together with the DSM-III-R criteria, however, these heuristic signs are very useful in identifying the BPD patient. One of the most obvious differences between the borderline category and other personality disorders is the large intradiagnostic variability of BPD patients (Beck et al., 1990). The borderline group does not have the easily identified, well-defined cognitive map or style that other Axis II disorders evince. Frequently, we have seen BPD patients meet diagnostic criteria for a host of other personality disorders as well; therefore, their range of symptoms is quite broad. Kernberg (1975, 1984) and Meissner (1988) have suggested that BPD is more of a spectrum disorder than a single discrete entity.

Along these lines, we suggest that the borderline diagnosis consists of at least three separate but related subtypes, distinguishable from each other by symptom constellation. In each of the subtypes that we describe later in this book, the individual patient meets the DSM-III-R criteria for BPD but would, in addition, be identified by a particular borderline spectrum type. These three subtypes are:

1. Borderline–avoidant/dependent
2. Borderline–histrionic/narcissistic
3. Borderline–antisocial/paranoid

Each of these three types of BPD has its own more clearly circumscribed clinical picture. For example, patients representing all three subtypes may be hypersensitive to interpersonal abandonment. However, the BPD–avoidant/dependent patient may demonstrate this symptom by fearfully clinging to a domineering significant other (achieving "safety" through subjugating the self to another), whereas the BPD–histrionic/narcissistic patient may become involved in numerous impulsive sexual relationships (achieving "safety" in numbers). By further contrast, the BPD–antisocial/paranoid patient may physically assault a loved one who is erroneously perceived to have been unfaithful (achieving "safety" by punishing the transgressor).

We have found these hypothetical subdivisions of BPD extremely beneficial in understanding such patients more clearly and precisely. In turn, these classifications also help us to provide interventions that are tailor-made for the patient. Our case chapters will address these issues in greater detail.

THE PHENOMENA OF SCHEMAS IN BPD

Definition of *Schema*

Standard cognitive therapy for acute Axis I disorders such as unipolar depression focuses a great deal of attention on two levels of patients' thinking; (1) automatic thoughts and (2) assumptions or beliefs (the terms *assumptions* and *beliefs* frequently are used synonymously). The automatic thoughts pertain to the running internal commentary in which patients engage in specific situations. An example is a person who unwittingly adds to his own anxiety and dysphoria as he works on a project by saying to himself: "I'll *never* get this done on time. What am I going to do? I'm going to lose my job if this keeps up!"

A deeper level of cognition is that which consists of assumptions or beliefs, which represent tacit rules that are hypothesized to give rise to automatic thoughts. The patients do not necessarily spell out the content of these beliefs in their minds, but their automatic thoughts, actions, and behaviors imply that such a deeper meaning exists. For example, the patient mentioned before exhibits patterns of automatic thoughts such as these:

- I have to get this work finished or I'll be in big trouble!
- If I forget to pick up my wife's coat from the cleaners today she'll kill me.
- I have to get this promotion. I simply must!
- (Upon having trouble assembling his son's bicycle) What the hell is wrong with me?!
- (Patient insults himself out loud after grounding out in a softball game.)

These automatic thoughts and behaviors suggest that some deeper beliefs exist that organize the way this man perceives himself. We may infer that these beliefs include:

- I need to succeed at whatever I do in order to like myself.
- If I fail, others will punish me.
- I am a good person only to the extent that I am competent.
- Being angry at myself helps to motivate me to succeed.

As we see here, these beliefs are not articulated in the patient's internal dialogue, but they seem to be the basis for many of his moment-to-moment reactions. Note that a preponderance of the beliefs are conditional if–then statements. The patient will maintain a critical view of himself unless certain conditions are met, such as succeeding at a task and thereby maintaining the approval of others.

These two levels of cognition, automatic thoughts and beliefs, are major targets of change in standard cognitive therapy. There is, however, a third, deeper, more fundamental level of cognition that is termed the *schema*. Schemas have been defined in a number of different ways by various authors. On one hand, the term *schema* has been used to refer to a hypothesized *structure* of cognition, such as a mental filter or template that guides the processing of information (e.g., Landau & Goldfried, 1981). A second definition of schemas holds that they are latent, core beliefs (Young, 1990). Here, schemas are identified by their content—for example, "I am a bad person" schema or a "Nobody can be trusted" schema.

In practice, we tend to use both definitions alternatively, depending on the phenomena we are describing. For example, when explaining that a person failed to perceive a compliment, we might say, "He couldn't hear that comment or incorporate it into his self-image because he doesn't seem to have the schema in which to fit such positive information." With such a patient, we endeavor to help him metaphorically to build a new schema, a mental cubbyhole for compliments that he didn't have before, so he can process, store, and retrieve positive information about himself and thereby improve his self-esteem. Here, we are using the term *schema* as if it referred to a structure of the mind.

More regularly, however, we use the construct of *schema* in reference to the *content of fundamental, core beliefs*: the basic rules that an individual uses to organize his or her perceptions of the world, self, and future, and to adapt to life's challenges. They are considered to be core cognitive material for the following reasons:

1. They are absolute, not conditional.
2. They give rise to other, higher level beliefs.
3. They are difficult to assess and to access in treatment.

With regard to the first point, schemas do not make if–then propositions. Although one person might have a belief that states, "I am not a good person unless I succeed," another, more disturbed person is more likely to have the unconditional, absolutist belief that "I am not a good person, period." This latter core belief is a schema.

Regarding point 2, schemas like the one given here give rise to other beliefs and thereby greatly influence a person's views of the world, self, and future. A person who has the schema "I am bad," will likely also have higher level (i.e., more situationally specific and more accessible to awareness) beliefs such as "No woman will ever want to marry me," or "I'll never get what I want in life because I'll just mess it up anyway."

Third, schemas are so fundamental to patients' perceptions that they rarely notice the influence of schemas on their lives. Whereas the therapist might show some natural curiosity as to how a patient functions and how she got to be the way she is, the patient who holds negative schemas initially may not be capable of such introspection. To her way of seeing things, everything about her and about life is simply bad, and that's that. For such a patient, a therapist's probing questions may seem completely off the mark. For example, after a therapy session (which the therapist thought was very productive) one of our patients indicated on the "Post Session Feedback Form" (which all patients at the Center for Cognitive Therapy fill out following sessions) that the therapist "totally missed the point." The next week, the therapist inquired about this surprisingly negative feedback and asked the patient what the point was that he had missed. The patient replied: "You were questioning the way I view myself. You were asking me questions about positive things about myself and about why other people think well of me. It was a complete waste of time! I told you I was an evil person, and you totally ignored me!" This patient met criteria for BPD.

It is at the level of schemas that the most meaningful work is done with BPD patients in cognitive therapy (Beck et al., 1990; Young, 1990). The BPD patient's schemas typically are extremely negative and have wide-reaching, pernicious effects on their lives. They influence the BPD patient's interpretations of incoming information so that it conforms to their negative status quo. It has also been proposed that the BPD schemas lead such patients to act on their environment in such a way as to confirm their veracity (Freeman & Leaf, 1989), a phenomenon commonly referred to as the self-fulfilling prophecy.

Characteristics of Schemas

There has been some disagreement over whether or not schemas necessarily are negative entities. It can be argued that all people hold core beliefs, some positive and some negative. For example, a person may have the schemas "I am competent" and "I am unlovable." This person may be successful and effective in the vocational realm but may struggle in relationships. Freeman (1987) has stated that schemas are neither positive nor negative but are to be interpreted in terms of their goodness of fit with life experience. To illustrate, a young child may have a dependency schema that is reflected by the hypothetical belief "I need others to take care of me and meet my basic needs." When a toddler accordingly acts in a way that demands attention and help, it is often thought of as cute. But when the same dependency schema is manifested at age 35, it is not cute, but dysfunctional.

Another example is reflected by two adults who exhibit unlovability schemas. One satisfies her potentially excessive needs for love and affection by becoming a nursery school teacher. The attention, admiration, and hugs and kisses that she receives regularly from the children fit well with her schema-based needs, and she feels that her job is rewarding. By contrast, the other person does not find an adaptive outlet to respond to his unlovability schema. Instead, he becomes extremely possessive and jealous in dating relationships, demanding that his partners show attention only to him. This leads to numerous conflicts and interpersonal losses, and the maladaptive aspects of the schema strengthen.

Another, more circumscribed usage of the concept of schemas has been put forth by Young (1990), who has outlined a series of early maladaptive schemas that predispose the personality-disordered individual to experience pervasive negative feelings and to behave in self-defeating ways. Many of these early maladaptive schemas are strikingly apparent in the BPD patient, such as schemas of unlovability, incompetence, lack of individuation, mistrust, emotional deprivation, abandonment, and dependence. Although we bear in mind that a broad interpretation of the phenomena of schemas allows for them to be positive core beliefs in people's lives, our use of the term *schema* in this book on BPD will reflect the specific area of early maladaptive schemas (Young, 1990).

Schemas can be either *dormant* or *active*. Schemas are dormant when patients are not confronted with life situations that tap into their individual areas of vulnerability. For example, a patient with an unlovability schema may be very content when she is at work. Her sense of industry and accomplishment encourages her to work to excess, and her colleagues see her as a very successful Type A personality. Because this patient's work life does not represent an area of vulnerability for her, her schema is dormant. If, however, she receives a surprise phone call from her estranged older sister, this same patient may become highly agitated because the contact with her sister activates the unlovability schema. Suddenly, years of early-life memories when the patient felt neglected, criticized, and shunned by her family of origin combine to arouse intense negative affect in this patient, perhaps inappropriate to the situation at hand.

In treating BPD patients, we have seen patients work very hard to keep their schemas dormant. Patients who have incompetency schemas underachieve because they are afraid to take on challenges. Similarly, patients who fear loss of individuation through intimacy avoid trying to establish romantic relationships. These avoidance strategies succeed in the short run by keeping these patients from experiencing their vulnerability. In the end, however, these strategies fail because the avoidance causes the patients to miss out on worthwhile opportunities for a higher quality of life. A BPD patient who is skilled at keeping his schemas dormant may not always appear to be a very distressed individual, but he is likely not very satisfied with his life either.

It follows, then, that the cognitive therapist must help BPD patients to learn the requisite skills to deal with the intense negative emotionality that emerges when schemas become activated. This is true primarily because it is therapeutic for patients to confront and deal with their most painful areas of vulnerability. We as therapists need to help them to cease avoiding their schemas at the expense of personal growth.

Secondarily, it is necessary to help patients to deal with their schemas because nobody (to our knowledge) has ever been able to go through an entire lifetime without having a schema become active through some sort of crisis. We witness these "accidental activations" of schemas when patients who seem to be doing well in treatment unexpectedly arrive at the therapist's office in a suicidal state. Less dangerously, but just as dramatically, we have witnessed the sudden activation of a patient's schemas in sessions when a seemingly innocent question or comment from the therapist stimulates an apparent overreaction on the part of the patient. As a case in point, Joan flew into a rage because her therapist showed some concern that she was keeping knives scattered about her house. Whereas the therapist simply was worried about possible accidents or the patient's potential for impulsive self-harm, Joan believed that the therapist was implying that she (the patient) shouldn't protect herself from victimization (Joan kept the knives in order to stab rapists who might break into her house). Joan's mistrust schema had been activated in grand style. In sum, schema activation is an important part of advanced cognitive therapy for BPD, although therapists must learn to handle such situations with sensitivity, confidence, and care.

Some schemas are more *compelling* than others. Those that are less compelling are somewhat more accessible and receptive to modification than those that are more compelling. This concept is similar to Kelly's (1955) observation that people's personal constructs may be "fixed" (i.e., rigid and resistant to change) or "permeable" (i.e., flexible and open to change). In general, none of the schemas of borderline patients are challenged or surrendered easily. Those that are most compelling of all, however, seem to be maintained at all costs by the patients. These schemas are as comparably ingrained as the beliefs of religious or political martyrs who would choose to be imprisoned or die rather than surrender their views. Fortunately, most BPD patients, unlike such martyrs, do not derive great satisfaction from their "missions" or "causes." On the contrary, their utter dissatisfaction with the state of their lives serves as an important motivator to enter therapy.

Many BPD patients exhibit a variety of early maladaptive schemas, but some of these may carry much more emotional weight than others. For example, BPD patients in the avoidant/dependent spectrum have compelling schemas of incompetence, dependence, and lack of individuation. Their schemas of unlovability and mistrust, while influential and important, tend to be less compelling. By contrast, BPD patients in the histrionic/narcissistic spectrum more often demonstrate compelling schemas of unlovability and abandonment. Schemas of lack of individuation, dependence, incompetence, and mistrust are somewhat less compelling. Finally, BPD patients in the antisocial/paranoid spectrum maintain extremely compelling mistrust schemas. Unlovability and abandonment schemas are quite important, but the patients work very hard to show that they are immune to these (they want to show how little they need others to care about them, but they "protest too much").

Another dimension of schemas pertains to how *pervasive* or *discrete* they are in the patient's life. The more pervasive a schema is in a patient's life, the wider the variety of situations that will tend to activate it. In general, patients who demonstrate a preponderance of pervasive, compelling schemas will be more severely troubled than those whose schemas are discrete and less compelling. The former group will be more difficult to treat and will experience more crises in therapy as well.

An example of a discrete schema is seen in a patient who functions fairly well at work and in friendships but who becomes depressed, agitated, and angry when he has any significant contact with his elderly parents. Here, his unlovability, lack of individuation, and dependence schemas are activated *within a circumscribed context*— in this case, by parents who continue to overcontrol and overcriticize him. A depressive episode becomes triggered when this patient spends Christmas with his family.

A more pervasive (and therefore more deleterious) schema is reflected by the patient who functions poorly across the board—at work, with friends, and with her family of origin. In this patient's case, her incompetency schema is so pervasive that she feels like a failure whether she is performing on a job, or mentally comparing herself to her successful friends, or dealing with her parents' thinly veiled comments of disapproval. This patient feels badly about her capabilities in almost all aspects of life and therefore has chronic low self-esteem, recurring depressive episodes, suicidal ideation, and a habit of avoiding opportunities to do something challenging in life.

Modifying Schemas

An important goal of therapy is to teach patients to identify their own schemas and schema-driven reactions to life's stressors, and to cooperate in efforts to change these negative schemas.

Therapists have several options in working with schemas. An ambitious option is to restructure the schema entirely. *Schematic restructuring* may be likened to urban renewal. Once a structure is determined to be unsound, the decision is made to tear down the old structure and build a new one in its place. Historically, this has been an explicit goal of psychoanalysis. We believe that it may be unreasonable to expect to achieve such dramatic change in most cases. An example of schematic restructuring would be to treat a BPD patient who has a very compelling, pervasive mistrust schema by attempting to transform her into a person who trusts all other people freely and easily. Achieving such a goal actually may be undesirable in that it substitutes one extreme for another, neither of which may serve the patient well.

A second option is *schematic modification*. This involves making more circumscribed changes in the patient's manner of responding to the world. An example would be to help a patient with a compelling mistrust schema to learn first to trust the therapist, and later to trust certain individuals who prove their mettle by meeting reasonable behavioral criteria for trustworthiness. In this manner, the patient may be able to establish a close friendship or romantic relationship that greatly enhances the quality of life, while still maintaining a background of characteristic cynicism that influences most casual interpersonal interactions. In clinical practice, when therapists describe their attempts to "restructure" patients' maladaptive schemas, they typically are referring instead to schema modification.

A third possibility for change is *schematic reinterpretation*. Here, therapists help patients to find alternative ways to view their schemas and their resultant life-styles. This typically involves working with patients to change their life situations so as to minimize the harmful effects of the schema, to make changes that will better satisfy the patient's excessive needs, and to reinterpret the schema itself so that it becomes less absolute. For example, a patient who suffers from an incompetency schema may be assisted in finding appropriate employment that will not force the patient to confront daily situations that will activate the schema. Or, as mentioned previously, a patient who has an unlovability schema may choose to teach preschool children, who give a great deal of innocent affection to their benevolent teacher, thus satisfying some of her needs for love on a regular basis. These changes will become beneficial to the patient if she is able to reframe the absolute belief that "I'm unlovable" to a more conditional belief, such as "I need a lot of love from many people in order to feel that I am lovable."

GENERAL RULES IN STARTING TREATMENT WITH THE BPD PATIENT

Treating the Axis I Problems

As previously noted, many BPD patients enter therapy in order to deal with their acute Axis I disorders. Although they may be relatively unaware of their self-defeating schemas and dysfunctional patterns in relationships, they may be very cognizant of an exacerbation in their anxiety and dysphoria. Therefore, it is often a good idea for therapists initially to help BPD patients to obtain some relief from their presenting symptoms. In helping the patients to begin to deal with their anxiety or depression, the therapists can teach them the basic cognitive therapy skills that are going to serve as the foundation for their work on the more difficult personality issues.

We have found that some BPD patients appreciate learning a few tangible skills right from the start, especially when they are able to identify a discrete problem or goal. For example, a BPD patient who had a myriad of complex problems in all facets of her life entered therapy with a primary goal of learning to deal better with her mother's criticisms. Although the therapist realized that this problem represented but a fraction of the patient's problems, she nevertheless spent the first few sessions teaching the patient the principles of assertiveness and rational responding (see Chapter 4). The patient was pleased to learn some techniques that she could use with her mother, and she admitted that she began to think that "maybe therapy has some usefulness after all." This small increment of change and relief served as a hook to gain the patient's involvement in a more complete course of treatment. Later, it became clear that this patient had a very compelling and pervasive mistrust schema that extended to dealing with therapists. When the therapist respected the patient's initial agenda for therapy and helped her to learn some practical skills, the patient began to trust the therapist, setting the stage for more intensive and extensive work. A little bit of therapeutic success at the start can foster a great deal of success down the road.

Educating Patients about Schemas

Some BPD patients decide to leave therapy after they have acquired a few technical skills and/or have noticed an improvement in mood. Such patients may be attracted to a short-term model of cognitive therapy, with its focus on acute symptoms and solving problems. They may have no initial intention to make broad, sweeping changes in their lives. Similarly, they may have no conception that their acute problems are fueled by more chronic issues. Here it is important for therapists to educate their BPD patients about the phenomena of schemas—that they are dysfunctional rules about living that some people grow up to believe implicitly, wreaking havoc on their well-being and on their ability to adapt to the changing demands of the world. These schemas negatively and chronically influence a person's self-esteem, coping skills, and interpersonal relationships. Furthermore, they are frightening to address and difficult to change without a serious commitment to therapy. The therapists then offer some examples of schemas, such as abandonment, unlovability, and incompetence, and discuss aspects of the patients' lives that exemplify these phenomena. When therapists explain the importance of working at the schema level, BPD patients who might otherwise have terminated prematurely sometimes choose to stay in treatment.

In many cases, it is appropriate (and perhaps necessary) to educate BPD patients about schemas very early in treatment. The following clinical situations offer therapists opportunities to do so:

1. The patient enters therapy stating, "I've seen therapists for years and years and nothing has ever helped."
2. The patient says, "I can't just change my thinking and make my problems go away. I can't be brainwashed into thinking positive thoughts."
3. The therapist attempts to teach the patient a self-help skill such as self-monitoring, scheduling activities, or rational responding, but the patient responds with extreme negative affect.
4. The patient acts in a hostile, disparaging manner toward the therapist, seemingly without provocation.
5. The patient refuses to speak.

In situations like these, therapists can openly hypothesize the patients' schemas that may be operating in the immediate present, and the ways these schemas may be causing the patient to feel hopeless, wary, and angry, and to experience other negative states of thought and emotion. The therapist then tries to engage the patient in the collaborative work of therapy by asking for feedback on these hypotheses. Here, patients' education about schemas serves as their primary introduction to cognitive therapy.

Conceptualization

When therapists elect to begin treatment with BPD patients by focusing on discrete complaints, they must bear in mind the importance of *conceptualizing* the patients' problems (cf. Persons, 1989). It is rarely sufficient simply to apply a rote set of techniques. This is true of all patients in cognitive therapy, not only those with serious personality disorders. The success of the implementation of "standard" cognitive therapy techniques (Beck et al., 1979) depends on the therapist's understanding the patient's idiosyncratic perceptions and needs.

For example, a therapist who understands that his BPD patient believes she is a "bad" person and does not deserve to feel better will not be stymied when the patient demeans the therapist's support. Instead, he may focus more attention on the patient's automatic thoughts when she hears a compliment directed toward her. Without this conceptualization, the therapist might try to teach the patient to respond rationally to upsetting thoughts, only to find that she summarily dismisses all of her own rational responses. The technique will then seem to have failed, and the therapist might be at a loss as to what to do next. (*Note:* In Chapter 4, we will outline and discuss in detail how to adjust "standard" cognitive therapy techniques in order to meet the needs of the BPD patient.)

Needless to say, some BPD patients enter therapy with their schemas blazing. For example, one of our patients telephoned her therapist three times with "emergencies" *before* the first face-to-face session was ever held! In such cases, it is almost impossible to proceed as one might with an Axis I patient. Here, therapists have the option of meeting the challenge by being attentive and available to help manage such emergencies (thus engendering trust), or of focusing immediately on hypothesized schemas that are part and parcel of the crises at hand. Either way, therapists can take the opportunity to ascertain quickly which schematic issues will need to be addressed in therapy.

The Therapeutic Relationship

The therapeutic relationship will be one of the key ingredients in the therapy of the BPD patient. The interactions between therapist and patient will be a microcosm of the patient's relationships with significant others outside the office. As BPD patients are extremely sensitive to signs of rejection and intimacy alike, the therapist must exercise extreme care in working with this patient group. Being even five minutes late for a session with a BPD patient may evoke anxiety about abandonment. The same five minutes will raise the specter of being taken advantage of (i.e., mistrust) in another BPD patient. Therapists need not capitulate to every BPD patient's needs and demands, but they should respond with sensitivity. In addition, therapists can use such incidents to initiate the process of learning about the patient.

It is essential that therapists work assiduously in fostering trust and collaboration in the therapeutic relationship. This is no small feat, as BPD patients often test the patience, skill, and commitment of therapists more than any other type of patient. For example, a BPD patient called his therapist at 3:00 A.M. to tell him that a woman had stood him up for a date. When the therapist groggily asked the patient what time the date had been set for, the patient said 9:00 P.M. the previous evening. The therapist asked the patient why he didn't call earlier, whereupon the patient replied, "I didn't want to bother you then." Perplexed and incredulous, the therapist asked the patient if he was aware of the time now. The patient retorted, "Of course, but you're supposed to be there for me whenever I need you."

In instances like this one, therapists must be aware of their own counterproductive reactions, lest they communicate hostility or other negative emotions in return. In this example, the therapist had to remind himself quickly that the patient's behavior, annoying and exasperating as it was, was a result of the patient's sense of unlovability and mistrust. It wasn't sufficient for him merely to call at 9:00 P.M. In order for the patient to test the therapist's trustworthiness—and, by extension, his own prominence in the life of the therapist—the patient had to resort to a phone call in the middle of the night. This was schema-driven behavior in all its dysfunctional glory. The therapist must nurture the formation and stability of the therapeutic relationship in the face of such behavior. Further, the therapist can focus on these reactions in order to facilitate understanding and change. Nevertheless, therapists need not endure such interactions silently. It is important to discuss a set of limits and guidelines to which both the therapist and patient will be expected to adhere (see Chapter 6).

Socializing the Patient into the Cognitive Treatment Model

Therapists must help BPD patients to appreciate the collaborative nature of cognitive therapy. They should explain to patients that both therapist and patient are mutually responsible for change, that both parties are expected to share ideas and feedback, and that the therapist supplies the support while the patient supplies the willingness to change. A typical explanation by the therapist is the following:

> We will be working together to help you with your problems. I'll probably ask you a lot of specific questions at times, but I'll also let you speak at length at other times. Also, I'll be open with you about my ideas and feelings, and I'll always be open to listen to yours. Even if we sometimes disagree, we need to respect each other's opinions. At those times when you ask me a direct question, I will do my best to give

you a direct answer. If you find the work of therapy to be scary or too difficult, I will do all I can to give you the necessary support to persevere and to move ahead. I will be here to help you as much as I can, but you will also have to be willing to learn ways to depend on your own resources so that you can feel better about yourself. I'll be responsible for making sure your treatment is suited to your specific needs, but you will be responsible for practicing your new insights and skills between sessions in your everyday life. In this way, you will have a better chance of remaining well even after therapy is completed.

Therapists may choose to break this monologue down into shorter segments or to add their own personal touches. Either way, it is imperative to ask the patients for their feedback on this information—an example of the process of collaboration in itself.

Therapists encourage patients to formulate a problem list and to set specific goals for treatment. Therapists then help to shape these goals so that they are achievable, proximal, and adaptive. At times, BPD patients will express goals that are inappropriate or unrealistic. Examples include a patient's wanting to have "perfect self-esteem" in twelve sessions, or desiring to "understand why I'm so screwed up so I can satisfy my curiosity before I kill myself," or asking the therapist to help find the patient a mate who will take care of the patient's every need. When this occurs, therapists must neither condemn nor accept these goals. Rather, the therapist sets the tone of cognitive therapy by *questioning* the BPD patient about the goals: the reasons for wanting them, the pros and cons of pursuing them, and the ideas for some alternatives. Therapists need to help their patients to take small, gradual steps toward discrete, specific goals such as accepting care and compliments from others, working toward graduating from school or finding a job, decreasing thoughts that are self-denigrating, learning how to be assertive without being overwhelmed by guilt, accepting invitations to socialize, understanding the feelings and thoughts that produce fear and avoidance and working to diminish them, and many, many more.

Patients who have read about cognitive therapy and expect to be "cured" in twelve to twenty sessions need to be apprised (in a sensitive, thoughtful way) of the greater severity and chronicity of their problems and hence the need for longer treatment. One to three years is a far more reasonable time frame for the treatment of BPD. Additionally, patients may believe that cognitive therapy never includes medication. Therapists should explain that research has indicated that some people respond very well to a combination of cognitive therapy and pharmacotherapy, and that such a treatment regimen might be appropriate in given cases (see Chapter 5).

The process of socialization includes fundamental information about the role of thinking in emotional distress and behavioral problems. Patients learn about the cognitive triad—their perceptions of self, others, and future—and how these perceptions may be dysfunctional. At the same time, it is made clear to patients that their *emotions* and *behaviors* will be important to examine as well. Further, unlike a "power of positive thinking" approach, cognitive therapy allows for the legitimacy of negative feelings and thoughts (Newman, 1991). For example, a BPD patient who never cried or spoke when his father died may need to cry and to experience catharsis in session. If this leads to a more positive outcome, then expressing the "negative" feeling of grief may be quite adaptive. In sum, BPD patients are to be accepted for themselves but encouraged to make the positive changes to which they will agree.

SUMMARY

The application of cognitive therapy to the treatment of BPD is a relatively recent development. In this book, we explicate the conceptual and technical advancements that have enabled cognitive therapists to achieve promising results in the treatment of this challenging population.

This therapy guidebook is geared toward those clinicians who understand and apply basic principles and techniques of standard cognitive therapy currently in their clinical work. While we describe some of the fundamental strategies, such as the assessment and modification of automatic thoughts, we emphasize a more advanced *schema-focused* approach to treatment (e.g., Beck et al., 1990; Young, 1990).

Chapter 1 has defined the term *schema* and demonstrated how it applies to the conceptualization of the borderline patient. We have discussed the general characteristics of BPD patients, and have hypothesized three specific subcategories of the disorder that serve to focus therapists on more idiographic aspects of symptomatology. We have underscored the central role of the therapeutic relationship in the treatment of BPD patients, and have offered initial guidelines for the earliest stages of treatment.

In the next chapter of our introductory section (Chapter 2), we present a developmental/historical perspective on the etiology of BPD, with an emphasis on understanding problems in cognitive development from both Eriksonian and Piagetian theoretical perspectives.

Part Two focuses on *clinical applications*. Chapter 3 focuses on the methods that therapists use in order to formulate a cognitive case conceptualization of the BPD patient. A sample report of such a conceptualization is presented as well. Chapter 4 spells out a variety of new techniques, as well as modifications of standard strategies, whereas Chapter 5 deals with the application of pharmacotherapy to the overall treatment plan. The important issue of the cognitive therapist's countertransference reactions is addressed in Chapter 6.

Our final section outlines the *three subtypes of BPD that make up our hypothesized borderline spectrum*. This is followed by five case studies that explicitly describe those techniques and concepts that have been reviewed in this book.

Chapter 2

Developmental Issues in Borderline Personality Disorder

One reason that it is often difficult to effect therapeutic changes in BPD patients is that many of their beliefs, emotions, and actions are rooted in schemas that were acquired and strengthened in early childhood. In order to treat early maladaptive schemas (EMSs; Young, 1990), we need to consider the following developmental factors:

1. The *content* of the schema
2. The *Eriksonian stages* of the patient's life relevant to the times when the schemas were acquired and reinforced
3. The *perceptual channels* through which the schema-building information was received and stored
4. The *Piagetian level* of cognitive processing relevant to the schemas

Therapists who ascertain the foregoing information are more likely to understand the process by which the patients' schemas developed. Furthermore, they will begin to find clues regarding the means by which patients continue to process information in the present time so as to fit the schemas. With this knowledge, therapists will be in a better position to form a healthy therapeutic alliance with their patients and to begin to generate powerful strategies for change.

CONTENT OF THE SCHEMA

As noted earlier in this book, schemas are unconditional, core beliefs. Unconditional beliefs are more firmly rooted and resistant to change than are conditional beliefs. For example, the following belief about competency is conditional: "I am a failure unless I do everything perfectly." This is a dysfunctional belief, but we can see how the patient who holds such a belief may still be able to feel competent, albeit under great pressure. By contrast, an unconditional belief (i.e., a schema) states, "I am a failure no matter what I do." Patients who hold such a schema never can negate the "truth" of the belief, and thus it is virtually impossible for them ever to feel competent.

In some cases, BPD patients avoid thinking about these schemas so that they do not experience the negative affect associated with seeing themselves as incompetent. In other cases or circumstances, the BPD patient may try to avoid situations or persons that threaten to activate the schema. These strategies may spare the patients some immediate anxiety and dysphoria but ultimately do not help them to dispute the veracity of the schema. In addition, BPD patients often avoid close, intimate relationships in an effort to prevent other people from coming to recognize their schematic deficiencies. Finally, the unconditional nature of the schemas provides no motivation for BPD patients to notice or collect perceptual data that contradict the schema. Therefore, a person with an incompetency schema, for example, is unlikely to attach any significance to a positive evaluation from an employer.

Young (1990), who has hypothesized that schemas are developed in the first few years of life, has identified fifteen early maladaptive schemas that are pertinent to the full gamut of personality disorders:

1. Independence
2. Subjugation/lack of individuation
3. Vulnerability to harm and illness
4. Fear of losing control
5. Emotional deprivation
6. Abandonment/loss
7. Mistrust
8. Social isolation/alienation
9. Unlovability/defectiveness/badness
10. Social undesirability
11. Guilt/punishment
12. Incompetence/failure
13. Unrelenting standards
14. Loss of emotional control
15. Entitlement/insufficient limits

Any of these schemas may be found in the BPD patient. The most frequently encountered tend to be *dependence, lack of individuation, emotional deprivation, abandonment, mistrust, unlovability,* and *incompetence.*

Two more reasons that BPD patients are so difficult to treat are that they generally maintain numerous schemas, and their schemas tend to be incongruent with or antagonistic to each other. This causes great conflict in BPD patients and frequently puts them in no-win situations. For example, a BPD patient simultaneously holds dependence and mistrust schemas. On one hand, she believes that she is incapable of taking care of her own needs without the total support of another person. On the other hand, she believes that it is very dangerous to trust anyone. If she seeks nurturance, she activates her mistrust schema and is likely to withdraw from or cause a rift with her significant other. If she seeks solitude, she begins to panic at the thought that she cannot exist on her own. Either way, the BPD patient is torn, unhappy, and unsettled. If therapists comprehend the conflicting nature of their BPD patients' schemas, they will be better able to empathize with the terrible pain and chaos that the patients experience. Additionally, the "crazy" behaviors of the BPD patient that once seemed inexplicable may now become "logical" to both the therapist and the patient.

STAGES OF DEVELOPMENT OF THE SCHEMAS: AN ERIKSONIAN MODEL

In a significant proportion of cases, BPD patients have experienced extreme difficulties early in life (Zanarini, Gunderson, Marino, Schwartz, & Frankenburg, 1989). In some cases, these difficulties are obvious incidents of abuse (Goodwin, Cheeves, & Connell, 1990; Stone, Unwin, Beacham, & Swenson, 1988)—for example, sexual abuse, physical beatings, or severe neglect. Many childhood histories of BPD patients are filled with stories of trauma. One of our patients ("Alice") recounted that she was often left alone, locked in a bedroom, while her schizophrenic mother and antisocial father went away for the weekend. As early as the age of three, Alice would be left with only a sandwich, a bottle of water, and a tin can in which to urinate. When the parents returned, they often beat her with a stick.

In other cases of BPD, the childhood difficulties do not appear at first glance to be so severe. However, the parents of these patients often lacked adequate understanding of the needs and the psychology of the child. As a result, markedly inappropriate parenting behaviors were repeated on a daily basis across many different situations. A case in point is "Helen," whose mother would tell her that she was so bad that she would be taken away forever by "Mrs. Smith." The mother would pack Helen's suitcase and pretend to phone "Mrs. Smith" to say that she should come and take the child away. Then the mother would go out the back door, walk around the house, and ring the front doorbell. Returning through the back door, she would lead Helen toward the front door until the child dissolved in tears. This was but one example of numerous, repeated, malevolent mistakes in parenting made by Helen's mother and father.

Sometimes the traumas consist of combinations of uncaring parenting and situational problems. This is exemplified by the case of "Evy," who was forced to relocate many times during her childhood as a result of her father's business moves. Not only was she continually hurt by the loss of friends (and concomitant loss of identity within a steady peer group), but her parents denied her the right to cry over her losses. They gave her no support at all and repeatedly criticized her for her "obstinacy" in not wanting to be uprooted year after year.

Childhood traumas such as these produce the schemas that are at the core of the borderline disorder. In examining the nature of the schemas that have developed in a BPD patient, therapists gain important information by ascertaining the corresponding stage of development of the child at the onset of these traumatic events. The developmental theory of Erikson (1963) is a useful reference in undertaking this task. According to the model presented here (Table 2.1), an individual who experienced mistreatment during infancy (e.g., approximately 0–1 years of age), in Erikson's stage of "trust versus mistrust," is likely to exhibit a schema of mistrust in adulthood. By contrast, a child is more likely to develop an incompetency schema in connection with failures and criticisms received during the early school years. We posit that the schema of unlovability may develop across any of Erikson's proposed stages but is more compelling and pervasive when the child experiences lack of caring from more significant others over longer periods of time (up to and including adulthood).

According to Erikson, the child learns to function in the world by mastering challenges. In each stage of development there are specific issues that are of critical importance and skills that must be learned in order to cope with those issues. Each stage is named for the pair of opposing learning experiences that are hypothesized to be critical at that point in life. The terms used to summarize each stage consist of a relatively healthy resolution of life crises and a relatively negative one (e.g., in infancy, trust versus mistrust). Favorable resolution of each developmental period is theorized to occur when a balance is struck that leans somewhat toward the positive side, but not at the extreme.

Borderline patients do not master such balancing acts. As an illustration, the all-or-none nature of BPD patients' thinking leads them to be either excessively trustful or totally mistrustful of others, including their therapists. Sometimes they will vacillate between these polar extremes with regard to a single person. When an adult BPD patient's main maladaptive schemas are dormant, they may show themselves to be capable of viewing things in shades of gray. When schemas are activated,

Table 2.1. Schemas Associated with Eriksonian Stages

Age	0 to 1	1 to 3	3 to 6	6 to puberty
Erikson's Stages	Trust vs. Mistrust	Autonomy vs. Shame and Doubt	Initiative vs. Guilt	Industry vs. Inferiority
Schemas	Mistrust Abandonment	Dependence Lack of individuation	Dependence Emotional deprivation Incompetence	Incompetence
	←——— Unlovability/Defectiveness/"Badness" ———→			

however, the BPD patients' thinking becomes polarized again. The middle ground or moderate approach that is most adaptive in solving most of life's major problems is unknown to BPD patients whose schemas are activated. For example, a BPD patient whose chief schemas are abandonment and unlovability may have no trouble evaluating new cars in a showroom. He or she can rate the products on a continuum and make a choice to buy one or another, on the basis of a number of factors. The same patient, however, may not be able to weigh the pros and cons in this manner when a lover proposes marriage. Here, the schemas are activated, leading to vacillations between fantasies of a perfect marriage and fears that marriage will necessarily lead to cruel abandonment. The resultant mixed emotions are quite intense, the indecision is agonizing, and a consideration of the pros and cons of the situation becomes virtually impossible.

Although Erikson proposes a discrete stage theory, his works imply that all of the developmental issues exist in varying proportions across the life span. The notion that all the issues (e.g., trust, autonomy, industry, intimacy, and others) are present throughout the life of the person means that the failure to resolve a crisis within a particular developmental stage is not irreversible. Resolutions of early crises that are less than satisfactory may be improved upon with the help of growth-enhancing experiences later in life. Therapy often serves this purpose.

Information about the age at which the patients experienced serious difficulties may give us an idea as to how challenging it will be to resolve their problems in therapy. Generally, the earlier and more continuous the negative experiences, the more difficult they will be to restructure or modify later. This observation appears consistent with clinical realities for a number of reasons. First, the younger child is more vulnerable and has fewer coping skills than the older child. Second, schemas developed very early in life are more difficult to access directly later in treatment. For example, a patient who suffers from an incompetency schema that traces back to grade school ridicule is likely to be more capable of expressing the specific nature of her dysphoria than a patient whose mistrust and intimacy problems trace back to sexual abuse that she vaguely remembers suffering when she was still in her crib. Third, the kinds of cognitive strategies that the younger child uses are less mature and lead to errors. For example, very young children have a primitive conception of attribution in comparison to older children. Therefore, all else being equal, a 10-year-old boy is less likely to blame himself erroneously for his father's leaving home than is his 4-year-old brother, who may develop a schema of "badness" or unlovability.

The life problems that contribute to the development of BPD often start before the age of 7, during the first four Eriksonian stages. Crises occurring later may produce other psychological disorders, but these are less likely to be BPD than when the crises occur very early. Consequently, in describing each of the Eriksonian stages, we will focus on these first four, which we hypothesize to be the precursor stages in schema development. We conceptualize the latter four stages as outcome stages, where the deleterious effects of the schemas become manifested in a variety of ways.

Precursor Stages

Trust versus Mistrust (Ages 0 –1)

The critical determinations in the first year of life are whether the world is a safe place and whether the people who populate that world can be trusted. It is of vital importance that the needs of the helpless infant be met with some consistency. The baby who is hungry needs to be fed, and the baby who is upset needs to be comforted. If the child learns to expect a benevolent world, one in which comfort and nurturance are forthcoming on a regular basis, the child will learn to trust.

Serious disruption in the life of a child during this period may foster at least two main schemas—mistrust and abandonment. Adult BPD patients who have suffered unduly during infancy often maintain unconditional beliefs, such as "All people will abuse me, hurt me, or manipulate me," and "Everyone I care about ultimately will leave me." Along with these core beliefs we see concomitant schemas of unlovability or "badness." A case example illustrates this point.

"Sally" was born to an unwed mother who put her up for adoption when she was born. Soon after the baby's placement with a family, her new father died suddenly. Sally then was placed with another family. Again, tragically and ironically, the adoptive father became critically ill, and she was removed from this household as well. At the age of 7 months, Sally was placed with yet another family, and her adoption was completed. When Sally was an adult, her mother (her *fourth* mother) casually remarked that for one year after the adoption Sally would scream and cry whenever someone put a coat on her. We might infer that it must have seemed to this child that each time a coat was put on her she lost a set of parents and a home.

As an adult, Sally demonstrated symptoms that reflected pronounced abandonment fears and distrusting of others. The abandonment schema generated extreme panic in what normally would be perceived as nonthreatening situations. As an illustration, a man she had dated twice left for a three-day business trip. This event triggered extreme emotions that clearly were unwarranted for the situation. For example, she became distraught and angry, assuming that the man would never return, or at least that he would forget about her, or that he would meet someone else while he was away and dump Sally. She felt as strongly as would a wife whose husband of twenty years had left her forever.

Sally exhibited all-or-none thinking in the area of judging other people's trustworthiness. Upon meeting someone for the first or second time, she would determine that the person was either completely trustworthy or totally treacherous. Consequently, she was continually disappointed by people's inevitable innocent inconsistencies or white lies, and she often felt disillusioned and stabbed in the back. This was especially true with regard to men, as she found it particularly difficult to trust the men that she dated. She drew firm conclusions that men were betraying her on the basis of the most meager of evidence. Also, her schema-driven behavior often was inappropriate—for example, clandestinely searching her boyfriends' mail for signs of deceit.

In treatment, the temporal remoteness of early life crises and trauma poses a formidable obstacle to the therapist's ability to gather relevant historical information. Patients do not have readily accessible memories of their infant years. The therapist may have to depend on information obtained from older relatives, or (less directly) from stories that the patients have been told by their elders.

Autonomy versus Shame or Doubt (Ages 1–3)

The child's initial development of a sense of mastery is the proposed critical challenge of this period. Children at this age need to begin to think that they can do things for themselves. Parents who do far too much or far too little for their toddlers foster a sense of doubt in the children. Caregivers who are excessively impatient and intensely belittling may produce a sense of shame in the child, particularly if the disparagement has to do with the youngster's toilet training or curiosity about his or her genitals.

During this period, children begin to develop an identity apart from their caretakers. Trauma at this stage is theorized to create a deficient sense of separateness. Therefore, it follows that it becomes difficult for the developing individual to learn about boundaries and limits in relationships. At one extreme, BPD patients frequently grow to resist becoming involved in relationships because of fears that their own personalities will be swept up or buried by the stronger identities of others. At the other end of the spectrum, they often become enmeshed in relationships and, indeed, lose their sense of differentiation between themselves and their significant others. Obvious examples of this phenomenon are the BPD patients who seek symbiosis with the therapist—for example, by wanting therapists to treat them as if they were the therapists' only patients, to spend all their time talking with the patients on the phone, and to make all the patients' decisions for them.

Traumas during this period often trigger excessive dependence as the child learns that he or she is neither allowed nor able to do things for him or herself. Parents who blatantly and repeatedly interfere with the child's attempts to do activities alone (e.g., dressing, eating, manipulating objects) may produce dependency schemas in their children. These schemas become even more pronounced and entrenched when the overprotectiveness described here continues through the child's adolescence and adulthood as well.

For example, "Gail's" mother was hypercritical, and her father was excessive in his attempt to care for Gail's needs. This was a double whammy that made it almost impossible for Gail to develop any self-confidence or autonomy. Even when she was an adult, Gail's father continued to be enmeshed with her and to involve himself in her daily life. Predictably, Gail's relationships with potential lovers were riddled with fears of being overwhelmed and suffocated by them. Although she was apprehensive about losing her sense of identity in relationships, she was double-bound by her simultaneous belief in her inability to perform routine daily tasks of living. This latter problem necessitated her dependence on others in order to cope with day-today survival. Both the dependence and lack of individuation schemas are evident in Gail's adult behavior.

Initiative versus Guilt (Ages 4 to 5)

Children who have gained a rudimentary sense of mastery from the previous stage are likely to initiate activities when they reach late preschool age. A feeling of capability and autonomy produces active exploration and task initiation during this period. Children for whom taking initiative leads to rejection, punishment, harm, or marked lack of responsivity from significant others learn to experience excessive shame and guilt. This may lead to the establishment of schemas in the areas of dependence, incompetence, emotional deprivation, and unlovability (the ubiquitous schema).

A pattern of dependence or a constant cycling between dependence and avoidance frequently is observed in the BPD patient who has had major difficulties during late preschool years. For example, Helen's mother was severely depressed during this period of the patient's childhood. As a result, she typically responded as if Helen were not there and gave her daughter almost no feedback or emotional support for her attempts to conquer tasks. As an adult, Helen entered therapy believing that she was incapable of taking care of her own life, and she craved excessive emotional investment from others. She had long periods of unemployment followed by periods of underemployment. In each case she would state her dissatisfaction with the situation but was unable to take even the most modest steps to initiate change. In addition, she wanted others to take over basic decisions, such as what she should eat, what she should wear, and how to decorate her apartment. Her initial "goal" for therapy was that the therapist would find her a man who would assume all her responsibilities. This need reflected her dependence, emotional deprivation, and incompetence schemas.

Helen's problems were compounded by the fact that she became frightened by close relationships, as her fragile sense of self was threatened. She then would avoid or leave relationships until her dependency needs were restimulated by loneliness and the need to make daily decisions. This cycle was vicious indeed.

Industry versus Inferiority (Ages 6–11)

In this stage, children engage in productive tasks and bring them to completion. They are beginning grade school and start to deal more directly with the practical tasks of everyday life. Failure and derision experienced during this stage may lead to a sense of inferiority. The long-term result is an incompetency schema.

To illustrate, Helen remembered going to school at the age of seven with the expectation that she could not complete her work satisfactorily. Rather than challenging that belief, her mother and grandmother (who was a professional writer) actively supported it. They wrote book reports for her that were of such quality that the young girl was placed in a class for the gifted. Helen felt grossly inferior to her classmates and frequently dealt with her emotional discomfort by feigning illnesses so that she would be allowed to go home.

When she became an adult, Helen's incompetency schema manifested itself in extreme self-doubt. When she was unexpectedly asked to learn a new task at work, she became so upset that she believed she should not only quit her job but should move out of town as well.

Outcome Stages

The outcome stages represent adolescence and adulthood, and demonstrate the cumulative effects that occurred in the precursor stages. Additionally, negative experiences during the outcome stages further compound the psychological problems wrought upon the child in the earlier stages. Difficulties that have accrued from early life crises impede the patient's ability to mature in a fulfilling and optimal way in adolescence and adulthood. The early maladaptive schemas are fixed in place by the onset of adolescence, serving to inhibit psychological growth as time goes on.

Ego Identity versus Role Confusion (Ages 12–18)

Successful negotiation of this stage requires the development of a sense of identity combined with a hopeful view of the future. It is at this time that persons are starting to formulate the answers to important questions and decisions in life, such as future career directions, sexual orientation, and choices of people with whom to have important relationships. Unfortunately, patients who are well on their way to being identifiable as BPD sufferers will likely have very unsatisfying teenage years. Their schemas of lack of individuation, mistrust, incompetency, dependence, unlovability, and abandonment engendered earlier in life inhibit their ability to develop healthy relationships or to conceive of educational or career fulfillment.

Intimacy versus Isolation (Young Adulthood)

The central task of this stage is to attain intimacy, to care about others, and to share one's life with another without feeling overwhelmed or engulfed. For BPD patients, there is a constant fear of loss of identity when involved in intimate relationships. The push–pull of dependency and avoidance developed during previous stages manifests itself in approach–avoidance conflicts in relationships. Often we see BPD patients operationalize the concept of *intimacy* as being synonymous with the act of sex. The result may be numerous impulsive, stormy relationships that go hot and cold very quickly, leaving the BPD patients feeling even more distrustful and unlovable than before.

Generativity versus Stagnation (Middle Adulthood)

During this period one's concerns ideally expand beyond oneself and one's mate to include society and future generations. Stagnation is witnessed in adults who are so caught up in their own day-to-day psychological needs that they do not progress in terms of emotional stability, wisdom, productivity, and contributions to the welfare of their descendants and to society. This phenomenon is seen commonly in middle-aged BPD patients who seem to lag far behind their cohorts in personal growth, family ties, and worldly experience.

Integrity versus Despair (Old Age)

Ideally, this is the time when one looks back over one's life with a sense of satisfaction, contentment, and repose. BPD patients who have not succeeded in overcoming their problems during young adulthood and middle age often feel embittered and believe that their lives were filled with missed opportunities, unfruitful efforts, and unmet needs.

Implications for Therapy

It is extremely important for therapists to obtain a thorough history on their BPD patients in order to formulate accurate case conceptualizations (Persons, 1989). One of the tasks involved in this process is to hypothesize the role of the various early maladaptive schemas in the patient's past and present difficulties. This task requires a good deal of exploration and perseverance because much of the information needed to identify the schemas is embedded in distant past events. Even if it is not possible to obtain a complete account of childhood events, it is still useful to gather as much information as possible. Therapists can ask their BPD patients to discuss and write about the following:

1. Their most important memories across successive age brackets
2. Descriptions of their relationships with their parents (how they were disciplined; what implicit or explicit family rules prevailed; how they were treated when they were happy, sad, angry)
3. Significant geographic moves
4. Significant separations from loved ones
5. Incidents of physical, verbal, emotional, or sexual abuse, and identification of the persons involved
6. Family history of substance or alcohol abuse
7. Family history of psychiatric problems
8. Relationships with siblings
9. The quality of the parental marital relationship (and incidents of divorce and separation between parents or stepparents)
10. Important memories about school (academics, social adjustment, level of confidence)

Exploring these areas in therapy will shed light on the nature of the crises that the BPD patients faced in their early developmental years. It is extremely important that therapists ask their patients to discuss not only the factual nature of the experiences, but the *personal meaning* that all of this information has for them. This is so because the childhood events in and of themselves tell only part of the story. The essence of the tale concerns how the patients construe these events.

When certain critical memories are identified, such as incidents of sexual abuse, the age of the child at the time of the trauma becomes a key to the assessment of schemas. As noted earlier, the traumas that occurred earlier and more continuously seem to be associated with more pervasive and compelling schemas. For example, we would expect that (all else being equal) the child who suffered sexual abuse from preschool age to the teenage years would evidence more severe pathology than the child who was molested on one occasion sometime during the same time frame.

Additionally, the tracing of discrete crises to a specific age identifies a particular stage of Eriksonian development, which provides a clue to the nature of the schema involved. For example, painful events during early school age are likely to have engendered a schema of incompetency. To use the example of the sexually abused child, we have treated a patient ("Hallie") who developed a compelling incompetency schema at the age of 7. At this time she was being molested periodically by an uncle. As a result, Hallie became preoccupied with thoughts of sex and began to do poorly in school. Her teacher and parents unwittingly compounded the problem by attributing the girl's failings to inattention, daydreaming, and laziness. (It is noteworthy that, in addition, Hallie's experiences of sexual abuse gave rise to a schema of mistrust as well. As we have noted, Erikson's model does not necessarily restrict the development of the child's senses of trust and mistrust to the first year of life.)

The gathering of data about childhood, adolescence, and more recent past events should be an ongoing process throughout therapy. Sometimes the patient's current symptoms act as a sign to look back at particular periods of life for key forgotten events that need to be discussed and processed in treatment. As a case in point, the patient with the compelling abandonment and mistrust schemas (Sally) could offer no explanation for her present behavior. The therapist, using the Eriksonian model as a guide, hypothesized that there might have been a serious disruption in the patient's life during infancy. Sure enough, when the patient's stepmother was consulted, it was learned that the patient had been a member of four households by the age of seven months. This information opened up new areas of understanding for the therapist and patient to pursue in treatment.

CHANNEL OF SENSORY INPUT

In treating BPD patients, therapists need to take into consideration the sensory modalities through which the patients learned the information that led to the development of their maladaptive schemas. In older children, information often is received verbally and stored in language memory. At younger ages, children may be relatively more dependent on visual inputs that are stored as images. At even earlier ages (e.g., in infancy), information is taken in via sources such as touch, body position, tone of speech sounds, and unformed visual inputs. These latter sources, should they prove noxious to the infant, later result in disorganized cognitions that we have dubbed "the cloud."

Although the activation of all schemas involve marked affect regardless of whether the schemas were learned through verbal channels, visual channels, or "the cloud," BPD patients often have a more difficult time identifying and articulating those schemas that are based in "the cloud." Instead, they experience a vague sense of distress that they have difficulty in describing clearly (thus contributing to their sense that others do not understand). Generally speaking, we have found that core beliefs that were engendered by preverbal sources of sensory input will be most resistant to therapeutic interventions that remain solely at the verbal level. This would account for the all-too-familiar BPD phenomenon whereby patients are capable of stating rational responses (see Chapter 4) but show no concomitant improvement in mood.

Infants are surprisingly sensitive in their ability to process the sensory stimuli with which they are bombarded. For example, vision develops quite rapidly. In the first few months of life, infants demonstrate depth perception (Gibson & Walk, 1960), show preference for forms that resemble human faces (Fantz, 1961; Freedman, 1971), pay an increasing amount of attention to a person's eyes (Hainline, 1978; Haith, Bergman, & Moore, 1977), prefer to look at photos of their own mothers over photos of strange women (Barrera & Maurer, 1981), can discriminate between different facial expressions (LaBarbera, Izard, Vietze, & Parisi, 1976; Young-Browns, Rosenfeld, & Horowitz, 1977), and are able to imitate facial expressions (Meltzoff & Moore, 1977). All these studies indicate a high degree of visual sophistication in the very young child.

Infants are sensitive to more than just visual cues. Babies respond preferentially to a soft human voice, especially that of a female, over other sounds (Freedman, 1971) and prefer to hear "motherese" (a high-pitched slow rate of talking with exaggerated intonations) spoken by a stranger over adult talk spoken by a stranger (Fernald, 1984; Fernald & Simon, 1984). By ten months, infants begin to respond to specific words. These studies indicate that children perceive verbal stimuli long before they can produce language and before the organizing advantages of language are available to them.

Infants' memories may be better developed than had been thought previously (Cohen & Gelber, 1975). Fagan (1973, 1977) found that 5-month-olds can remember briefly exposed stimuli for up to two weeks. Their cognitive strategies, however, are relatively primitive, so that although they may be able to receive and retain significant amounts of sensory information, their ability to manipulate the information mentally is limited (Appleton, Clifton, & Goldberg, 1975; Flavell, 1970; Flavell, Beach, & Chinsky, 1966). It is clear that children at this very young age do not possess the cognitive strategies for solving problems, nor do they demonstrate semantic grouping skills.

Nevertheless, the main thrust of our argument is that infants are extremely sensitive to the stimulation that they are receiving. These early visual and auditory inputs, together with kinesthetic cues, form the basis of "the cloud." Although they perceive the sensory information, infants have difficulty organizing this stimulation and making sense of it. They do not have the cognitive wherewithal to understand the motivations and intentions of the adults who are so vital to their survival.

Early maladaptive schemas that form from information in "the cloud" typically result from a lack of adequate caregiving in these early stages of life. This may include physically rough or abusive behavior (e.g., shaking a child violently) or consistent neglect and unresponsiveness to the child's signals of need (e.g., hunger, thirst, diaper discomfort). In addition, significant inconsistency (e.g., double-bind messages) and emotional unavailability from caregivers may produce early maladaptive schemas. Examples include parents suffering from clinical depression who demonstrate emotional and behavioral retardation, and parents who demonstrate prominent features of narcissistic personality disorder, for whom the child's needs are considered as competition to the parent's needs and who therefore respond with hostility toward the child. The most obvious examples of dysfunctional parental behaviors that produce negative schemas in the child are physical and sexual abuse. Under such harmful conditions, the child learns that the world is not a benign place and that people cannot be trusted. These children may also conclude that they themselves somehow are bad and unlovable.

The information contained in "the cloud" provides few retrieval cues that the patient can use to gain access to the relevant memories. A mother who stiffens her body, as if repulsed, each time her baby is laid in her arms sends a powerful negative message to the infant. That information is stored neither as a word nor as a picture but, rather, as a kinesthetic cue that carries vague meaning. As a result, adult BPD patients often have trouble articulating their thoughts when they are visibly upset. Instead, they either feel physically sick or become numb, "spacy," or depersonalized (Young, 1990). These patients frequently note that they do not understand their own responses. Some patients have even used the phrase, "It all seems cloudy," when describing their reactions to situations that stimulate those very early schemas of mistrust and abandonment.

As a child grows older, visual inputs become better organized and understood, thus producing more efficient retrieval cues for later recollection. Schemas that are based in experiences where clear visual stimuli were involved are more readily accessed in treatment than are schemas based in "the cloud." Therapists help their patients gain greater awareness of their core beliefs by teaching them to pay close attention to the spontaneous flashes of images that occur when they become very upset. For example, a BPD patient whose mother had been severely depressed when the patient was 4 years old regularly experienced flashes of her mother's passive, unresponsive, uncaring face. These flashbacks tended to occur when she believed that someone important to her was rejecting her. The early maladaptive schema of unlovability formed by these repeated passive responses from her mother still was producing strong negative emotional reactions in adulthood. Until she came into therapy, this patient had not been able to recognize and assess the images, nor had she been able to trace their origins or understand how they pertained to her problematic reactions in relationships today.

As the child continues to grow and become more verbal, schemas become increasingly based in language. The crises or trauma associated with these schemas are more easily remembered and described by the BPD patients. Retrieval cues that activate the schemas at this age are more likely to be verbal. An 8-year-old child, for example, is less dependent on tactile cues from the parent than on verbal cues. "June," a BPD patient who suffered from profound feelings and beliefs of incompetency, was able to remember verbatim statements that her hypercritical and belittling father made to her on a routine basis when she was in grade school.

These aforementioned channels, tactile, visual, and verbal, are not mutually exclusive. In many cases information is processed from each of these sources at the same time. The 8-year-old child who has verbal skills does not cease being visual and tactile but, rather, has added important new sources of sensory input. As a result, schemas often have verbal, visual, *and* cloud components. As the child grows, a greater proportion of information is ascertained from the verbal source (Figure 2.1). The upshot is that therapists must pay attention to all of the BPD patient's channels of sensory input. Well-articulated memories have a preponderance of verbal sources and probably took place later in childhood or adolescence. On the other hand, verbal interventions that produce little therapeutic impact signal to therapists that they must focus more on images. When images are insufficient and the patient is somatisizing or depersonalizing, "the cloud" must be tapped.

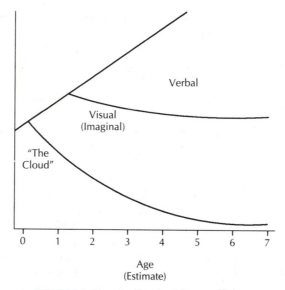

FIGURE 2.1. Channels of Input and Storage of Schema

Implications for Therapy

As therapists plan interventions to modify patients' schemas, they must consider the sensory modalities through which the schemas most likely were formed. Purely verbal interventions (e.g., Socratic questioning; Daily Thought Records or DTRs; see Chapter 4) will be useful in modifying schemas that were formed primarily on the basis of language-based information processing. Schemas that consist of mental images will be less changeable through strictly verbal interventions unless imagery techniques are included. Schemas that are based in "the cloud" will require interventions that tap into more primitive sensory inputs, such as tonality of interpersonal communication and kinesthetic/tactile variables (e.g., posture, degree of warmth). Because many of the BPD patients' problems can be linked to experiences that involve powerful images and sensory stimulation, we hypothesize that *interventions that utilize only normal spoken language will be less effective in the long run than techniques that utilize imagery, dreams, tone of voice manipulations, and kinesthetic elements as well.*

In order to tap into the patients' subverbal experiences, therapists must take note of the patients' emotional and somatic responses in addition to their thoughts. This is particularly salient when a patient's schemas are activated in the therapy session, as demonstrated by a sudden intensifying or diminishing of affect.

Clinical Examples

In one case, a therapist responded to a patient's unexpected angry outburst by asking about his emotions, spontaneous images or memories, and bodily sensations. The patient focused on the fact that his face felt "red hot," the same feeling he used to have as a child when his father would humiliate him in front of houseguests. This discovery led to the patient's understanding that his incompetency and (to a lesser degree) his unlovability schemas became activated anytime he blushed as a result of an interpersonal interaction. One intervention that the therapist devised in order to deal with this problem involved a role-play exercise in which the therapist pretended to insult the patient. As the patient noticed his face become hot, his task was covertly to utilize relaxation techniques in order to release the tension in his jaw and neck. Further, the patient was to imagine looking into a mirror and seeing that his face was of normal color again. This technique was quite useful in diminishing the effects of a stimulated incompetency schema and the concomitant anger. Verbal techniques such as the DTR then were used to supplement and reinforce the gains that had been made through visual and sensory channels.

In another case, a patient became stone-faced and silent in session. The therapist inquired about her emotions and bodily sensations, whereupon she stated that she felt "nothing ... totally cold and numb." Upon further exploration, the therapist and patient noted that she tended to feel this way whenever she sensed that someone cared for her. It would have been unhelpful for the therapist in this instance merely to explain verbally that he did care about the patient and that there was nothing to fear. Instead, it was necessary for the therapist and patient to focus further on the feelings of numbness, where they originated, and what function they served in protecting the patient from imagined harm. After many sessions, the patient was able to piece together memories of making her body become numb when she was sexually assaulted by her stepbrother many years ago. This sensory strategy had overgeneralized to the point that she would dissociate when she sensed that a man (in this case, the therapist) had positive feelings about her. Naturally, this response style greatly disrupted her personal relationships. As a result of these revelations, the therapist and patient agreed that when the patient would become "numb" in session, she would attempt to "concentrate and get some of the feelings back and to see what happens." To facilitate this process, the patient brought a warm blanket to session. She was instructed to wrap the blanket around herself when she felt "cold and totally numb." The blanket helped to keep her warm and aided the process of voluntarily making herself feel things again. The long-standing therapeutic relationship enabled this patient to trust the therapist just enough to begin to practice extinguishing her dissociative responses. Eventually, the patient began to engage in low-risk, step-by-step experiments of this sort in everyday life.

A PIAGETIAN EXPLICATION OF COGNITIVE DEVELOPMENT IN BPD

Piaget (1952) proposed that children are born with relatively immature cognitive processing skills that become more sophisticated qualitatively over time. As children interact with the world, and as their brains develop, they learn to become more effective problem solvers. In BPD patients, we have noticed a phenomenon whereby they solve certain complex problems in life very well, whereas other problems reduce them to using extremely immature and maladaptive cognitive processing strategies. This disparity is quite striking. Repeatedly, we have seen that *the problems that cause this apparent cognitive regression are those that stimulate early maladaptive schemas.* In Piagetian terms, a BPD patient may be quite capable of utilizing formal operations in handling tasks at work and in performing intellectual skills. Yet this same patient may seem to regress to preoperational thought when relationship problems occur. In treatment, therapists sometimes are caught off guard when their seemingly logical and rational patients unexpectedly react to a given problem in the way that a helpless, wounded child might. When this happens, it is certain that a schema has been tapped. Therefore, cognitive therapy techniques that utilize formal operations will be rendered almost useless if used alone at these times.

For example, "Wendy" believed that she was a "bad" person, and seemed hell-bent on proving this fact to her therapist. The therapist, in turn, attempted to use Socratic questioning (which presupposed that the patient could engage in formal logic or metathought) in order to help Wendy challenge her deleterious suppositions about herself. The therapist asked Wendy for evidence in support of her "I am bad" schema (an extreme version of the unlovability schema). Wendy proceeded to list a number of relatively minor faults. Then the therapist asked Wendy to name a person that she believed was "good." After naming her friend Pam, the therapist then asked if Pam had any of these "faults" that Wendy had listed for herself as evidence of her badness. Wendy admitted that Pam seemed to have all of these flawed qualities as well. The therapist believed that she had achieved a breakthrough—after all, she had just demonstrated that Pam had the same human failings as Wendy, yet Pam was "good." Surely now, the therapist thought, Wendy would use her powers of formal logic to see that she must be judging herself irrationally harshly. Instead, Wendy exclaimed, "What's your point here? Don't you get it? I'm *bad!*" The therapist was forced to confront the fact that Wendy's ability to engage in formal operations was seriously impaired *in response to the activated schema.*

Consistent with this clinical vignette, Rosen (1985) has explained that although patients may have developed to a stage of formal operations, they may not utilize this higher order cognitive style in all domains of their lives. He adds that patients are most likely to fail to activate their full cognitive capabilities in those areas of life that involve emotional and interpersonal strife. Thus, we see patients who may be quite logical in discussing financial matters, but who may regress to lower order cognitive processes when experiencing marital discord. Extrapolating from this, we say that BPD patients may no longer believe that they control the moon because it appears to move along with them, and they may not believe that an object ceases to exist if it goes out of sight. Nevertheless, there are significant remnants of prelogical thinking that still exist in their personal areas of vulnerability—where early maladaptive schemas come into play.

Sensory-Motor Stage (0 to 2 Years Old)

A central characteristic of the sensory-motor stage is profound egocentrism. By *egocentrism* Piaget does not mean selfishness but, rather, a deficiency in differentiating subject from object. Most fundamentally, the baby does not perceive the physical boundaries between itself and the mother. To progress from this stage, children must undergo a "Copernican revolution" (Rosen, 1985, 1989) in which they begin to realize that they are neither the whole universe nor even the center of the universe. In the BPD patient, this revolution is incomplete. It manifests itself in the BPD patients' tendency to enmesh with others, whereby they become extremely dependent on others for all of their basic emotional needs. Likewise, it is seen in the BPD patients' fears that they will lose their identities if they become intimately involved with others.

Borderline patients also often demonstrate a sense of entitlement that is born of cognitive egocentrism. They tend to see themselves as the focus of others' attention, and expect that they will be given special personal consideration. These patients believe that others will *want* to satisfy their needs, and they assume that their own wishes and the wishes of others are one and the same. For example, a BPD patient may wish to go to a particular restaurant and may assume that her date wants to go there as well. When the date suggests an alternative place for dinner, the BPD patient may become outraged. This may seem incomprehensible to the date, but it is understandable from the phenomenology of the patient. Here, the patient expected that the date would agree to the same thing that she wanted. When this expectation was confounded, it meant that the date was *deliberately* denying her something he "knew" she wanted. Further, the patient's unlovability schema may have been aroused. After all, from the patient's point of view, someone who cared would always be able to know how to (and want to) satisfy the patient's each and every need, spoken and unspoken.

The therapist witnesses this egocentrism in the form of the BPD patients' demands for special appointment times or repeated calls at all hours of the night. The BPD patients in such cases often do not consider that what is convenient for them may not be convenient for their therapists. Such cognitive deficits lead to major rifts in the patients' relationships outside of therapy as well.

Egocentrism appears in speech as well. In the same way that a child often does not understand the needs of the listener, BPD patients frequently fail to provide vital information that is needed to be understood. This is manifested in the BPD patients' tendency to engage in mind-reading and to expect that significant others and the therapists can read their minds as well. Needless to say, this leads to many instances of miscommunication, thus adding further frustration and strife in the relationships of BPD patients.

Likewise, BPD patients have difficulty understanding points of view that differ from their own. We have been struck by the numerous times that we as therapists will painstakingly explain our conceptualizations of the patients' problems, only to be met with blank stares or the curt question, "What do you mean?"

All of the cognitive deficits that we describe in this section vary from case to case, depending on the level of severity of the borderline disorder. In other words, the degrees to which different patients will engage in prelogical thought lie on a continuum. Those cases that we refer to as "low functioning" demonstrate a greater preponderance of primitive processing than those cases that are higher functioning. Therefore, we emphasize that the BPD qualities that we describe under the rubric of "sensory-motor" cognitive processing occur with much more frequency in the lower functioning BPD patients.

Many BPD patients are similar to the sensory-motor child in that they have difficulty empathizing with others. They are acutely aware of their own needs, so much so that it precludes their attending to the needs of others. Additionally, they do not readily understand other people's differing views but instead believe that others must see things the way the patients themselves do. Therefore, BPD patients frequently project their intentions onto others. For example, a BPD patient who is both fearful and needy in a newly formed love relationship may falsely conclude that the significant other is fearful of intimacy and wants to break up, when in reality it is the patient who is the one looking to escape.

Borderline schemas strongly influence these patients' processing of information. The fact that they feel something makes it self-evident and factual to them. They forget, misinterpret, or fail to attend to life events that are contrary to their core beliefs about themselves and others. Borderline patients are prone to negative tunnel vision—they have difficulty seeing alternative, more positive explanations for events.

Another characteristic of the sensory-motor stage that parallels BPD perceptual processing is the relative absence of object permanence. Objects, including people, that are out of view are assumed by the sensory-motor child to no longer exist. This often triggers separation anxiety in the very young child. In the adult BPD patient, these perceptions are manifested as abandonment panic. Relatively minor situations of separation can activate abandonment schemas, leading to intense, negative, dysfunctional reactions. Our patient Helen had an argument with her lover in a park. When he walked away, she experienced a torrent of emotion. As the man rounded a curve and moved out of the patient's sight, Helen feared that the relationship had been lost forever. With the lover out of sight, Helen was not able to consider the possibility of reconciliation, and she became suicidal.

Another patient of ours, "Eric," demonstrated similar problems with object (person) permanence. One day, he left an unopened can of soda in his female therapist's office. Although their next appointment was not to be held for another week, the therapist deliberately left the can of soda in its place until the following week. When Eric returned, the therapist pointed out that he had left his soda in the office, and that she had left it as it was. As predicted, this was a very meaningful event for the patient. When he got teary-eyed, the therapist initiated a discussion about Eric's fears of "lack of permanence in relationships." She added that the can of soda was a symbolic gesture that said that she would be there for Eric, even if she wasn't always in sight or reachable by phone. The therapist's understanding of the patient's abandonment schema enabled her to find a creative way to solidify the therapeutic relationship, while at the same time raising the issue of the need for appropriate degrees of separation in relationships.

Preoperational Stage (2 to 7 Years Old)

Symbolic and representational thought begin to emerge during this period, with children starting to be able to comprehend (imperfectly) the notions of past and future. "Centering" is a characteristic of preoperational thought in which the child focuses on only one aspect of an object or an event and is unable to deal with two or more simultaneously changing or interacting characteristics. For example, a child at this stage of cognitive development is fooled into believing that the amount of water in a tall, thin jar is greater than that in a short, wide jar, even though the *same* amount of water was poured backed and forth between the two jars. The child is aware of the dimension of height, but is unable to consider the second dimension of width in calculating the volume of water.

In the adult BPD patient, centering appears in a number of ways. One cognitive manifestation is the phenomenon of overgeneralization, whereby different situations or people that share one common element are regarded erroneously as being equivalent. This is seen most dramatically in the therapeutic relationship when BPD patients reenact child–parent conflicts with their therapists, solely on the basis of the fact that the therapists share the parental characteristic of being guiding authorities in the lives of the patients. Transference overgeneralizations provide therapists with rich material for schema identification. At the same time, it is important that therapists help their BPD patients to learn to *differentiate* the therapeutic relationship (and other significant relationships) appropriately from the child–parent relationship.

Consequences of centering also can be seen when patients mistakenly equate sex with intimacy and love. Once again, one element is held in common between the two. Sexual relationships and love relationships both may involve intercourse. However, the two situations may not share commitment, intimate conversation, and trust. Whereas a patient may regard sex and intimacy as identical, the sex partner may not. Accordingly, we maintain that one of the reasons that some BPD patients are characterized by numerous stormy relationships is that the BPD patients continuously search for love by engaging in sex with a succession of partners. When the partners do not necessarily show the same assumption of long-term commitment, the BPD patients feel betrayed and abandoned, which leads to interpersonal conflict and reinforces the patients' schemas of mistrust, unlovability, and abandonment.

Another characteristic of young preoperational children is an inability to seriate. They struggle to order objects along quantitative dimensions (e.g., larger to smaller, longer to shorter). They make few, if any, stepwise shadings or gradations. This process of thinking appears in the adult BPD patient in the following ways:

1. *Dichotomous, black-and-white thinking,* in which things are either all or nothing, is an example of the inability to seriate.
2. *Catastrophic thinking* and perfectionism also are examples of dichotomous thinking. Patients who catastrophize frequently call their therapists in states of "crisis" that may seem trivial to others (e.g., a patient who called her therapist in a suicidal state as a result of a "bad haircut").
3. *Perfectionism* is witnessed in the BPD patient who wants a "perfect love," or else life is deemed to be meaningless.

Because schemas are by nature all-or-nothing propositions, the BPD patients' difficulties in seriating tend to support these maladaptive core beliefs. A central task of therapy, therefore, involves teaching BPD patients to judge situations, people, feelings, and other variables on *continua*. If successful in learning this skill, BPD patients will be less prone to make such cognitive mistakes as judging themselves to be totally unlovable, or others to be completely untrustworthy.

A further characteristic of preoperational children's thinking can be seen in the unsystematic nature of their logic. Preoperational children use transductive reasoning, which is neither inductive nor deductive, neither moving from the general to the specific nor moving from the specific to the general. In classifying objects, they may start to group according to one characteristic and then shift midstream to classify by another characteristic. In this way, they move from the specific to the specific. This pattern of thinking accounts for the adult BPD patients' deficits in generalizing conclusions properly from one situation to a similar new situation. In therapy, conclusions drawn from discussions and homework assignments must be repeated over and over again by therapists.

As a result of transductive reasoning, BPD patients often are slow to learn from their painful mistakes and failures. Instead, they tend to repeat the same maladaptive patterns again and again. Similarly, they do not readily learn from positive experiences that might otherwise lead them to become more hopeful and empowered in choosing new directions in life. Therapists who work with such patients must ask them frequently, "What is the main *principle* that you have learned from this situation, and how can you apply this knowledge to similar situations in the future?"

Transductive reasoning also helps to account for the rapid vacillation between different schemas that is seen in BPD patients. As one schema is activated, the patient may be propelled to act in a particular direction (e.g., approach). At this point, another schema may become activated that produces motivation to act in the opposite direction (e.g., avoid). This roller coaster ride of acting and negating actions is emotionally draining for both BPD patients and their significant others. Unfortunately, this does not compel the BPD patients to reconsider or ponder their modes of operation in the same way that it would an individual who is processing information at a more sophisticated level.

An additional characteristic of the preoperational child is "affective realism." The child believes that if one feels something, then it must be true. A rather clear connection can be drawn between affective realism and what has been called "emotional reasoning" (Burns, 1980) in an adult. This is especially dangerous in the BPD patient, as such patients often "feel" that life is not worth living and may impulsively conclude that suicide is the only answer. This phenomenon is particularly striking when the patient's emotions vacillate. A BPD patient may be content one day, suicidal the next day, and happily taking a trip the next day. Each day is a new "reality" for such a patient. Therefore, another important goal of therapy with BPD patients is for the patients to investigate and construe the realities of their life situations *apart from their acute emotional states*.

We must reiterate an important point at this time. The aforementioned cognitive deficits that BPD patients exhibit *manifest themselves when schemas are activated*. It is, perhaps, impossible to teach a preoperational child the skills of formal logic. However, it is quite possible to teach a BPD patient such adaptive cognitive skills, because the patient likely is utilizing those very skills of formal logic in nonschema areas of life or when schemas are dormant (i.e., the patient does not feel vulnerable). *The therapist's task is to help the patient to generalize advanced cognitive skills from nonschematic domains of life to schematic areas.*

We now present the final two stages of Piagetian cognitive processing. These stages, concrete operations and formal operations, represent the skills that therapists endeavor to help their BPD patients to develop, practice, and utilize in the areas of the schemas.

Concrete Operations (7 to 11 Years Old)
and Formal Operations (12 Years Old to Adulthood)

Concrete operations are characterized by the ability of the child to produce internal thought that is consistent and logical. The formal operational child not only thinks logically but can produce theories based on collected data. In addition, formal operational thought includes the ability to think about thinking, which is known more formally as *metathought*. By contrast, BPD patients who are dealing with schema-based reactions seldom think about their thinking, rarely review their strategies of reasoning, and neglect to draw conclusions that are consistent with the overall data. These characteristics of thinking make cognitive therapy—with its emphasis on self-monitoring and modification of ingrained, maladaptive thoughts— a challenging proposition for BPD patients. On the other hand, cognitive therapy forces BPD patients to stretch their cognitive capacities and to transcend the "immature" status quo.

As children move from concrete to formal operations, their processing becomes less tied to actual situations and becomes freer to consider the possible—the hypothetical. They are able to entertain thoughts about how things could be different and how to achieve these changes. Again, by contrast, BPD patients are hard pressed to imagine how their schema-based reactions could ever be different. They generally do not explore hypothetical new possibilities for their lives, instead clinging to familiar but dysfunctional patterns. One patient, "Trudy," professed to be unable to imagine how she might present herself as a less cynical and caustic conversationalist. Even when the therapist wrote a script for her to read (one in which she would speak in a friendly and confident manner), Trudy could not progress beyond the first sentence. She wanted to be more lovable, but she simply could not and would not allow herself to perceive herself any differently than she already was, and she refused to go on with the exercise. Thus, Trudy was forced to acknowledge her resistance to change—a breakthrough in and of itself—as she previously had maintained that her problems were outside of herself.

Table 2.2 shows the parallels between Piagetian stages and borderline characteristics.

Assimilation and Accommodation

Assimilation occurs when new external information is sorted and stored into mental categories or "cubbyholes" that already exist (analogous to schemas of the structural sort). The outside stimuli seem to fit the internal organizing structures; therefore, there is no need for change. On the other hand, accommodation occurs when the incoming information will not fit readily into the mental categories as they exist. This necessitates a change in the mental "structures" (schemas) themselves, an adaptive reaction when schemas are maladaptive and information is positive. For many BPD

Table 2.2. Parallels and Differences between Piagetian Stages and Borderline Characteristics

Piagetian Stages	Cognitive Characteristics	Corresponding Borderline Characteristics
Sensory-motor	Egocentrism	• Enmeshment • Fear of engulfment • Fear of loss of identity • Dependency • Sense of entitlement • Assumed clarity of speech
	Lack of empathy	• Lack of awareness of others' needs • Lack of awareness of effect on others • Excessive demands on others
	Lack of object permanence	• Abandonment fears
Preoperational	Centering	• Overgeneralization • Confusion of the "then" with the "now" • Confusion of sex and intimacy
	Lack of ability to seriate	• Dichotomous thinking • Catastrophizing • Perfectionism
	Transductive reasoning	• Lack of ability to learn from mistakes • Vacillation between opposing schemas
	Affective realism	• Emotional reasoning
Piagetian Stages	Cognitive Characteristics	Dissimilar Borderline Characteristics
Concrete and formal operations	Logical thinking Theoretical thinking Metathought	• Lack of deductive and inductive reasoning • Lack of theory construction • Lack of metathought • Lack of ability to see alternatives • Lack of ability to see hypotheticals

patients, however, the confrontation between schemas and discrepant external information does not lead to accommodation. Instead, the schemas demand complete assimilation, thus discrediting potentially useful environmental feedback and reinforcing primitive, negative core beliefs about the self, others, and the future. It therefore becomes imperative for therapists to assist their BPD patients in learning to reconcile conflicts between positive facts and negative schemas by redefining their most deeply held beliefs. This involves a long and arduous process in treatment, making use of many of the techniques and strategies that follow in successive chapters of this volume.

Implications for Therapy

Therapists must bear in mind the patients' deficiencies in cognitive processing when introducing interventions. Early in therapy, techniques such as the use of Socratic questioning and guided discovery (see Chapter 4) may have no therapeutic impact if the patients are not yet adept at utilizing formal operations (Rosen, 1989). The woman presented earlier (Wendy) who demonstrated the "I am bad" schema is a case in point. Logical discourse alone was ineffective in helping this patient to reconsider her negative core beliefs about herself. In dealing with such BPD patients early in treatment, it is necessary to emphasize methods that communicate professional involvement and positive regard. Although it is a truism that the establishment of a healthy therapeutic relationship is important in all cases, we emphatically state that this is of paramount importance (and difficulty) in the initial stages of treatment with BPD patients.

In addition, until the BPD patients learn to use formal logic more consistently, therapists may need to be more directive than they might ordinarily be with other patients. When we say "directive" we do not mean that the therapists act in a bossy manner with their BPD patients, telling them everything that they should do in a patronizing fashion. Rather, we mean that therapists must carefully spell out their clinical hypotheses to the patients, then ask for feedback and discussion. In this way, therapists may stimulate the BPD patients' thinking without necessarily having to wait for them to arrive at adaptive conclusions that may be outside their cognitive grasp. At the same time, therapists who ask for feedback, summary statements, and collaborative discussion avoid the trap of allowing the patients to remain as passive recipients of information that they likely will distort anyhow. The following brief dialogue serves as an example:

T: "Ben," it seems to me that each time we begin to talk about times you've had success at school or at work, you tend to change the subject.

P: Yeah, so?

T: (Rather than Socratically asking, "What does this suggest to you?"—the type of question that typically elicits a disdainful "I don't know!" from Ben, the therapist directively states ...) Do you think it might suggest that you are either uncomfortable with focusing on your success, or that you are ignoring the information altogether, or that you don't believe what I'm saying? Do any of those reasons strike a chord with you?

P: (Sarcastically) You're my therapist. I pay you to say nice things about me. It doesn't mean shit.

T: So you think that my focusing on your successes is insincere?

P: Hey, it's not your fault. You've got to do what you've got to do.

T: But you're still unconvinced that my focusing on your successes has any merit, right?

P: I'm a failure, goddammit! And you're not going to shrink my brain into thinking otherwise.

T: Ben, my goal is not to shrink your brain, and my goal is not to patronize you, nor is it to convince you of things of which you don't want to be convinced. I'm glad that you're being honest with me about the way you feel. It helps me to understand you better, and I appreciate it. I'm interested in hearing about the events in your life that seem to have proved to you that you're a failure. Would you feel comfortable talking about this? I really want to understand what you've gone through in life that makes you feel so strongly about this issue.

Notice that in the foregoing example, the therapist does the following:

1. Focuses the patient's attention on a maladaptive response
2. Provides a clinical hypothesis
3. Avoids arguing with the patient (but doesn't agree, either)
4. Asks the patient for his opinion
5. Subtly interjects a compliment
6. Provides support and empathy
7. Entreats the patient to provide more information pertinent to the incompetency schema

In sum, the therapist was directive, nurtured the relationship, set the stage for the gathering of more information, but did not demand that the patient engage in formal cognitive operations at this stage. The therapist in this example chose to postpone the use of cognitive restructuring techniques until later in treatment. Little by little, the therapist hopes to provide a safe enough environment, combined with a few thought-provoking hypotheses, toward the goal of teaching the patient to engage in and practice higher order cognitive skills (the likes of which will be discussed in successive chapters).

SUMMARY

This chapter has focused on the following developmental issues in the conceptualization of BPD:

1. The content of schemas
2. The Eriksonian stage model of schema development
3. The perceptual channels through which developing children incorporate schema-producing information
4. The Piagetian model of successive levels of cognitive sophistication in developing children, as they pertain to the dysfunctional cognitive styles of BPD patients

An important responsibility of the therapist is to identify the schemas that fuel the BPD patients' maladaptive thoughts, emotions, and behaviors. Examination of the themes in the current life crises of the BPD patients, along with an exploration of the critical incidents of their developmental years will help the therapist identify the content of the schemas.

The Eriksonian model is a useful heuristic in discovering the nature and the chronology of various negative experiences in the patients' lives that have fostered the formation of early maladaptive schemas. In general, we propose that the earlier the traumas (i.e., the earlier the Eriksonian level of development), the more compelling and pervasive the resultant schemas will be. This, in turn, will partly determine the degree of difficulty in working with a given BPD patient. As a caveat to the Eriksonian stage model (which presents specific developmental issues at discrete stages), we have found that the unlovability schema seems to transcend stages and may arise out of crises at any point in childhood or adolescence.

The therapists' choices of interventions are partly governed by the sensory channels (e.g., verbal, imaginal, or "the cloud") through which the patients received and stored schema-related information. For example, if information is stored linguistically, then verbal techniques will be efficacious. If the schema information is stored primarily in the form of mental pictures, then imagery techniques will play an important role in treatment. Schema information based in "the cloud" is the hardest to identify and to modify, requiring therapeutic ingenuity and creativity (e.g., using a blanket to warm a patient whose "cloud" involves becoming cold, numb, and amnestic as a result of schema activation). As schema information and memories often are stored across more than one sensory channel, a great diversity of techniques may be called for.

Finally, the Piagetian model of cognitive development is useful in understanding the areas of cognitive unsophistication on the parts of BPD patients. Therapists endeavor to use techniques that are within the cognitive conceptual grasp of the BPD patient, and try to teach the patient (over the course of treatment) to develop higher order cognitive skills in order to improve coping and all-around adaptive functioning. Typically, it is those areas of problematic functioning that are identified by a troubled stage of Eriksonian development in which cognitive processing is most rudimentary. Therefore, if a BPD patient suffers from an incompetency schema as a result of early negative experiences in grade school, we can expect that he will be prone to prelogical thinking regarding his sense of adequacy and capabilities in adulthood.

Furthermore, the intense negative emotions that are stimulated as a result of schema activation tend to inhibit the patient's use of formal logic to solve his or her problems. Therapists must be prepared to spot and address the BPD patient's "affective realism" (emotional reasoning) at such times.

In sum, a longitudinal understanding of the critical events and perceptions of the patients' lives, and their impact on the patients' core beliefs and cognitive development, is a vital aspect of cognitive therapy with BPD patients.

PART TWO
Clinical Applications

Chapter 3
Case Conceptualization

The cognitive therapy of BPD begins with a conceptualization of the patient's problems and general modes of operation in living. To understand BPD patients satisfactorily, therapists must assess not only their patients' automatic thoughts and concomitant behaviors and distressing emotions, but their underlying assumptions and schemas as well. We agree with Young (1990) that the most frequently encountered schemas in BPD patients are those of:

1. Unlovability/defectiveness/badness
2. Incompetence
3. Mistrust
4. Abandonment
5. Lack of individuation
6. Dependency

When patients demonstrate numerous schemas, and when these schemas are compelling and pervasive in the patients' lives, it is likely that the patients' functioning will be highly impaired, especially if they possess relatively few compensatory strengths such as intelligence, social support networks, and economic stability.

In general, BPD patients have some basic core features in common. For example, it is typical for BPD patients to believe that they are "bad" or unlovable and that they are inept in dealing with the major tasks they confront in everyday life. They regularly wreak havoc in their personal relationships by alternating between loving and hating, trusting and suspecting, wanting and fearing, and pursuing and rejecting their friends, family, and lovers. In addition, they frequently present with crises, which may represent either exaggerated reactions to objectively mild stressors and/ or realistic self-imposed threats to their safety and health.

However, as we have mentioned, BPD patients are a diverse lot. Therapists must go beyond the common characteristics mentioned here (and in DSM-III-R) to understand each BPD patient idiographically. In order to achieve this end, therapists must attempt to solicit a great deal of information about the individual BPD patient. We say *attempt* to solicit because BPD patients may be highly reluctant to divulge the most important facts about their lives to therapists in whom they have not yet established the requisite amount of trust. Also, the traumatic backgrounds frequently encountered in BPD patients often render them virtually amnestic with regard to critical incidents in their lives. These incidents, such as early childhood abandonment or abuse, are crucial to understand and to discuss in therapy if the BPD patient is to receive the optimal individualized care.

Starting from the first session, therapists should work assiduously to obtain information from the patients about the following aspects of their lives:

1. Family history of mental disorder, substance or alcohol abuse, and suicide
2. Details about their family structure, such as:
   a. Birth order
   b. Circumstances surrounding the patient's birth (e.g., was the patient adopted, unwanted, fatherless?)
   c. Parental divorces, remarriages, strife, violence
   d. Persons living with the patient in the household
   e. Significant separations from loved ones
3. Quality of relationships with each parent or with other important caregivers
4. Episodes of emotional, physical, or sexual abuse while growing up (also other traumatic events, such as rape, untimely deaths of loved ones, unwanted pregnancies, and other forms of victimization or sources of extreme guilt)
5. Memories of school years, including peer relations, sense of competency, years of education

(*Note:* For assessment items 1 through 5, it is important to ascertain the patients' *ages* at times when critical incidents occurred. This helps in the formulation of hypotheses about the developmental issues and schemas discussed in Chapter 2. See Tables 3.1 and 3.2.)

6. Role of religion in the patient's upbringing
7. Employment history (stability, appropriateness to level of education and intelligence, sense of direction and progression, quality of interpersonal relations with co-workers, employers, and employees)
8. Significant romantic relationships (frequency; longevity; common patterns in establishing, maintaining, and ending such relationships)

Table 3.1. Critical Life Events: Hypothesized Developmental Issues

Name of patient:

Critical event (description):

Chronological age(s):
Eriksonian stage/task:

Piagetian level of cognitive operations:

Perceptual channels involved:

Schemas:

Associated beliefs:

Table 3.2. Critical Life Events: Hypothesized Developmental Issues

Name of Patient: "Sally"

Critical event (description): Patient was adopted shortly after birth. Within months, she was removed from the home of her adoptive parents due to the illness of the father. Months later, this happened again with the next family.

Chronological age(s): 0–1 year of age

Eriksonian stage/task: Trust versus mistrust

Piagetian level of cognitive operations: Sensory-motor

Perceptual channels involved: "The Cloud" (kinesthetic, visual, olfactory)

Schemas: Mistrust, abandonment, unlovability

Associated beliefs:
1. Men will leave me and I'll be all alone.
2. I can't count on people to keep their promises to me.
3. I have to take any and all measures to make certain that people are being honest with me.
4. I have to take any and all measures to make certain that people will not leave me.
5. Men never stay commited to me because I'm defective.
6. People lie to me because they don't care about me.
7. I can't tolerate being apart from the person I love.

9. History of use and abuse of psychoactive substances (alcohol, nicotine, prescription medications, over-the-counter medications, illicit drugs)
10. Legal difficulties
11. Medical history (illnesses, accidents, chronic conditions) and psychiatric history (number of treatments, settings, progress, medications)
12. Current life situation:
    a. Common daily routines
    b. Quantity and quality of friendships
    c. Marital status, quality of marriage
    d. Employment status, satisfaction with job
    e. General stressors
    f. Hobbies
13. Analysis of the patient's *strengths* and *compensatory strategies* (e.g., intelligence, creativity, ambition, kindness toward children, willingness to engage in self-improvement programs, success in attracting friends, and others)
14. Mood states and suicidality in the present
15. Automatic thoughts that emerge spontaneously in everyday life and in therapy sessions
16. Patient's current assessment of:
    a. Self-worth and the worth of other people
    b. The meaning of his or her life
    c. Views of the future (the *cognitive triad;* Beck, 1976)
17. The *patient's* evaulation of how developmental/longitudinal items 1 through 11 have translated into present-time items 12 through 16.

To obtain and organize all of this information into a thorough, internally consistent case conceptualization requires much diligence. It may take the therapist many months to obtain sufficient data to understand the patient and to ascertain the operative schemas. This does not mean that meaningful therapeutic work cannot be done in the interim; on the contrary, many BPD patients have benefited from learning some standard coping skills—such as rational responding, scheduling activities, increasing mastery and pleasure in daily activities, and assertiveness—*before* significant schema work has begun in earnest. Once the therapist and patient have succeeded in organizing and understanding the 17 points listed previously, however, they greatly multiply their chances of making significant and lasting changes through therapy.

The following is a sample case conceptualization that incorporates most of the 17 points that are pertinent to this particular patient. Drawn from our case files, with details altered to preserve the anonymity of the patient, this profile is constructed on the basis of information from the intake report as well as a year's worth of therapy sessions.

CASE EVALUATION (THE CASE OF "HALLIE")

Objective Measures at Intake

Beck Depression Inventory: 34 (severe depression)
Beck Anxiety Inventory: 35 (severe anxiety)
Hopelessness Scale: 11 (moderate to severe hopelessness)

Objective Measures after One Year of Weekly Sessions

Beck Depression Inventory: 11 (mild depression)
Beck Anxiety Inventory: 8 (mild anxiety)
Hopelessness Scale: 4 (mild hopelessness)

Presenting Problems at Intake

Hallie is a 28-year-old, previously married woman who holds a college degree. She works as a free-lance journalist and photographer and lives alone. When she initially entered treatment, she complained of a pervasive depression and sense of agitation and dread that had plagued her since adolescence. She claimed that she had no idea why she felt this way, although she was able to link the onset of her mood disorder to her first sexual relationship. This man rejected her shortly after they became sexually involved. In the present, she stated that she was very confused about her direction in life and that she was disturbed by her inability to like herself or control her moods. She admitted that she often scratched herself on the arms and legs until she bled whenever she would feel overwhelmed with dysphoria, anxiety, anger, and/or shame.

Along with these affective symptoms Hallie experienced severe tension head-aches, difficulty breathing, and frequent laryngitis. Behaviorally, she often withdrew to her "study" at home, where she would alternately compose and destroy new works of fiction. She was able to earn a living through her photography and journalistic reports, but her real desire was to become a poet and novelist. Nevertheless, her attempts to write fiction led only to self-hatred and avoidance of social interaction.

When asked about her automatic thoughts and general beliefs when she felt dysphoric, Hallie was able to identify the following:

"I hate myself."
"I'm a fake, a sham."
"I'll ultimately sabotage anything good in my life."
"I've wasted my talents."
"I'm out of control."

"Who could possibly love such a basket case?"
"I'm frightened by anyone who appreciates me."
"I'd rather hurt myself first before somebody else gets the chance to do it to me."

It was of note that Hallie reported all of this through a curious mixture of crying and laughter. Eye contact was minimal.

Medical History

Hallie reported that she had recently had a complete medical workup as a result of her headaches, and all results were within normal limits. She reported no known allergies to foods or medications. She had suffered from no serious illnesses or injuries in her life, although she had some superficial scars from her scratching.

Hallie sought treatment from a psychiatrist at the age of 17 following the breakup of her first relationship. In addition to focusing on her sense of unlovability and abandonment, she surprised herself by admitting for the first time that she harbored a great deal of anger toward her parents. She also reported that although she felt ashamed of her sexual activity, she never felt comfortable enough to discuss this with her therapist. At the age of 23, following her divorce (after a one-year marriage), she sought treatment with a psychologist. Again, her main source of distress seemed to be her sense of utter rejection and worthlessness. At this point, however, she also had begun to withdraw from people and to scratch herself as a response to emotional upset. Three years later, she entered therapy with another psychiatrist who prescribed a tricyclic antidepressant medication for a period of six months.

Hallie was unaware of any particular pattern in these treatments until the current therapist asked her to reflect on the common elements of her psychotherapy history. In each case she dealt with themes of abandonment, unlovability, incompetence, and mistrust. Furthermore, she tended to terminate prematurely rather than get into issues regarding her sexuality. Hallie inevitably relapsed within weeks of ending her therapy sessions, but she would never contact her doctors thereafter.

Hallie denied ever having any serious intentions of killing herself, although she did admit to fantasizing about the way that she would ultimately die.

Historical/Developmental Information

Hallie was the youngest of four children born to a religious Catholic couple. She remembered her father, now deceased, as having been very punitive. Her mother alternated between being very loving and supportive and being irritable and critical.

As a youngster, Hallie enjoyed school and did very well. When she was in third and fourth grade, however, her grades plummeted for a period, which led to her parents becoming more critical and punishing. Hallie's talents for writing and photography became apparent when she started secondary school. She recalled that her mother often gave her a confusing mixed message. On the one hand, the mother extolled the virtues of being a top-notch student. On the other hand, she told Hallie never to show off her abilities to others, lest they become jealous and hateful toward her. This led to Hallie's becoming more reclusive in school, as she wanted to perform well but believed she had to maintain a very low profile. Later in adolescence, the patient's mother was horrified to see that Hallie's writings and photos contained strong sexual themes. The mother made it clear to Hallie that such activity and thinking were sinful. Hallie came to believe that she was bad because she found that she could not bring herself to cease infusing sexual imagery into her works.

When she was 22 years old, Hallie married a co-worker at the newspaper where she worked. The marriage was very brief and very stormy. She blamed the deterioration of her marriage on her depression and on her husband's professional jealousy. Since then she had been involved with four men, three of whom she believed had never had intentions of long-term commitment, and the fourth of whom she was seeing as she entered the present treatment at the Center for Cognitive Therapy.

During the course of cognitive therapy, a number of other vital historical facts came to light that led to a new understanding of the patient's chronic symptoms of depression and BPD. First, Hallie admitted that she was still haunted by an abortion that she had during the last months of her marriage. At the time, she rightly foresaw the end of her marital relationship and decided to terminate her pregnancy rather than give birth to a child into a ready-made broken home. Although the patient had disavowed her family's strict Catholic beliefs, she continued to have flashbacks and an overwhelming sense of guilt, badness, and the "necessity of suffering."

Another compelling and startling revelation was that Hallie had been repeatedly sexually molested by her uncle when she was 7 to 8 years of age, a fact that she had kept to herself all these years. Hallie cried to the current therapist, "My parents told me never to trust strangers. But they never warned me about my own relatives. Why?"

Case Conceptualization

Despite her intelligence and creativity, Hallie was the black sheep of her family. Her talents represented a double-edged sword: She was asked to perform well as a student—but not *too* well, as this might bring the wrath of the less gifted upon her— and not to stray from conventional, conservative work lest she fall from grace. Hallie alternated between isolative underachievement (which disappointed herself and her parents alike) and avant-garde demonstrations of precocity and brilliance that were roundly chastised as "bad" and "blasphemous." To this day, she strives for success but destroys much of her work before anyone ever has the chance to see it. In this manner, her schemas of incompetence and badness do battle with each other in cyclical fashion. In order to build a good therapeutic relationship, the present therapist will need to show a genuine interest in Hallie's writings and photos, and to encourage and accept her artistic expressions.

Hallie's experiences of sexual abuse were particularly devastating (Table 3.3). Her trust in her family (and in her sense of safety among "loved ones") was badly damaged, including her trust in her parents for failing to warn her, to see what was going on, or to protect her. Hallie's experiences, frightening though they were, led her to become preoccupied with sexual thoughts at an age when she was ill prepared to cope with or understand the concomitant emotions. Her grades in school took a nose dive, which only compounded problems as she received further criticism from others and herself alike. Her schemas of "badness," mistrust, and incompetence were taking shape and solidifying at this time. As her abusive uncle had threatened to hurt her if she told anyone what was going on, she could not receive corrective and supportive feedback from others, and she continued to believe the worst and to feel confused and unsafe. Later, the patient was able to see how her breathlessness and laryngitis problems in the present were associated with her involuntary physiological reactions to the sexual abuse and her attempts to "keep the horrible secret," respectively, in the past.

Table 3.3. Critical Life Events: Hypothesized Developmental Issues

---

Name of patient: "Hallie"

Critical event (description): Patient was sexually molested by an uncle who tricked her into sex play. This occurred on a number of occasions and may have involved sexual intercourse. The patient was very confused, scared, and alone with her "bad secret."

Chronological age(s): Age 7

Eriksonian stage/task: Industry versus inferiority

Piagetian level of cognitive operations: Preoperational to concrete operations

Perceptual channels involved: Verbal, kinesthetic, visual

Schemas: Incompetence, unlovability/"badness" (also mistrust)

Associated beliefs:
1. I hate myself.
2. I'm a fake.
3. Nobody could ever love me.
4. I'm a basket case.
5. Anyone who cares about me or shows appreciation for me is scary. Such a person could hurt me very badly.
6. I should hurt myself.
7. I'm a disgusting person who has disgusting thoughts.

Her first consensual sexual relationship was a further source of schema reinforcement for Hallie. Although she initially believed that the relationship was "good," she
quickly condemned herself when the boyfriend lost interest. Instead of finding a
fulfilling outlet for her sexual desires, Hallie had found abandonment and a reminder that sex was "bad."

When Hallie married, her hopes were heightened yet again. Unfortunately, the
specter of her mother's beliefs about "being hated by others who envy your talents"
arose when her husband could not cope with her journalistic success. Hallie blamed
herself once again: for hurting her husband, for disobeying her mother's edicts, and
for sabotaging a relationship that she valued. This further convinced her that she did
not deserve to succeed, that interpersonal rejection was inevitable, that she was a bad
person, and that her mother was right about everything. Shortly thereafter, when she
made the agonizing decision to have an abortion, her sense of badness deepened.
Her self-harming habit of scratching herself also began after the divorce.

In the years that ensued, her schemas of unlovability and badness showed
themselves in her reluctance to become involved with men who demonstrated
serious emotional involvement. Unfortunately, this fed into her schema of mistrust,
as she believed that the uncommitted men she did date simply were using her for
sex. Hallie's tendency to stifle and destroy her own creative works because of their
sexual content led to an exacerbated schema of incompetence, and she began to
despair of ever realizing her artistic potential. Her avoidance of close relationships,
her ambivalence about her current boyfriend, and her habit of terminating therapy
prematurely all were examples of the patient's attempts to protect herself from
abandonment. As a result, her personal life was arid, unstimulating, and unfulfill-
ing, and her schema of unlovability strengthened. It was no wonder that Hallie was
so deeply and chronically depressed, yet she seemed to have little understanding of
her problems at the start of cognitive therapy.

POSTSCRIPT TO CONCEPTUALIZATION

The foregoing case formulation provides a blueprint for the course of cognitive
therapy. The patient's basic maladaptive assumptions and schemas are well elucidated, and the therapist is able to understand, appreciate, and empathize with the
patient in an accurate way. In addition, both the patient and the therapist are in a
better position to make sense of (and change) the otherwise confusing and self-
defeating patterns in the patient's functioning. Furthermore, the review of past
traumatic events helps that therapist to anticipate when therapeutic interactions
might inadvertently inspire fear and avoidance in the patient. For example, a
therapist who is aware that his BPD patient had been raped repeatedly by a man who
said to the victimized patient, "Now just relax and I won't hurt you," would
understand the inadvisability of suddenly suggesting a relaxation induction as a
means to cope with acute anxiety.

Properties of Schemas

The case conceptualization also demonstrates the pernicious ways in which schemas operate in the BPD patient. As typified by Hallie, the core beliefs that BPD patients steadfastly maintain often conflict with each other, a phenomenon we call *schema antagonism*. For example, Hallie believed that she was a fraud as a writer, a point of view over which she agonized. When she found the courage to allow herself to write with creative abandon, however, she became horrifed by the erotic nature of her poetry and prose. Her sense of badness discouraged her from engaging in the very activity in which she demonstrated the most talent, thus perpetuating her incompetency schema. This dilemma is just the sort of no-win situation in which BPD patients often find themselves every day of their lives as a result of schema antagonism. Therapists who are attempting to formulate a case conceptualization for a BPD patient need to be alert to the existence of these conflicting schemas.

A related phenomenon is *schema vacillation,* in which BPD patients experience the activation of conflicting schemas in a rapid, oscillating fashion. For example, a BPD patient may mistrust those who are closest to him and therefore act in a hostile and rejecting way toward family and friends. When the significant others comply by distancing themselves from the patient, the patient's abandonment schema may become activated, thus compelling him to act out in ways to gain attention and nurturing. When the significant others begin to attend to the BPD patient, he may revert back to feeling threatened as his mistrust schema once again comes to the fore. Schema vacillation is clearly demonstrated when BPD patients habitually run extremely hot and cold in relationships, and when they shift back and forth between opposing emotions and sensations such as pain and numbness. This phenomenon is also at least partly responsible for BPD patients' ill-defined sense of self, as they have terrible difficulty in ascertaining a consistent set of wants, needs, desires, and goals. Therapists can do their BPD patients a great service by explaining that the behaviors that others may have told them seem "fickle" or "crazy" actually are the result of schema antagonism and schema vacillation.

Level of Functioning

As mentioned earlier in this chapter, BPD patients enter treatment at diverse levels of functioning. Axis V of the DSM-III-R, known as "Global Adaptational Functioning," is one way to measure such levels of functioning qualitatively. Another way to conceptualize whether BPD patients are relatively high or low in functioning is to assess the nature of their maladaptive schemas. Are they numerous? pervasive? compelling? antagonistic or vacillating? and so on. The more definitively and consistently one answers "yes" to these questions, the more that the patient is likely to evince a lower level of overall functioning in life and in therapy.

Other factors that diminish the BPD patient's level of functioning (and, along with it, their receptivity and potential responsivity to therapy) are:

1. A history of severe, ongoing childhood and adolescent traumas, such as sexual abuse [lower functioning is more likely when the traumas occurred earlier in life, over a longer period of time, were perpetrated by persons who were psychologically close to the patient (e.g., parents), and when the patient attributes the traumas to the self (e.g., "I'm bad")]
2. Early negative life experiences that cannot be described verbally (i.e., "the cloud"), as evidenced by major somatic reactions to schema activation, such as nausea and depersonalization
3. Few social, physical, and economic buffers in the patient's life, past and/or present
4. Significant family psychopathology, past and/or present
5. Unsatisfactory psychotherapy experiences in the past
6. High-level general life stressors, such as family or marital dissolution, loss of employment or financial support, medical illness, and sexual and/or racial discrimination
7. Low level of intellectual resources, leading to poor problem-solving skills and low self-efficacy
8. Low level of physical attractiveness, leading to social ostracism and loneliness

The patient's level of functioning is an important variable to consider when formulating therapeutic interventions. For example, a therapist who introduces the topic of early maladaptive schemas to an intelligent, employed, therapy-wise BPD patient may inspire interest and hope in the relatively long process of therapy. The same agenda may inspire mistrust, misunderstanding, and a premature flight from therapy in a patient who is poor, is medically ill, and is seeking moral support and concrete answers as a primary goal of an intended short-term treatment. In general, cognitive therapists must ask themselves the following questions in order to formulate a treatment program that will fit the needs and the level of functioning of the individual BPD patient:

1. What are this patient's personal and environmental resources on which he or she can rely in order to accomplish the intended therapeutic tasks and goals?
2. How emotionally vulnerable (labile, suicidal, etc.) is the patient at this time?
3. How much general reassurance does the patient require at this time?
4. How much confidence does the patient have in himself or herself right now? How much confidence or trust in others in general? In me?
5. What immediate life crises or negative life conditions need attention right now? How can I begin to address these?
6. What are the patient's expectations about therapy? Does the patient understand the appropriate role that he or she will play in treatment?
7. To what degree is this patient feeling overwhelmed with burdensome tasks? How much energy is available for the work of therapy?

8. Does this patient have any meaningful interpersonal relationships on which to rely *outside* of treatment? How can we begin to maximize these relationships in a healthy way?
9. How willing and able is the patient to engage in the process of therapy?
10. Do I have an understanding of this patient that is sufficient to proceed with specific interventions?

By applying these questions, therapists will be more apt to pace the course of treatment in a way that maximizes the patients' available resources without going so far as to unduly overwhelm or frighten them into leaving therapy.

Finally, it is important to add that the cognitive conceptualization of the BPD patient must not remain static throughout the entire course of treatment. As new information comes to light that contradicts or supplements the therapist's conceptual hypotheses about the patient, the case formulation must be reevaluated and modified when appropriate to fit the data. Furthermore, as the patients learn new methods for coping and for enhancing self-understanding and self-acceptance, these compensatory strengths must be figured into the case conceptualization as well. An ideal outcome of therapy is not only a positive change in this "story of the patient's life," but a change in diagnosis as well, such that the patient no longer meets criteria for BPD.

Chapter 4
Clinical Strategies and Techniques

Advanced cognitive therapy for BPD is comprised of four broad types of interventions:

1. Establishing, nurturing, and learning from the *therapeutic relationship*
2. *Crisis intervention strategies*
3. *Standard cognitive therapy self-help and self-monitoring skills*
4. *Schema-focused conceptualization and intervention*

All these components of treatment may be utilized at any point during the course of therapy, depending on the needs and the level of cognitive maturity of the individual patient. Typically, however, there is greater emphasis on the therapeutic relationship early in therapy. Crisis management and schema work receive greater emphasis when patients are lower in functioning and/or unfamiliar with the process of therapy, whereas standard cognitive therapy skills are more prominent with higher functioning patients and/or those who are well socialized into the cognitive model of treatment. There may be significant overlap between these elements of treatment as well, as when a suicidal crisis emerges because the patient has misconstrued a therapist's comment to mean that the therapist doesn't care.

Issues regarding the *therapeutic relationship* with BPD patients arise regularly, as a consequence of the patients' problems with mistrust, dependence, overidealizing and undervaluing, dichotomous thinking about relationships, and the therapists' frequent feelings of frustration. Ideally, over the course of therapy, the therapist will gain an optimal measure of the patient's trust, and the work of therapy can focus more directly on issues of self-esteem and day-to-day problem solving.

Crises occur readily in the lives of BPD patients and therefore become an important part of therapy. Therapists must be prepared to help their BPD patients to mobilize their cognitive skills, affect-modulation skills, and problem-solving skills at these times so as to avert the patients' engaging in self-defeating or self-harming behaviors, and to build their confidence in dealing with practical difficulties and emotional pain. Even when BPD patients seem to be making excellent progress, they are still prone to sudden regressions in functioning. Therefore, therapists must remain vigilant to crises, and will need to formulate well-defined strategies for handling the various problematic scenarios that we will describe.

Both *standard cognitive therapy techniques* and *schema-based cognitive strategies* can be used at any point in therapy depending on the individual patient's needs, capabilities, and personal agendas for treatment. For example, a BPD patient may have a clear goal in mind—for example, that she wants to learn to assert herself better with her hypercritical mother—but may have no desire to deal with her sense of inadequacy in the work world or with her sexual fears. In this case, it is probably a good idea to collaborate with the patient by helping her to develop the requisite skills in rational responding and assertiveness in order to ameliorate her situation with her mother, *before* asking the patient if she wants to go further in treatment—perhaps into the previously forbidden areas of her incompetency and unlovability schemas.

In another case, a patient may enter therapy in such a highly intense emotional state that he does not want to examine his thoughts or feelings in any way. He simply wants relief, but he has no idea how to achieve this when his psychic pain seems so overwhelming and out of control. Here, it may make sense to address the schema level from the outset (as schemas are most accessible during periods of high emotionality) in order to understand his acute distress. Much of this work may overlap with the areas of crisis intervention and the building of the therapeutic relationship as well. Later in treatment, when the patient has learned about schemas and schema activation, and knows how to modulate his emotionality, he may agree to work on some more specific and goal-directed skills.

Another important factor to consider is the patient's capacity for engaging in the logic of formal operations (see Chapter 2). A patient who demonstrates an advanced level of cognitive operations at the start of treatment often will be more receptive to learning the self-help techniques of standard cognitive therapy than will the patient whose cognitive capabilities initially are limited. In the case of the latter patient, schema work typically precedes the learning of specific skills.

THE THERAPEUTIC RELATIONSHIP

The interpersonal interactions between therapists and their BPD patients are as much a rich source of conceptual information as they are a source of emotional highs and lows for both parties. There are three main goals in establishing therapeutic relationships with BPD patients: (1) to connect, (2) to develop mutual trust and positive regard, and (3) to learn about the patient's major modes of operation in life as a function of how he or she deals with the therapist.

To *connect,* the therapist will need to be a consistent, benign, sincere, level-headed, interested, and unthreatened helper to a patient who at times may seem inconsistent, malevolent, deceptive, impulsive, unengaged, and highly threatened. It is a safe bet that BPD patients experience other people with some degree of trepidation, partly because of the wrongs that others have wrought upon them and partly as a function of the boomerang effect of their own noxious interpersonal behaviors. It is also likely that the BPD patient rarely if ever experiences someone who is a constant source of support in the face of such patient turmoil. When therapists succeed in providing their care and involvement on a consistent basis over time, BPD patients may begin to trust their therapists. Along with this, they begin to devote themselves more fully to the work of therapy.

Another important task is the therapist's recognizing that BPD patients are acting out their extreme emotional pain and trying to communicate their thoughts in the only ways they know how. We address the issue of the therapists' challenges in coping with their BPD patients later in our chapter on countertransference (Chapter 6).

Trust and positive regard, if they are to develop in any kind of meaningful and lasting way, develop slowly over time. It is insufficient for a therapist simply to say to a BPD patient, "You can trust me." Actions speak louder than words, and trust must be earned, not asked for. Therapists need to demonstrate a genuine interest in their BPD patients' lives. This is demonstrated by the following approaches (among others):

1. Pay close attention to the patient in session.
2. Work to remember important information as well as minor details about the patient from session to session.
3. Acknowledge that therapy is often difficult and painful, that it will take some time before the patient will feel comfortable with the therapist, that the patient may experience a *heightening* of anxiety as vital issues are addressed, and that the patient's discomfort is understandable and reasonable.
4. Avoid judgmental comments. Instead, look at the relative merits of and drawbacks to the BPD patient's behaviors that the therapist deems harmful.
5. Speak the patient's language. Avoid unnecessary jargon, and use imagery or metaphors that have personal meaning to the patient (e.g., telling a patient who loves classical music that her shrieks of despair are unheeded by others not because she is unloved, but because she is "playing a potentially heart-rending symphony at *200 decibels,* where nobody can hear the subtleties or beauty of your music as they're covering their ears").
6. Be willing to confront unpleasantness in the therapeutic relationship. If the patient accuses the therapist of counterproductive intentions or behaviors, the therapist must be willing to take a closer look at the situation and to own up to the kernel of truth in the matter, if that is the case. Feel free to apologize, if appropriate (see Chapter 6).
7. Don't skirt uncomfortable issues. Provide the BPD patient with a coping model for dealing assertively with difficult problems. For example, if the patient hints that she has been opening and reading her adult daughter's mail, the therapist

may note (humbly and gently) that although he generally supports the patient, he wonders whether this secretive behavior might lead to some serious problems. The therapist then may ask the patient if she'd be willing to discuss the matter at greater length.

8. Be careful with compliments. BPD patients may construe positive feedback as a sign that the therapist doesn't really understand or that he or she is deliberately manipulating the patient with false praise. *In the early stages of treatment, compliments are best directed toward the patient's efforts in doing the work of therapy, rather than the patient's personal characteristics.*

9. Ask for feedback. Be willing to listen to criticism. Be willing to repeat things again and again until the patient understands. Similarly, *give* feedback freely, always checking to see how the patient is interpreting this information. Do not remain silent to let the patients flounder on their own for prolonged periods of time.

10. Remain calm and collected, even as the patient may be expressing high-intensity emotionality. Check to make certain that the patient does not misinterpret this response to signify therapist indifference.

The third goal of the therapeutic relationship involves *the use of the interactions (both overt and suggested) between therapist and patient as important sources of information about the psychological life of the patient.* To do so requires that the therapist be adept at monitoring the *process* of therapy that underlies its content. One such scenario involves a therapist who is teaching her patient a series of questions that she can ask herself in order to respond rationally and adaptively to upsetting thoughts. The patient, typically a very talkative woman, remains dead silent and politely nods her head. The therapist, noting this out-of-character behavior, asks the patient if she has any hesitation or concerns about applying the technique she has just been taught. The patient begins to cry. The therapist gently asks what the patient is thinking and feeling, and if this reaction has something to do with the task that she reviewed. The patient responds, "My problems are *real*. I'm not going to be able to talk myself out of them. You must think my problems are really stupid and minor if you think that I can solve them just by asking myself questions!" The therapist responds by saying, "I'm truly sorry if that's the way it came across. I'm really sorry [appropriate apology]. I *do* take your problems seriously, and my only intention is to teach you a skill that can be very helpful if used regularly and properly [clinical rationale]. It doesn't mean that I think your problems are minor or not real. I wonder if this situation reminded you of other situations in life when you believed that your pain and suffering weren't being taken seriously [links therapeutic relationship to other relationships in the patient's life]?"

By keeping tabs on the process of the therapeutic interactions, the therapist was able to ascertain an important interpersonal pattern in the patient's life. Indeed, this patient had grown up in a household where she was not allowed to show her sadness and grief at having to move to new homes and cities with her parents every year.

Instead, she was told that she was "lucky" compared to most children, and that she should count her blessings and stop complaining. Now as an adult, this patient was hypersensitive to indications that others were minimizing her problems, a pattern that interfered with many of her potential relationships in the present, and a pattern that arose during an otherwise innocuous skill-teaching portion of a therapy session.

DEALING WITH CRISES AND LACK OF FOCUS

We have previously touched upon the importance of providing structure for BPD patients in session. Likewise, we have explained that it is vital that therapists sensitively and gradually facilitate positive working relationships with their BPD patients. Although these may appear to be straightforward tasks for any compassionate, competent therapist, they are made most difficult by the BPD patients' propensity for intense emotional reactions and impulsive acting-out behaviors. Before engaging in any specific, circumscribed techniques, it is useful for therapists to conceptualize those BPD emotions and behaviors that otherwise would seem to interfere with the process of therapy.

For example, a therapist attempts to review the patient's homework assignment from the previous week. In response, the BPD patient shows the therapist the marks on her arm where she cut herself with glass during the week. Rather than trying to stick to the homework agenda in a rigid fashion, or conversely becoming completely sidetracked by the need to do crisis management, the therapist chooses to help the patient understand the psychological process she went through in hurting herself. They discover that she cut herself when she believed that she was deserving of punishment. They conceptualize this harmful behavior as being tied to a schema of "badness," and begin to look at the etiological factors as well as the current sources of schema activation.

When therapist and patient collaborate to make sense of the patient's maladaptive responses, the stage may be set for building more specific skills. In this example, the therapist suggested that the patient's self-harming actions were understandable in light of her belief that she was morally defective and deserved to be punished. She (the therapist) suggested that they explore the patient's schemas thoroughly before concluding that they truly were warranted. In the meantime, she entreated the patient to crunch a raw egg on her body instead of cutting her arms with glass when she felt compelled to harm herself.

Parasuicidal Behaviors

When BPD patients engage in self-harming behaviors, it is imperative that their therapists address such actions immediately. Slashing, burning, overdosing, and the like represent potentially suicidal behaviors and therefore must become top-priority items for discussion in session. Linehan (1987) notes that the "parasuicidal" behaviors of her BPD patients at the very least threaten the work of therapy (if not the lives of the patients themselves). Therefore, she contracts with her patients that the general process of treatment must come to a halt in order to deal with these self-destructive acts as they arise. Linehan is very direct with her BPD patients, explaining that therapy cannot be of benefit to patients who are no longer alive (in contrast to the morbid surgeon's joke that "the operation was a success but the patient died").

We agree with Linehan (1987), but we would add that it is potentially very fruitful indeed if the patient and therapist address the patient's self-harming behaviors in the context of the patient's core issues—namely, schemas. For example, in the aforementioned example of the BPD patient who cut her arms, much progress was achieved when the therapist helped the patient to understand the association between the activation of the latter's "badness" schema as a precipitant of her self-slashing. In this instance, the therapist succeeded not only in setting firm limits and standards regarding the patient's actings-out, but also taught the patient to recognize the cognitive triggers that might put her at risk for further self-harm.

Patients who engage in parasuicidal behaviors often report that their intention is *not* suicide but, rather, to punish themselves (as in the case of the activated badness schema), or to utilize physical pain as a preferable distraction from emotional pain. Here, therapists can empathize with the patient's plight, but can suggest alternative (less harmful) ways to deal with the need to self-stimulate. Such options include the following:

1. Telephone the therapist or the professional on call.
2. Telephone a sympathetic friend or relative.
3. Go to the emergency room of the nearest hospital.
4. Hit oneself with pillows.
5. Use a water-soluble red-felt tip pen to write on oneself as an alternative to cutting with a sharp object.
6. Immerse one's hand into cold water.
7. Crunch raw eggs on oneself.
8. Spend an hour reviewing an audiotape from a therapy session (preferably one in which the patient expressed some hope and in which the therapist was particularly supportive).
9. Spend an hour reviewing old homework assignments (kept in a therapy notebook or folder) in order to switch one's mindset into "problem-solving mode" as opposed to "catastrophe mode."
10. Spend an hour applying various self-help skills (to be described later in this chapter and in subsequent case chapters).

Behaviors that are less acutely dangerous, but nonetheless represent chronic threats to health and safety, can be dealt with in similar fashion. For example, BPD patients who binge and purge or who engage in reckless sexual behaviors or spending sprees will need to have the dangers of these actions spelled out for them promptly and directly. Furthermore, the therapist should endeavor to help these patients to ascertain the schema or schemas that trigger such responses. Additionally, therapist and patient can work together to generate a list of activities in which the patient can engage as alternatives to the chronic crisis-producing behaviors.

In contrast to the serious self-harming actings-out just discussed, BPD patients also present with many and varied pseudocrises from week to week. The therapist may work on a particular "crisis" (e.g., harsh criticism from the patient's employer) in a given session and may believe that further sessions will be needed to resolve the problem. In the ensuing session, however, the BPD patient may want to discuss an entirely new "crisis" in life (e.g., dental problems and fears of treatment). Again, the therapist often will perceive the need for a great deal of concentrated work over an extended period of time in order to deal adequately with the new issues. Again, the patient confounds this plan with a new problem the following week. These "crises du jour" often are experienced as major frustrations by therapists who would like to help the BPD patient to make steady progress on consistent themes but, instead, spend all their time in session putting out therapeutic brushfires. In such cases, therapists often become frustrated, as they may feel that they are on nightmarish merry-go-rounds with their BPD patients and that no real therapy is being accomplished at all.

One useful strategy for dealing with these crises in a productive manner is to identify the common themes that connect the seemingly disparate upheavals from week to week. For example, a single issue—a schema of mistrust—may underlie a series of separate conflictual crises with a spouse, employer, neighbor, and friend. If therapist and patient agree that this is an accurate assessment of the problem, they may begin to work more efficiently by tackling the patient's pervasive sense of mistrust. As one therapist said, "If you have to fight an octopus, it makes more sense to attack the head than to try to fend off all the tentacles one by one."

It goes without saying that a BPD patient who harbors a schema of mistrust may direct this toward the therapist and therefore be less than willing to collaborate in treatment. Here, therapists must be patient and flexible in their approach. It does little good to engage in a power struggle with the patients, to force-feed them standard techniques for improved coping, or to try to cajole them into trusting the process of therapy before they are ready to do so. The standard therapeutic skills of accurate empathy, genuineness, warmth, and reflection are extremely important to utilize at such times. In addition, however, the therapist can still begin to try to help the patients to make sense of their problems, to begin the process of explaining the cognitive model of psychotherapy, and to agree on a preliminary list of goals and targets for intervention.

Combatting Overwhelming Feelings

Borderline patients often find it difficult to identify the thoughts and emotions that they are experiencing. They may be overwhelmed by a flood of emotions and physiological arousal that is both confusing and aversive (e.g., "the cloud"), or conversely they may become numb and amnestic. When this happens, the patients often are rendered unable to contribute to the constructive activity of the session. As a result, therapists must be somewhat more directive and didactic in treating BPD patients than they might ordinarily be with patients who suffer from disorders such as simple unipolar depression. Certainly, we do not mean that the therapist should lecture, exhort, or badger patients. What we are advocating is for therapists to be active in the following ways:

1. *Educate* the BPD patients about the nature of their disorder and about the cognitive model of therapy.
2. *Offer hypotheses* about the psychological phenomena that are taking place in the life of the patient.
3. *Make suggestions* to the BPD patients about how they might make some positive changes.
4. *Elicit feedback* from the BPD patients to show that you value their input and to emphasize the importance of their active participation in treatment.

All of these points can be made in a gentle, open-minded manner, especially if the therapist consistently shows an interest in the patient's reactions to all of the therapist's hypotheses and suggestions.

Acting Out toward the Therapist

Another variation on crisis management occurs when patients act out in session or abuse telephone contact privileges with their therapists. We have personally witnessed the following behaviors (among others) from our BPD patients:

1. Patient crawls under the therapist's desk.
2. Patient screams at the therapist.
3. Patient throws and breaks the therapist's coffee mug.
4. Patient refuses to leave the therapy session at the end of an already extended "hour."
5. Patient hyperventilates and becomes faint.
6. Patient becomes unwilling to speak.
7. Patient abruptly leaves the therapist's office before the session is over.
8. Patient calls the therapist five times in one day, including twice after midnight.

Unfortunately, there are no foolproof formulas for dealing with these types of crises, and no ironclad measures that therapists can take to prevent such situations from occurring. However, we have found the following general guidelines useful in minimizing the fallout of such occurrences and in reducing the chances of repeated crises:

1. *Remain calm, nondefensive, and empathic.* Do not punish the patient, as this will only fuel the fires of mistrust and abandonment. For example, when a patient screamed at one of us, the therapist placated the patient by saying, "It's okay that you're upset with me. I know you're only trying to protect yourself, and you have a right to protect yourself."

2. *Negotiate with the patient to set mutually agreeable limits.* For example, the therapist can state, "In order for us to respect each other and to protect each others' rights, I pledge never to force you to engage in any therapy assignment unless you understand adequately how it may be of some help to you. In return, I ask that you pledge neither to leave the therapy session prematurely, nor to prolong it without my cooperation." Other agreements can be made in similar fashion. If the patient reneges, the therapist can politely remind the patient that it is very important that both the therapist and patient honor their agreements. If this proves insufficient, the therapist has the prerogative to institute tangible (ethical) consequences, such as promptly ending a session, or agreeing to schedule further sessions only *after* the patient renews his or her commitment to the agreement (offering a suitable referral if the patient chooses not to cooperate).

3. *Help the patient to ascertain the issues that sparked the crisis and to deal with the issues themselves, rather than focusing on the maladaptive behavior per se.* For example, rather than scolding patients for throwing mugs, crawling under desks, or making repeated phone calls, therapists can discuss the *schemas* that sparked such behaviors, and question the patients about more self-enhancing and self-confident ways to express the concomitant thoughts and feelings. For example, one patient refused to leave the therapist's office because she reported that she was afraid to drive home. She insisted that the therapist drive her home! Rather than focus on the inappropriateness of the request (which could always be spelled out later, at a less volatile time), the therapist reflected on the patient's dual schemas of dependence and abandonment. The patient admitted that she believed that a person who would decline to "be there for me at all times" must not really care about her. The therapist reaffirmed his care for the patient, suggested that he was showing his care by trying to strengthen her self-esteem and autonomy (e.g., by giving her heartfelt encouragement to drive herself home), and gave her the assignment of reflecting on alternatives to her beliefs about love and dependency (which would be discussed at the next session).

Separation from the Therapist

One of the most prevalent types of crisis involves the patients' separation from their therapists, because of either temporary breaks or termination from treatment. For example, a therapist may find it necessary to postpone a BPD patient's sessions for two weeks as a result of a vacation or professional conference. This temporary separation may activate abandonment or dependency schemas in the patient that lead to angry outbursts and statements of rejection aimed at the therapist, or to desperate attempts to keep the therapist nearby. It is no coincidence that BPD patients often present with crises or other forms of behavioral regression when they learn that their therapists will be away.

If the therapist initiates a temporary break from therapy, it is valuable to plan for the interruption well in advance. Therapists should forewarn their BPD patients early enough to assess thoroughly and address the patients' thoughts and feelings about the matter. The therapist then will have the opportunity to allay the patient's idiosyncratic concerns. For example, does the patient believe that the therapist is showing a lack of care and commitment? that the therapist is trying to get rid of the patient? that the therapist finds the patient unlovable, defective, too dependent, bad, and so on? that the therapist is making the patient a very low priority compared to almost every other activity in life? that the therapist is giving up on helping the patient? These are important rhetorical questions that BPD patients often implicitly ask themselves. They are rhetorical because, left unaddressed, BPD patients may assume that the answers to all of the above are a resounding YES!

When breaks from therapy activate the BPD patients' schemas of unlovability, badness, abandonment, mistrust, and dependence, the therapist will need to deal with this problem in two ways: psychologically and practically. *Psychologically,* the therapist helps the patient to identify the schemas that have been activated and to begin a process of reattribution. Together, patient and therapist examine the state of the therapeutic relationship through objective eyes. For example, they may review as many instances as they can remember when the therapist *was* available to the patient, and when the patient *benefited* from coping *on his or her own* for a period of time. Also, they may discuss the phenomenon of "object permanence" (see Chapter 2) as it applies to interpersonal relationships. In this case, a sign of progress in treatment is the patient's recognition that even though the therapist is out of sight, he or she is not out of the patient's life. The commitment, concern, and involvement that the therapist has in the patient's treatment does not disintegrate when sessions are temporarily discontinued. Further, this concept can be applied to other important relationships in the patient's life as well, so that the patient can come to see the benefits of combatting his or her own general separation anxiety.

On the *practical* side of the matter, the therapist will need to arrange for professional coverage for those patients who truly may need to be supervised very closely during the therapist's absence. One possibility involves the use of a substitute therapist during the hiatus. Ideally, the patient can meet with this substitute therapist in a co-therapy session before the regular therapist leaves. At the very least, the fill-in therapist needs to be thoroughly apprised of the case. Later, it is often useful to enlist the services of this same substitute therapist regularly when the primary therapist is unavailable to the patient.

Patients also need clear guidelines on how to proceed if a crisis should occur in the therapist's absence. Helping the patient predict what these crises might be and working through strategies to deal with them in advance is excellent practice for the future goal of termination from therapy. Patients will need to formulate a series of coping activities in which to engage if their affect takes a turn for the worse. If these strategies are insufficient, the patient will need to know who to contact and will need to have a clear plan for self-admission into a hospital if suicidal impulses become out of control. It is wise for therapists to explain that discussion of these measures is merely *preventive* and that they do not reflect a vote of no-confidence from the therapist.

Patients sometimes flee from therapy when they believe that their therapists are uncaring and unhelpful. They may also leave treatment out of fears of addressing painful topics and of the process of change itself. Additionally, BPD patients occasionally drop out of sight in order to test their therapists' motivation to resume contact. *When patients unexpectedly miss sessions, or report that they want to end therapy, therapists should not blithely agree to terminate therapy without first investing some time and energy in understanding the schemas that are behind the patients' intentions.* This strategy holds the best promise for offering evidence against the patient's mistrust and abandonment schemas, as well as for keeping patients engaged in a process that may be on the brink of effecting positive changes in their lives. It also helps demonstrate that adversity can be overcome and that good communication can resolve seemingly hopeless interpersonal situations. These are extremely valuable lessons for BPD patients to learn.

When BPD patients suddenly insist that they want to end therapy, the therapist should try to encourage at least one final face-to-face session in order to explore the issue. Should the patient absolutely refuse to return, the therapist should still communicate good will by offering a referral and perhaps by noting that the door is still open for future resumption of treatment.

As the patient and therapist work toward ultimate termination, the frequency of therapy sessions should be reduced slowly. The exact rate of tapering from therapy should be a collaborative decision between the patient and therapist. Sometimes this may be achieved over the course of a few months. On the other hand, it may take years to wind down from weekly to biweekly to quarterly to semiannual sessions.

We believe strongly that the therapist's suddenly putting an end to therapy or refusing to have any future contact with the patient following official termination is ill advised with most BPD patients. Schema modification is a revolution of the mind and needs to be handled with care over a period of time. As the patient tapers off of therapy, he or she may begin to gain more and more confidence to apply new skills and new mindsets in an independent fashion. At the same time, it is appropriate for therapists to be available for consultation in the event of renewed crises or lapses. At such times, it is important for the therapist to assess whether the lapse is due more to objective stressors or more to a subjective sense of helplessness without the therapist. In either event, it is fitting and proper to review the methods that patients may use in order to combat such problematic reactions in a more autonomous fashion in the future.

If the termination of therapy must occur suddenly as a result of a geographic move, it is imperative that the issue of coping with separation and loss be addressed far in advance (if foreseeable). If there is to be a transfer or referral to another therapist, it is often helpful to hold one or more joint sessions before the separation from the original therapist occurs (an arrangement that presents logistical problems when therapists are in individual private practice, but that can be accomplished readily in group practice or clinic settings).

STANDARD COGNITIVE THERAPY TECHNIQUES

A thorough review of standard cognitive therapy is beyond the scope of this handbook and is well described elsewhere (Beck et al., 1979; Beck et al., 1985; Newman & Beck, 1990; Newman & Haaga, in press). However, we present an overview of some of the most important ways to utilize the basic repertoire of cognitive therapy techniques in the treatment of BPD patients.

Anxiety Reduction Techniques

As we have discussed, BPD patients often fear the process of change. Similarly, they often find the emotional reactions associated with discussing core issues in their lives (that frequently provoke schema activation) to be highly aversive. In order to minimize the likelihood that patients will avoid engaging in the work of therapy, we advocate spending a good deal of time focused on teaching the patient *nonavoidant* methods for reducing anxiety (cf. Beck et al., 1985; Newman, in press a).

For example, we often teach BPD patients to utilize progressive muscle relaxation and controlled breathing exercises in order to reduce physiological arousal. These techniques are especially useful in helping patients to modulate and moderate their intense emotional reactions. As a caveat, therapists must check to be sure that the BPD patient has a modicum of trust in the therapist before introducing these exercises. In some cases, patients associate the relaxation induction with being out of control or being manipulated or "hypnotized" by someone. If this indeed is the belief, the issues can be discussed without necessarily diving directly into the relaxation and breathing interventions themselves. Another alternative involves giving patients an audiotape of a relaxation or controlled breathing induction to practice in the privacy of their own homes.

Another useful anxiety reduction intervention is *distraction techniques*. Here, patients are taught to counteract their volatile emotions and desires to flee from threatening situations by focusing their attentions on any number of neutral or positive thoughts. Such thoughts may include nonsense games such as "How many of my family's and friends' birthdays and middle names can I remember?" to meaningful positive memories, to images of pleasant scenes such as a warm day on a quiet beach. Although this intervention does encourage a form of cognitive avoidance, we make it clear to our BPD patients that the technique is intended to help them reduce their anxiety *in order to prime them to deal with the major issues of their lives.*

Problem-Solving Skills

Borderline patients often present with numerous life problems, a function of their noxious environments, their impulsivity, their self-defeating tendencies, and their senses of incompetence in ameliorating their difficult situations. In this context, the acquisition of problem-solving skills (D'Zurilla & Goldfried, 1971; Nezu, Nezu, & Perri, 1989) can be a tremendous boon to their self-images and lives.

The components of problem solving include the following: (1) defining the problem, (2) brainstorming methods to deal with the problem, (3) weighing the relative pros and cons of each method, (4) choosing and implementing the best method, and (5) evaluating the results. When our BPD patients present with pseudo crises or otherwise feel overwhelmed, we gently ask them, "Can you switch from 'catastrophe mode' to 'problem-solving mode' right now? I'd be more than happy to help you deal with your concerns, but we need to be in a more constructive state of mind to make it work. Is that okay with you?" By teaching the skills of problem-solving, therapists can begin to help their BPD patients to be more deliberate and open-minded about interpreting and handling their difficulties, as opposed to their more characteristic impulsivity and tunnel-vision responses. Naturally, schemas of dependence or incompetence will prove formidable obstacles to the implementation of these skills. Nevertheless, we have found problem-solving techniques to be a valuable part of advanced cognitive therapy for BPD, especially as a means for combatting hopelessness and suicidality.

Communication and Listening Skills

As we have noted previously, BPD patients characteristically have major difficulties in interpersonal relationships. Part of the problem, in addition to the activation of schemas such as mistrust, unlovability, and abandonment, is a deficiency in basic communication and listening skills. As noted, their Piagetian egocentrism contributes to their lack of ability to understand or empathize with the needs of the listener.

We have been struck by how some BPD patients are completely unaware of the aversive quality of their communication style. Rather than eliciting sympathy and nurturance from others (which often is their primary intention), BPD patients more often *repel* others by coming across as critical, guilt-provoking, and/or manipulative. An example is the patient who would like to communicate the following idea to her therapist, "I'm really frightened right now, and I'm looking to you for guidance more than ever. Can you help me?" but instead says, "I don't know what to do! I don't know what to do! And you're not helping me! I don't know why I even bother to come here! What am I going to do? I'm falling apart and you're supposed to be helping me!" Therapists, who are professionally trained to cope with such demands as well as to weed through the patient's hostility in order to hear the plea for help, still may feel put off by such communication. One can readily imagine how people in the BPD patient's personal life react to such outbursts.

There are some basic, fundamental communication skills that therapists can teach their BPD patients. These include:

1. *Change accusations into requests.* For example, don't say, "You're never there for me when I need you!" Instead, say, "I really need you. Please try to be supportive. It would mean a great deal to me."

2. *Don't assume what the other person means. Ask for clarification first.* For example, one of our patients thought that the therapist had insulted him by calling him "scattered." Instead of assuming that he had heard correctly, he asked the therapist exactly what she meant by "scattered." As it turned out, the therapist had called *herself* "scattered" in jest because she had momentarily forgotten the patient's lover's name.

3. *Neither give someone the silent treatment nor talk excessively.* Instead, take the middle ground, and try to have an even-handed exchange of thoughts and feelings with the other person.

4. *Use more "I" statements and fewer "you" statements.* For example, say, "I feel very hurt because I think I'm not very important to you," instead of, "You don't care about me at all!"

5. *Modulate tone of voice. Neither yell nor speak meekly.* This helps to instill confidence and to keep the other person engaged.

6. *Reflect back what the other person is saying before responding.* By starting a sentence with a phrase such as, "If I've got this straight, you're trying to tell me that . . ." before giving a retort, the patient may demonstrate a willingness to understand, which in turn may make the other person more receptive to what the patient is trying to say.

7. Related to these communication skills is the skill of *assertiveness.* Therapists teach their BPD patients that to be assertive they must demonstrate respect for *themselves* as well as respect for others. This involves standing up for themselves in a friendly, nonthreatened, humble, confident way (e.g., "I'm really sorry, but I'd prefer not to do what you're asking me to do. I hope you're not offended, because I really don't want to cause a problem between us, but I feel strongly about the matter and I've learned that it's best if I follow my conscience"). Such an approach is far

preferable to the passive approach taken when the dependency and abandonment schemas are activated (e.g., "I'll do whatever you say as long as you don't leave me"), or the aggressive approach taken when the mistrust schema is activated (e.g., "Get away from me. I hate you!").

After discussing these principles of good communication and assertiveness with patients, therapists can help them to consolidate their newfound knowledge by role playing various scenarios where they would have to utilize these skills. It is sometimes useful to audiotape or videotape these role plays in order to give the patients objective feedback on their behavioral changes. Later, when the BPD patients feel reasonably ready, they can begin to use these techniques in everyday life (first with "safe" others, such as a close friend, and then progressively with others who are more and more intimidating to the patients, such as an employer or a critical parent).

Rational Responding Skills

Perhaps the single most identifiable hallmark of standard cognitive therapy, rational responding skills help patients to view their lives more objectively, less catastrophically, and with greater ability to find solutions to real problems. Therapists teach their patients to use their emotional upset as a cue to ask themselves, "What am I thinking right now?" These thoughts, called "automatic thoughts" (Beck, 1976), often evince perceptual biases that are associated with the patient's distress and lack of constructive focus.

Once patients become comfortable and adept at monitoring their automatic thoughts, they are taught to generate objective, adaptive answers ("rational responses") to these upsetting thoughts by asking themselves the following questions:

1. *In what other ways can I view this situation?* This question helps patients look at different perspectives to an issue or problem, thus helping them to make their thinking more *divergent,* as opposed to tunnel-visioned or locked into one (usually defeatist) mindset (Newman & Haaga, in press).

2. *What concrete, factual evidence supports or refutes my automatic thoughts on this matter?* Here, patients are encouraged to pay less attention to their hunches or intuition (which often are negatively slanted and foster hopelessness) and more attention to the actual data of their lives. When patients pay less attention to their *conjectural* thinking and pay more attention to those ideas that have been *confirmed,* there is less chance that they will blindly act in self-defeating ways or engage in self-fulfilling prophecies of gloom and doom (Newman, 1988).

3. *Realistically, what is the worst that could happen, and how would it ultimately affect my life?* This question helps patients to decatastrophize even the worst-case scenario. For example, one of our BPD patients received a promotion at work that

entailed greater responsibilities. She not only fretted that she would not be able to carry off the job, but she catastrophized that she would have to quit the job and move out of town! By asking herself the preceding question, she was better able to understand that the worst that could happen was that she would be demoted back to her old position again, and that her life would go on as usual.

4. *What are the pros and cons of continuing to think the way I do?* This question encourages patients to consider the harm that they do themselves by insisting on seeing things in the worst possible light. On the other hand, it elucidates schema-driven "reasons" that BPD patients may erroneously feel that it is in their best interest to think the worst. For example, one patient expected that her husband would soon suddenly die and leave her all alone. Although this expectation caused her daily (anticipatory) grief and even some marital discord, she believed that it was in her best interest to continue to catastrophize. This belief was based on a superstition that she held, a superstition that maintained that, "I'm bad. I deserve to be punished. Therefore, as soon as I let myself feel happy with my life, Fate will punish me and take it all away. Therefore, if I relax and enjoy my marriage, my husband will surely die." On the other hand, this question helped the patient to realize that there were compelling *disadvantages* to her catastrophic thinking.

5. *Now that I have considered all of the above, what constructive action can I take to deal with the problem at hand?* This is the question that focuses patients' attention on solving problems, rather than merely feeling bad about them. This call to action is intended to combat the patients' helplessness, to increase their self-confidence, and to teach them to handle actual crises in a much more productive way.

A convenient method for organizing this process is the Daily Thought Record or DTR, shown in Figure 4.1. (For more details on the uses of the DTR, see Beck et al., 1979; Burns, 1980; Newman & Beck, 1990; Newman & Haaga, in press). In addition, patients may choose to write their favorite rational responses on index cards or in a notebook for easy reference during times of rampant dysfunctional thinking.

Another technique to help patients respond rationally involves *teaching them to turn their rhetorical questions into literal questions*. For example, when patients desperately throw up their hands and say, "Oh, what's the point of going on?" the therapist should respond by saying, "That's a good question. Tell me, what *is* the point of going on?" Similarly, when a patient asks, "What am I going to do?" (implying that he or she hasn't a clue about what to do, and that there may be no solution anyway), the therapist should respond by saying, "That's an important question to address. Let's think; what *are* you going to do?" This technique serves the ever-useful function of helping patients switch from "catastrophe mode" to "problem-solving mode."

DATE	SITUATION Actual event leading to unpleasant emotion.	EMOTION(S) 1. Specify sad/anxious/angry, etc. 2. Rate degree of emotion, 0–100%	AUTOMATIC THOUGHT(S) 1. Write automatic thought(s) that preceded emotion(s). 2. Rate belief in automatic thought(s), 0–100%	RATIONAL RESPONSE 1. Write rational response to automatic thought(s). 2. Rate belief in rational response, 0–100%.	OUTCOME 1. Rerate belief in automatic thought(s), 0–100%. 2. Specify and rate subsequent emotions, 0–100%.

FIGURE 4.1. Daily Thought Record

We have also found it helpful to teach patients to identify certain classes of common cognitive distortions, such as these:

1. Minimizing the positive and magnifying the negative
2. Labeling (e.g., "I'm bad")
3. All-or-none thinking
4. Jumping to conclusions
5. Overgeneralizing
6. Mind-reading
7. Fortune-telling
8. Emotional reasoning

We often encourage patients to read Burns's (1980) *Feeling Good,* which spells out clearly the ways to spot and combat these problematic styles of thinking.

One particularly useful method for modifying an all-or-none thinking style is *continua ratings.* Here, patients are encouraged to rate the *degree* to which a thought or emotion is true. On the DTR, patients are instructed to indicate on a scale of 0 to 100 how much they believe a given automatic thought or rational response, and how intensely they feel their emotions. An obvious goal is to achieve a lower rating of belief in the automatic thoughts, a lower degree of intensity of maladaptive emotions (e.g., rage), an increased rating of belief in rational responses, and an increased intensity of adaptive emotions (e.g., appropriate grieving, pride, etc.). Therapists help their BPD patients to strive for these positive *modulations* in thinking and feelings, instead of demanding that their lives change from black to white. Similarly, BPD patients are taught to rate themselves and others on continua of personal qualities. Therefore, instead of seeing themselves as being *totally* bad, or someone else as being *completely* untrustworthy, the patients learn to set up a graded hierarchy of criteria on a continuum. Once having done this, they can ascertain more objectively where they or others fit on the scale.

For example, Dr. Aaron T. Beck (personal communication, 1990) has recounted an experience in his work with a depressed man whereby the patient believed that his loss of a professional promotion was an "utter disaster." A facsimile of their dialogue follows:

Dr. Beck: On a scale of 0 to 100, how much of a disaster was the loss of this promotion?
Patient: Definitely 100. It's a crushing blow. I can't get over it.
Dr. Beck: I know it's very upsetting to you, but if you could just bear with me for a moment, let's see if we can put this in perspective. You say that the loss of the promotion is a 100 percent disaster. What rating on the disaster scale would you give to a situation where you were in an accident and everybody in your family died?

Patient: That would be 100.

Dr. Beck: Is the loss of the promotion as bad?

Patient: No. Of course not. I see your point.

Dr. Beck: What would you rate the loss of the promotion now?

Patient: I'd give it a 90.

Dr. Beck: OK. That's a start. (Pause) How would you rate the situation where you got into an accident and became paralyzed for life?

Patient: I'd give it a 95.

Dr. Beck: So the loss of a job is only 5 points less noxious than losing the use of your legs?

Patient: Not when you put it that way.

Dr. Beck: How would you rate the loss of the promotion now?

Patient: Maybe a 75.

Dr. Beck and his patient continued along this path until it became apparent to the man that his initial negative appraisal of the loss of his promotion was vastly overblown. This vignette highlights the utility of teaching patients to make scaled ratings of their upsetting thoughts and feelings.

Behavioral Skills

Common self-statements for many depressed patients (including those who also suffer from BPD) include, "I'm overwhelmed," "There aren't enough hours in the day to do all that I need to do," "Given my inability to do what needs to be done I might as well just die," "I just sit around all day doing nothing, so what's the use of going on?" "I'm just a waste."

These individuals, who feel overloaded and unable to cope with what they perceive as insurmountable demands, rarely consider the potential benefits of *scheduling* their time. The goal of activity scheduling is not simply to maximize the patient's productivity, but to increase his or her sense of accomplishment and hopefulness. By utilizing the activity schedule (see Figure 4.2) as an assessment device early in therapy, the therapist can do the following:

1. Assess the patient's present use of time.
2. Help to plan better and more productive use of time to attack the patient's hopelessness.
3. Begin to socialize the patient to the idea of homework.
4. Work with the patient to test the idea that he or she is doing "nothing."

Patient and therapist can also use the activity schedule prospectively to *plan* activities so that the patient has specific goals on a daily basis. A common patient belief that interferes with compliance is the notion that activities *shouldn't* have to

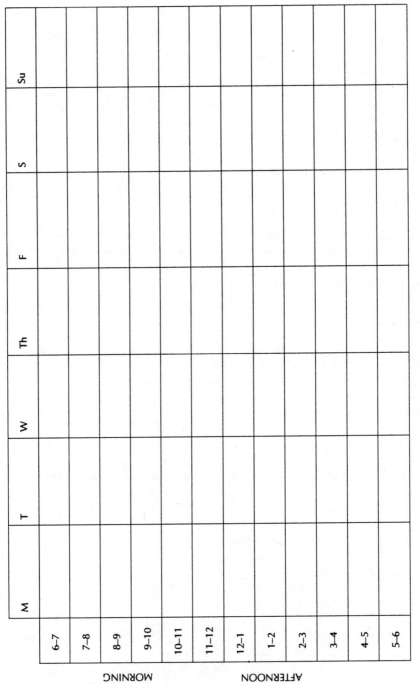

FIGURE 4.2. Weekly Activity Schedule

	M	T	W	Th	F	S	Su
EVENING							
6–7							
7–8							
8–9							
9–10							
10–11							
11–12							
12–1							

Remarks:

Note: Grade activities M for Mastery and P for Pleasure 0–10.

be scheduled but that activities *should* happen naturally and spontaneously. These beliefs are best addressed promptly in session.

A further use of activity scheduling is to have patients self-monitor and rate (from 0 to 10) the sense of *mastery* and of *pleasure* that they derive from each activity. Inasmuch as suicidal patients report that they rarely experience either mastery or pleasure, it is vital to help such patients to focus on activities that bring joy or a sense of accomplishment, meaning, or value as a means by which to reduce suicidality.

Graded-task assignments are useful for BPD patients who feel helpless in making behavioral changes in their lives. Graded-task assignments are derived from behavioral "shaping" strategies wherein each small, sequential step approximates the eventual goal and helps the patients to begin to expand their activities in a gradual, nonthreatening manner.

For some BPD patients, especially those who are demanding and perfectionistic, their response to small sequential steps may be, "So what?," "Big deal," or "It's not enough." For example, the patient who berates himself for being unable to find a lover may scoff at the idea of taking the small step of working on building communication skills with acquaintances, yet it may be this very skill that remains a formidable obstacle to his ultimate goal. Nevertheless, the therapist can point out that the patient's insistence in getting everything he wants in one leap has not worked, and that he has little to lose by trying something new.

The foregoing example illustrates a common difficulty in working with personality-disordered patients, especially those with BPD. *Their resistance to demonstrably helpful cognitive therapy techniques becomes a focus of therapy unto itself.* In such cases, it is a mistake to conclude that "cognitive therapy won't work with this patient." Rather, cognitive therapy must then focus on the manner in which patients' problematic beliefs and schemas are activated by the interventions themselves. Also, as explained in Chapter 2, the patients may not be adept at intellectually processing schema-based information at a level mature enough to be responsive to the interventions. Here, the long-range challenge is to teach patients to use concrete and formal cognitive operations in response to schema activation.

Homework

Therapists can help their BPD patients to begin the process of ordering and gaining some control over their lives by assigning homework. Therapists should stress to their BPD patients that their commitment to doing these between-session assignments is a good prognostic sign inasmuch as it signals their willingness to apply skills learned in therapy sessions to their everyday lives. Furthermore, patients who invest time in therapy homework tend to make swifter progress, and to maintain their gains more readily in the months and years following the completion of treatment (Burns & Auerbach, 1992; Elliott, Adams, & Hodge, 1992; Newman, in press b; Persons, Burns, & Perloff, 1988; Primakoff, Epstein, & Covi, 1989).

Therapists must be alert to their BPD patients' schema activation as a result of their being given a homework assignment. Patients may believe that they are incapable of following through with the self-help or self-monitoring tasks that have been assigned (incompetency schema), and therefore may feel overwhelmed, belittled, or misunderstood. It is very useful at these times to reassure the patients that they will not be criticized or penalized for having difficulty with the assignment, and that their self-doubts are no reason to feel hopeless about therapy. In addition, the therapist can ascertain the BPD patients' hot cognitions at this time in order to begin to shed light on the nature of their schemas.

Another related complication occurs when patients' mistrust schemas become activated as a result of the therapists assigning homework. The patients may believe that the therapists are trying to control, manipulate, or humiliate them. Therapists can address this in the same manner as described above—with sensitivity, reassurance, and a thoughtful probing of the patients' beliefs and schemas in the session.

Yet another potential problem arises when BPD patients maintain strong dependency schemas. In such cases, the prospect of acting independently during the week (without the therapist's direct guidance) may be very threatening. Here, it is appropriate for therapists to acknowledge that taking a step such as doing homework would be very frightening indeed. Still, the therapist should encourage the patients to go ahead with the assignment as part of a behavioral experiment. If the patient succeeds, an important step toward greater self-efficacy and self-sufficiency will have been achieved. If the patient falters, nothing is lost as the therapist and patient will work together to understand the psychological obstacles that interfered with this potential independent behavior.

SCHEMA-FOCUSED COGNITIVE THERAPY TECHNIQUES

Many standard cognitive therapy techniques are only partially effective with some BPD patients early in treatment. This is so in part because most of this repertoire focuses on the verbal level, whereas many of the BPD patients' problems may require techniques that involve imagery, kinesthetic components, or other aspects of "the cloud." In addition, many BPD patients fight against therapeutic techniques by virtue of their fears of change, their mistrust of the therapist and the process of therapy, their belief that they do not deserve to feel better, and their misunderstanding of skills that require sophisticated cognitive processing. In response to this sort of resistance, cognitive therapy has added to its repertoire in order to meet the challenge of Axis II patients, especially BPD patients. The initial work of the schema-focused component of treatment is largely directed by therapists. Later, as the patients develop the ability to assess and modify their schemas through the use of mature cognitive operations, the patients themselves become more active in directing their own treatment.

Schema Identification

It is the therapist's task initially to hypothesize the schemas that are present in the BPD patient. The most common schemas relevant to this population are badness/ unlovability, incompetence, mistrust, abandonment, lack of individuation, and emotional deprivation. Some BPD patients evidence only one or two of these schemas, some demonstrate the full complement, and some show themselves to maintain additional schemas that are more closely associated with other Axis II disorders (e.g., sense of entitlement; cf. Young, 1990). All hypotheses regarding the patients' schemas should be viewed as preliminary; therapists are advised not to become wedded to their initial theories about a given patient. Instead, therapists must maintain open minds and be prepared to amend their conceptualizations as the data become available.

Therapists reflect on three main sources of clinical data in order to begin the process of hypothesizing the BPD patients' relevant schemas. These are as follows:

1. The presenting problems
2. The types of crises that emerge during treatment
3. A review of the patients' most critical negative experiences in the past (e.g., in childhood)

When the patient describes the presenting problems or lapses into "catastrophe mode," the therapist can begin to gain a better understanding of the problems by pondering, "What basic, core beliefs about herself and the world might induce the patient to react in the way that she has?" For example, it may appear on the surface that a patient's quitting a job just after receiving a well-deserved and well-paying promotion is an act of sheer lunacy. On the other hand, it might make "sense" if the patient believed that she were a fraud as an employee and that her fundamental incompetence would no longer remain "concealed" if she accepted the promotion. Thus, rather than remaining puzzled or assuming the patient will spontaneously change her mind on her own, the therapist may instead hypothesize that this patient has a compelling schema of incompetence. Naturally, it is useful to present this sort of hypothesis to the patient to see if it rings true. Also, the therapist may ask the patient to hypothesize on her own what her beliefs and schemas might be in a given problem situation. Even if the patient has no immediate answers, the questioning process will plant the seeds for later self-exploration as her skills improve. Furthermore, the patient will begin to get the message that she needs to be an active participant in the treatment process.

In discussing traumatic or otherwise critical incidents in the patients' distant past, it is useful to ask them what the "child" (themselves) must have been thinking and feeling at the time. Such memory work begins the process of reconstructing the etiology of schemas. For example, Hallie (Chapter 3) never conceptualized her problems as involving a schema of mistrust until she focused her memory on the sexual abuse she had suffered at the hands of her uncle when she was 7 years old. Although she *was* aware that she felt "bad," she was surprised to remember that she thought to herself, "I know I'm not supposed to trust strangers, but now I know I can't even trust people I know." Her blanket mistrust for everyone in the present began to make sense in the context of these early childhood experiences.

Once the therapists begin to formulate their hypotheses about the patients' schemas, they can begin to look for opportunities to share these thoughts with their patients in order to get feedback. The best opportunities occur either when patient and therapist are talking about an instance of great emotional upset or when the emotional upheaval takes place live in session. For example, a therapist formulates a hypothesis that her patient manifests a compelling abandonment schema. Later, when the therapist mentions her upcoming vacation, she notices that the patient becomes very withdrawn and sullen. The therapist, seizing the chance to assess the abandonment schema as it occurs, asks the patient: "Are you having some upsetting thoughts about my being away on vacation? Are you thinking that I'm leaving you in your hour of need? Is this something that is very familiar to you in your life?" This questioning opens the door to addressing the patient's most core beliefs in a very powerful, meaningful way. Note that the questioning methods presented here are more directive and leading than are typical of standard cognitive therapy, where Socratic questioning is the preferred mode of inquiry (Beck et al., 1979). Still, an ultimate goal is to make more and more use of the higher level Socratic method as treatment progresses (see Chapters 8 to 12 for clinical examples).

Another way in which therapists focus on hypothesized schemas is by noting common themes that run through a number of situations that patients describe within a session or over a number of sessions. For example, the therapist might say: "It seems to me that each of these three problem situations you've mentioned have something very important in common. In each situation you felt like a victim—that everyone was abusing your good will and trust, taking advantage of you, and not caring about the consequences for you. Does that seem accurate to you? Is this part of the difficulty that you have when it comes to trusting others? I'd like to hear your opinions on the matter if you feel up to discussing this with me." Some patients may respond with immediate recognition of the schema when it is presented to them. Others may not be so sure. Schemas may not be stored in the patient's memory in the form of words, so the presentation of a verbal descriptor may not instantly strike a chord. The therapist may opt to allow the patient time to consider the ideas and return to it later.

Schemas may be recognizable in nonverbal forms, such as mental pictures, tone of voice, kinesthetic cues, olfactory sensations, or temperature. An example is a patient who went outside on the first springlike day of the season, took a deep breath of clean, warm air, and promptly broke down and cried inconsolably. At first, this patient could offer no explanation for her reaction, except to say that she suddenly felt all alone in the world. The therapist, suspecting a nonverbally stored abandonment schema, asked when she had previously experienced interpersonal loss on a warm, beautiful day. After much probing of her memory, the patient was able to recall two critical events. First, she had gone boating on just such a sunny, warm day when she was a child, just hours before her father died of a sudden heart attack. Second, her most beloved boyfriend had broken off their relationship five years earlier during a spring break vacation in Florida. In the present, the sensation of deeply inhaling warm, clean air had triggered memories of two of the most traumatic episodes of abandonment she had ever experienced.

A useful aid for identifying schemas (and for ascertaining their effects on the patients' lives) is the Cognitive Conceptualization Diagram, developed at the Center for Cognitive Therapy in Philadelphia by Dr. Judith S. Beck (see Figures 4.3 and 4.4). Using this form, the therapist and patient identify critical childhood incidents, core beliefs that are associated with these incidents, the patient's conditional assumptions, and their compensatory strategies, as they affect several notable situations that epitomize the patient's current difficulties. Each situation is broken down into automatic thoughts, meanings (beliefs), emotions, and behaviors. Depending on the level of the patient's cognitive sophistication, the therapist may opt to assist the patient in some or all of this diagram.

Schema Modification

Verbal

Once the therapist and patient have identified the patient's relevant schemas and have understood the ways in which the patient's schemas typically become activated, the next step involves schema modification and restructuring. For schemas that are readily accessible to verbal recall and description, interventions that utilize verbal challenges are appropriate. We use a number of paper-and-pencil forms to facilitate this process.

The Core Belief Worksheet (developed by Dr. Judith S. Beck, see Figures 4.5 and 4.6) helps the patients to articulate their beliefs and schemas, and to rate the fluctuations in their degrees of certainty about these beliefs and schemas over the course of a week. Patients then generate new, therapeutically desirable beliefs and, likewise, rate their degrees of certainty regarding this new way of thinking. In order to solidify this proposed cognitive shift, patients are encouraged to document evidence that contradicts the old, dysfunctional core belief and supports the new, adaptive belief. Additionally, patients are to *reframe* positively any actual evidence that supported the dysfunctional belief in the past. The two-pronged approach of strengthening the new belief and weakening the old belief produces a stronger therapeutic effect than either method used alone.

We also recommend that therapists make use of the DTR, a technique that many BPD patients find difficult to apply effectively in the early stages of treatment when their cognitive processing skills are still relatively underdeveloped. However, since the patients' use of the DTR is part of their process of developing higher order cognitive skills, it is advisable to test patients' ability to benefit from their use of the

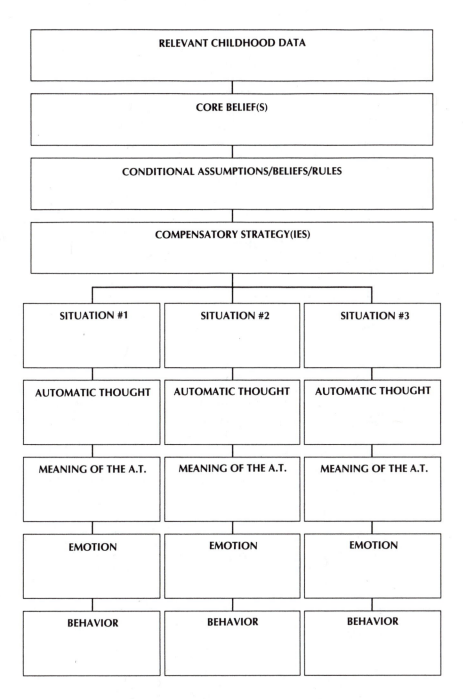

FIGURE 4.3. Cognitive Conceptualization Diagram

83

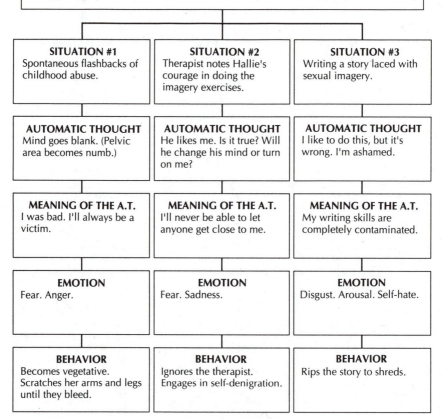

RELEVANT CHILDHOOD DATA
Sexually abused (repeatedly) by an uncle when she was 7 years old.

CORE BELIEF(S)
I'm bad. I'm disgusting. I'm damaged. I hate myself. I'm a fraud. I must be punished. It's dangerous to trust.

CONDITIONAL ASSUMPTIONS/BELIEFS/RULES
If I write stories that involve sex, it proves I'm a bad person. If I accept someone's attention, I will be vulnerable.

COMPENSATORY STRATEGY(IES)
Engages in sexual fantasies where she has control. Spends a great deal of time alone, taking photographs.

SITUATION #1	**SITUATION #2**	**SITUATION #3**
Spontaneous flashbacks of childhood abuse.	Therapist notes Hallie's courage in doing the imagery exercises.	Writing a story laced with sexual imagery.
AUTOMATIC THOUGHT	**AUTOMATIC THOUGHT**	**AUTOMATIC THOUGHT**
Mind goes blank. (Pelvic area becomes numb.)	He likes me. Is it true? Will he change his mind or turn on me?	I like to do this, but it's wrong. I'm ashamed.
MEANING OF THE A.T.	**MEANING OF THE A.T.**	**MEANING OF THE A.T.**
I was bad. I'll always be a victim.	I'll never be able to let anyone get close to me.	My writing skills are completely contaminated.
EMOTION	**EMOTION**	**EMOTION**
Fear. Anger.	Fear. Sadness.	Disgust. Arousal. Self-hate.
BEHAVIOR	**BEHAVIOR**	**BEHAVIOR**
Becomes vegetative. Scratches her arms and legs until they bleed.	Ignores the therapist. Engages in self-denigration.	Rips the story to shreds.

FIGURE 4.4. Cognitive Conceptualization Diagram

Judith S. Beck, Ph.D

Name: _____

Old Core Belief: _____

How much do you believe the old core belief right now?   (0–100) _____

What's the most you've believed it this week?   (0–100) _____

What's the least you've believed it this week?   (0–100) _____

New Belief: _____

How much do you believe the new belief right now?   (0–100) _____

Evidence That Contradicts Old Core Belief and Supports New Belief	*Evidence That Supports Old Core Belief, with Reframe*

FIGURE 4.5. Core Belief Worksheet

Judith S. Beck Ph.D

Name: _____ "Hallie" _____

Old Core Belief: _____ "I'm a bad, disgusting person." _____

How much do you believe the old core belief right now?   (0–100) __80__

What's the most you've believed it this week?   (0–100) __100__

What's the least you've believed it this week?   (0–100) __80__

New Belief: _____ "I have a mixture of positive and negative personal qualities." _____

How much do you believe the new belief right now?   (0–100) __50__

Evidence That Contradicts Old Core Belief and Supports New Belief	*Evidence That Supports Old Core Belief, with Reframe*
1. Other photographers and writers that I know seem to like me and admire my work.	1. Although I indulge in sexual fantasies, I do not act them out.
2. I'm kind to animals and children.	2. My preoccupation with sex is normal in light of the incest that I suffered at an early age.
3. I have been successful as a journalist in the past.	3. Although I may *feel* bad and disgusting, this does not mean that I *am* bad and disgusting.
4. My therapist has been willing to confront me when I do things that are maladaptive. Therefore, his positive comments about me are credible. He sees things in me that are both negative and positive. I'm not 100% bad.	4. I do have faults, but I've been unwilling or unable to focus my attention and memory on truly good things about myself.

FIGURE 4.6. Core Belief Worksheet

DTR, rather than assume that they cannot learn this powerful self-help tool. If they react adversely to the introduction of this technique, therapists have the option of helping the patients to understand the schemas responsible for their negative responses, or shelving the technique until a later time.

Imaginal

Imagery techniques are used to combat beliefs and schemas that have a significant pictorial component, such as vivid visual memories of early life events that were particularly upsetting for the patient (Edwards, 1990). We use imagery exercises for three main purposes. The first of these is assessment. By exploring memories and images of critical incidents in the past, therapists and their BPD patients can gain a better understanding of the types of schemas that may have formed. For example, as the patient closes his eyes (perhaps following a brief relaxation induction) in order to visualize a humiliating moment in his childhood, the therapist asks the "child" in the image what he is thinking and feeling. Therapist and patient then examine what the "child" is concluding about himself, other people, and his future as a function of the visualized event. Further, the "child" is asked to offer his idiosyncratic explanation for why the remembered event is happening, and what lessons in life he is learning as a result of the negative experience.

A second function of the imagery exercise described above is to modify therapeutically the "child's" self-defeating interpretations about the remembered situation. To illustrate, the adult patient may be able to state logically that he doesn't blame himself for the sexual abuse that he suffered as a child, but he still may carry a great deal of residual self-hatred and guilt that are born of early maladaptive schemas (e.g., "I'm bad, unlovable, worthless"). Metaphorically speaking, the "child" still remains convinced that the abuse was his fault, therefore the intervention must attend not only to the adult patient in the here and now, but the "child" of many years ago as well. Once the therapist ascertains that the adult patient is capable of understanding rationally that he is not to blame, and that he is indeed a worthwhile and lovable person (as indicated by his responses to standard techniques such as the DTR), the process of trying to convince the "child" of his innocence via imagery exercises may begin.

While the adult patient keeps his eyes closed (and remains in a relaxed state), the therapist provides empathy to the "child" and asks him to consider other ways to understand the upsetting event (e.g., reconstruing the child's father's drunken rage from "It's all my fault. I'm a bad boy and I upset Daddy." to "I'm upset because my father is not a well man. It affects my life but it's not my fault at all"). The therapist actively assists in this process of modifying and restructuring the meaning of the visual memory.

Third, the therapist can use the image to help the patient "reenact" the past in a healthier way. This is accomplished by asking the patient to take control over the image, to manipulate the events in a way that he could not when the event really happened, and to produce a more favorable outcome. This technique is *not* intended to deny the past but, rather, to help the patient gain a sense of empowerment.

Imagery techniques often produce strong affect in BPD patients. The therapist, therefore, should explain the possibility of adverse emotional effects, provide a clear clinical rationale for the procedure, gain the patient's permission in proceeding with the exercise, and brainstorm ways to moderate and modulate the intense affect after the procedure is over.

We explain to patients that a primary goal of the exercise is to modify the schema by empowering the "child" patient with the knowledge, rationality, and compassion of the adult patient. We note that, as a result, the adult patient may be better able to accept and cope with the traumatic memories and to modify the emotional reactions so that they are less harmful to the patient in the present time. Imagery exercises are powerful tools and should not be used toward the end of a session or with a fragile patient who has not yet demonstrated at least a moderate degree of trust in the therapist. For that reason, we often make arrangements in advance with BPD patients before going ahead with imagery exercises. Then we structure an entire session, or entire *numbers* of sessions, to give full attention to both the induction and the debriefing.

In order to choose appropriate subject matter for the imagery exercises, we follow these general guidelines:

1. Focus on past events that the patient has identified as critical in his or her life (e.g., memories surrounding the traumatic, premature death of a parent).
2. Focus on a current event in the patient's life in which the patient's emotional responses seem highly pronounced, more than the situation would seem to suggest. Link this to similar events in the past.
3. Focus on an issue in response to which the patient has shown exaggerated affect in the therapy session itself (e.g., patient cries when the therapist makes a seemingly innocent remark). Link this reaction to the patient's reactions to other people outside of therapy, in the present and in the past.

In general, schema activation can be observed in a patient when a topic evokes strong affect and/or impulsive behaviors that seem inappropriate to the situation at hand. Sometimes this occurs "accidentally" during the course of the session; at other times the therapist and patient can plan ahead to activate schemas by deliberately focusing on images and memories of these provocative situations. The therapist should follow by asking the patient to focus on the emotions (and their physiological concomitants as well) for a full minute or two. Then the therapist makes the link by asking, "When have you experienced these feelings in the past?" or "When was the first time that you can recall feeling this way?" If the patient is able to remember, therapist and patient then make a short list of such past experiences. We often attempt to focus as far back in time as possible, realizing full well that patients may have only fragments of relevant memories. We ask the patients to close their eyes so that they may elaborate on their memories. It is important to ask for as many peripheral details as possible, such as where they are, what they are seeing, whom they are with, what colors and textures they can see, and so on. For example, a patient who at first was unable to articulate a vague memory about a humiliating beating he had taken was able to remember much more about the feelings and thoughts that were central to the event when he elaborated on the sights and sounds surrounding him in the memory.

Therapists then follow by asking the patients to describe the most upsetting moments of the memory in as much detail as possible. By doing so, patients may have greater access to their feelings, thoughts, and schemas in the memory. A sample of prompts that therapists can ask their patients during imagery exercises are listed as part of Table 4.1.

During the height of the negative memory, therapists ask the patients what the "child" (or "younger person," if the memory is more recent) is learning from the critical event—about him-or herself, about other people, and about life in general. At such times it is common to hear patients articulate schematic beliefs such as, "I feel like a worthless nothing" ("badness," unlovability, incompetence) or "I feel all alone in the world" (abandonment, unlovability). The therapist must be especially supportive of BPD patients at these times in order to keep them actively engaged in the imagery long enough to explore all the relevant feelings and beliefs that emerge.

Once the therapist and patient have ascertained schematic information from the imaged event, the therapist asks the patient if he or she holds these core beliefs in the here and now as well. For example, patients who have experienced sexual abuse in their childhoods may have concluded that they were to blame, that they enjoyed it and wanted it to happen, and that they are "bad." After reviewing such traumatic situations imaginally, the patients may recognize that they still maintain this sense of their badness.

Our patient Hallie was able to state rationally in the present that she realized that she was an innocent victim of her uncle's abusive behavior. Nevertheless, in her current-day heterosexual relationship she still experienced feelings of guilt and revulsion. Hallie and her therapist conceptualized this as signifying that although the "rational adult" in her understood she was blameless and safe, the childlike memories within her would not let her senses of guilt and danger rest. Hallie and her therapist agreed to spend a full session in which the patient would reevoke a memory of her being molested by her uncle. The goal was to reevaluate rationally the situation from the perspective of Hallie as a *child*.

Hallie at first feared the proposed exercise, in the belief that it would cause her to remember even more horrifying aspects of the abuse that she had forgotten. For example, she did not remember experiencing forced intercourse, but she wondered if the imagery work would uncover this, a memory she did not particularly want to reawaken. After taking a week to think it over, however, Hallie agreed to go ahead with the imagery exercise. She reasoned that her current depression and low self-esteem were cues that she had some important unfinished business to take care of. Thus, she consented to the imagery work but added that she did not want to undergo a preparatory relaxation induction, as this would make her feel that her body was out of her control. The therapist respected Hallie's wishes.

In the image, Hallie was asked to close her eyes and to go back to the scene of the abuse. In order to make the experience of the image more vivid, the therapist asked Hallie to describe her surroundings, including the room, the paintings on the wall, the color and texture of the walls and rugs, and any sounds and smells of which she was aware. Then the therapist asked Hallie to recall how the uncle summoned her to his "office." Hallie began to cry as she recalled how she was tricked into fondling the

Table 4.1. Eliciting and Modifying Schemas from Childhood Memories (Sample Method)

1. Schema activation signals
    a. High affect
    b. Affect is inappropriate in intensity and content for the situation described.
2. Sources of information used to hypothesize the schemas
    a. History
    b. Current problems in living (general)
    c. Patient's presenting complaints (specific)
    d. Emergent crises
3. Induce imagery. Visualize current situation. Assess affect.
4. Focus attention on the emotions and physical sensations.
5. Ask, "Do you remember when you first felt this way?"
6. Focus attention on images, thoughts, and fragments thereof.
7. Elaborate content of the memory.
8. Elaborate thoughts and emotions experienced by the "child."
    a   What is the child thinking?
    b. What is the child feeling?
    c. What meaning does the child attach to this event?
    d. Why does the child think this is happening?
    e. What does the child expect to happen in the future as a result of this event?
    f. What does the child think about him- or herself as a result of this event?
    g. What does the child think about other people as a result of this event?
    h. What "rules for living" is the child constructing?
    i. What interpretations is the child making about his or her lovability, competency, sense of control, and so on?
9. Summarize the patient's personal meaning attached to this memory.
10. Assess the adult patient's thoughts (e.g., ask, "Do you still believe these things?").
11. Engage in rational responding with the adult patient.
12. Modify the child's beliefs.
    a. Bring adult patient into the image.
    b. Bring "safe" person into the image (e.g., Grandma, teacher, therapist).
    c. Ask the child, "With whom in the image would you like to communicate?"
    d. Ask the child, "What do you need to hear from them?"
13. Assess modifications in the child's belief. Ask the child: "What are you thinking now?" "What are you feeling now?"
14. Modify the events of the image so that the child is empowered and feeling better about him- or herself.
    a. Ask the child, "What do you want to happen?"
    b. Change the behavior of others in the image.
    c. Change the behavior of the child (greater control).
    d. Change the consequences of the event (more positive).
15. Assess the adult patient's postimagery thoughts and feelings.

uncle's genitals. Throughout the imagery, the therapist openly empathized with Hallie as a child. He asked her to express her feelings and thoughts, as the following dialogue indicates:

T: As you are touching him, what is going through your mind?

H: I'm curious. I don't know what's going on. I can't figure out what he wants me to do, but I want to be cooperative or he'll get angry with me.

T: It's absolutely normal for a child to be curious about anything new, especially something sexual. There's nothing wrong with your being curious. There's also nothing wrong with your wanting to be cooperative. You're trying to be a good girl. You couldn't possibly realize the full extent of the way that your uncle was taking advantage of you.

H: I'm feeling sick to my stomach. I feel nauseous. I don't want to touch him anymore. He's saying okay, but now he says he wants to touch me.

T: How does that make you feel about yourself, Hallie?

H: I'm disgusted with myself. I feel bad, dirty, but he isn't letting me go.

T: This is terribly painful for you. It's not right that this is being done to you. But you are *not* bad or dirty, Hallie. You are a good and honest child. Someone is abusing your trust. He's the one who should be feeling badly about himself, not you.

As the exercise progressed, the goal was to have the child Hallie begin rationally to challenge her own sense of badness. In order to achieve this, the image was manipulated so that the child Hallie could see the present Hallie come into the image.

T: Hallie, I want you to see the "adult you" coming into the room with Hallie the child and her uncle. I want you to talk to Hallie the child and tell her what you think of her, from the point of view of an understanding adult.

H: Hallie, I'm so sorry this is happening to you. It's not your fault. You would never do this if you realized what was going on and if you were big and strong enough to defend yourself.

T: Is Hallie the child a bad and dirty little girl?

H: Hallie, you're a good girl. You're bright and you're happy and trusting.

T: Does Hallie the child believe you?

H: She's trying to, but she's still confused.

T: Help her some more.

H: Hallie, I love you. You're kind and sweet. You're just trying to be obedient. You're good, and nothing can change that, not even what our uncle is doing to us.

T: I want Hallie the child to say something back. Does she understand? Speak in a child's voice so I know for sure that Hallie the child is speaking.

H: (As a child) I'm not bad. I just feel bad. It's not the same thing.

T: Are you still worthy of being loved?

H: Yes.

T: Are you still worthy of liking yourself?

H: Yes.

T: Tell me more about it.

H: This is a bad experience. It doesn't make me a bad person. I still deserve to feel good about myself. I still deserve to have people love me. I just want to be able to trust them back.

Hallie underwent a significant modification of her badness schema as a result of this exercise. If Hallie the child had not been able to articulate the kinds of adaptive responses recorded here, the therapist could have made use of some other options in the imagery exercise. For example, a "safe" person could have been brought into the image as Hallie's protector. Because of the flexibility of the intervention, the safe person could be someone who might not have been actually available in the real event. For example, if Grandma was a safe and trusted person but had died before the time the abuse occurred, the therapist could still choose to summon her into the image. This safe person can be directed to comfort the patient (as a child), talk to her, or take her to safety. The safe person may also be directed to hold and hug the child. The therapist can ask the patient to put her arms around herself in session to enhance this effect. After each attempt to restructure the schema, the therapist should ask the child how she is feeling and thinking to assess the degree of schema modification.

Another variation of the imagery exercise would have Hallie the "child" become empowered enough to speak out against the perpetrator. The therapist should ask the patient what she would like to be able to do, given this chance to "relive" the experience. In cases of sexual abuse, we have found that some patients simply want the abusers to own up to their behavior and apologize. In other cases the patient wants to lash out verbally and physically at the perpetrator. The therapist should try to induce in the image whatever the child patient asks for. Care must be taken here, however, as the patient may conclude that he or she is bad for having violent thoughts or for not having rescued him- or herself in like fashion during the actual episodes of abuse. As a rule of thumb, the therapist should check in with the patients (adult and child) to see how they are feeling and thinking at various points in the exercise. If the intervention is causing too much distress, the therapist can reduce the stress level by speaking to the adult patient, thereby establishing a little more safe distance from the memory.

Sometimes the patient wants to make a symbolic gesture in the image. It might be an act that indicates that the patient is powerful and not helpless, or lovable and not bad. Patients may want to knock down walls, break chains from their wrists, be hugged by teddy bears, or hear God telling them that they are good, to name a few possibilities.

Because the changes in imagery may need to be repeated, one particular scenario may be the focus of a number of imagery inductions. Likewise, several different critical memories may need to be tapped before schema modification can begin to take place. Once the most important images have been restructured, other images may then be restructured with verbal techniques.

Because schemas often are antagonistic, creativity is needed in formulating imagery exercises so that the changing of one schema does not worsen another. For example, patients may want to punish a parent-perpetrator in order to feel less dependent and incompetent. At the same time, the patients may be yearning for love from the same parents. The image of punishing the parents may inadvertently strengthen the unlovability and badness schemas. Therapists should be active guides in these imaginal excursions in order to circumvent problems like this. For example, the therapist could introduce into the image a "good father" who would punish the abusing father and then come back and care for the child patient.

Imagery exercises can be quite powerful for changing schemas. We have used such interventions not only to deal with memories of childhood abuse, but also in the following ways:

1. To help a patient speak to her deceased father, whom she believed she had "abandoned" when he lay dying in the hospital (thus to combat her "badness" schema)
2. To assist a patient in getting accurate feedback from a new set of parents (the real parents had taught this patient that he was the devil incarnate)
3. To relive an early love relationship that had soured as a result of the patient's mistrust; this time the patient would nurture the relationship imaginally (from Newman, 1991, the case of "Ms. B")
4. To "rectify" experiences of failure in the past by enabling the patient to use skills he had learned as an adult in order to succeed (thus giving life to the often-used phrase, "If only I knew then what I know now...").

"The Cloud"

As noted in Chapter 2, the schemas that make up "the cloud" are encoded during the first few years of life. These schemas may be activated by nonverbal cues such as temperature, smells, physical sensations, posture, and tone of voice. For example, one patient's abandonment schema was activated when the heat in her apartment went out. The temperature dropped to a point that felt similarly cold to the drafty Victorian house in which she lived with her neglectful parents during her years as an infant and toddler. Another patient who was abused by a babysitter who forced him to perform fellatio later developed an aversion to many foods, as well as an inability to open his mouth wide enough to speak loudly. A third patient, whose mother had been hypomanic and hypercritical, would have her unlovability schema activated whenever the therapist would speak to her in a hurried fashion (e.g., on the phone, or when trying to wrap up a session that had already gone well over time), even if the content of the interaction was friendly. A final example is that of a patient who could not tolerate sitting or standing too close to other people without having a great sense of mistrust. This person had spent his early years sharing a room with a number of unruly children in a foster home.

The first step in modifying the schemas of "the cloud" is to identify the nonverbal cues that cause hot affect in the patient (usually indicative that a schema has been aroused). This can be accomplished by carefully assessing those situations both in session and out of session (in the present and in the past) to which the patient seems to be "hypersensitive." By looking at all sensory modalities across all of these situations, patterns will emerge that suggest that certain nonverbal cues trigger the schemas.

Therapists use a *combination* of verbal, imaginal, and physical methods in order to challenge the schemas of "the cloud." In the case of the patient whose unlovability schema was triggered by the therapist's pressured speech, the therapist informed the patient that she would be deliberately speaking in a rushed manner in order to activate the schema. However, she encouraged the patient to listen carefully to the overt content of the message. The therapist's hurried monologue was a stream of automatic thoughts about being short of time. The following is a facsimile of the actual intervention:

"I'm really late today. I never seem to have enough time to do all the things I need to do. I really want to help 'Anna' but I'm in such a hurry I'm not sure I can do an effective job. Oh, why can't there be more time? Anna deserves my undivided attention. Anna deserves to feel good about herself. She's very lovable and often she doesn't know that. Now she may think because I'm pressed for time that I don't care about her and that she's not lovable but that's not true. She's very lovable. Oh, darn, why can't there be more time?"

The therapist then asked Anna for her thoughts and feelings. Anna admitted that she felt very agitated by the therapist's rushed monologue, but that she was able to hear some of the supportive content. Interestingly, Anna claimed that she had to work very hard to stay focused on what the therapist was saying, as the patient's feelings of nausea and urge to cry were very distracting. She indicated that the therapist's warning to listen carefully to the words was the only reason that she was able to hear them. Such is the power of schema-driven reactions that are based in "the cloud."

The therapist's clinical rationale for this procedure was to focus Anna's attention on verbal information that was incompatible with her cloud-based sense of unlovability. This would cause a form of cognitive dissonance that would provide the impetus for Anna to reevaluate her negative visceral reactions to the therapist's pressured speech. Indeed, Anna was able to see for herself that her sense of unlovability came automatically from within herself and was not actually based on what the therapist was saying. Further, Anna demonstrated to herself that with cognitive effort she could focus her attention on the overt verbal content of the communication.

This technique alone was not wholly sufficient to modify Anna's unlovability schema. Therefore, the therapist instituted some imagery/memory exercises as well. For example, the therapist asked Anna to remember a time when she was a little girl when her mother was *not* hypomanic. Anna was instructed to imagine those times when her mother held her and spoke gently to her. The therapist asked Anna to wrap her own arms around herself and to say aloud the nice things that her mother was saying to her in the memory. When Anna's memory would fail, she was encouraged to continue reciting the kinds of things that she would *like* for her mother to have said to her. Another exercise involved Anna's cuddling a stuffed animal that she liked, pretending that it was herself as a baby, and saying a number of affectionate and nurturing statements.

As highlighted by the case of Anna, the method of modifying or reconstructing "cloud"-based schemas involves:

1. Identifying the nonverbal cues that activate the schemas
2. Articulating the types of schemas that are evoked
3. Deliberately activating the schemas using the appropriate nonverbal cues
4. Using words, images, and physical sensations to combat the content of the schemas

We have also seen that it is possible to counteract the activation of a "cloud"-based schema by utilizing a nonverbal stimulus that represents comfort for the patient. For example, the patient whose abandonment schema was activated by a cold house was instructed to wrap herself in an electric blanket while she worked on her standard cognitive therapy homework assignments such as her DTRs. Another patient was able to remember that the only times he felt safe and loved as a very young child were when his "nanny" would wash his hair and powder him after a bath. In the present, he found relief from extreme negative affect by washing his hair with the same baby shampoo and by using the same brand of talcum powder, whose fragrance he associated with being loved. After shampooing and applying the talcum powder, this patient reported that his abilities to perform his cognitive therapy homework assignments were greatly enhanced.

Behavioral Tests

Some BPD patients are uncertain about how to translate their new, positive beliefs into new behaviors. For example, a patient who has worked hard in therapy to modify a schema of mistrust may have little concept of how to interact with others in a more trusting fashion. Likewise, a patient who has always expected to be unloved and abandoned may have no experience in behaving as a person who demonstrates a sense of self-worth and security in relationships. This is so because of the chronic nature of BPD, especially when the schemas have been operative since very early in life as they are with "the cloud." In many cases, there is scarcely a premorbid history of adaptive functioning to which the patients can return.

In order to facilitate the BPD patients' translating their schematic and affective changes into appropriate behavioral changes, the therapist can do the following:

1. Instruct patients to self-monitor any naturally occurring adaptive behaviors that are born of new, positive beliefs, and to keep a journal of these behaviors for future reference.
2. Role-play various scenarios with patients in session in order to help them gain some experience in positive interpersonal interactions.
3. Ask patients to examine the behaviors of persons that they would like to emulate (assuming that these persons are happy and productive individuals!).
4. Model positive behaviors for the patient. For example, ask the patient, "Do you remember how I handled those moments when there was some tension between us? Do you recall how we were able to reaffirm our commitment to a positive working relationship? What can you derive from that experience that you can use for yourself in your everyday relationships?"
5. Utilize behavioral experiments.

This latter point warrants some extra discussion, as it is a staple of both standard and advanced cognitive therapy. Behavioral experiments involve patients formulating hypotheses about their behavior and then, between sessions, acting in such a way as to test these hypotheses. One of our patients, who had worked hard to combat her schemas of unlovability and abandonment, used to create ugly scenes in public when she thought she noticed that her boyfriend was looking at other women. Now, after over a year of therapy, she wondered how she would react if she caught her boyfriend's wandering eye. She believed that she could cope better if she told her boyfriend exactly what she was experiencing at such moments in a calm fashion. However, she believed that he would ignore her or make fun of her, which would precipitate a full schema activation crisis.

In order to address this, the therapist role-played this scenario with the patient in preparation for the actual event. Then, the patient's task was to test her hypothesis by actually telling the boyfriend that she was prone to feeling rejected when he would glance at another woman, and that she really needed him to pay more attention to her. When she actually did this, she was pleasantly surprised to find that her boyfriend was quite receptive and understanding. To him, this reaction was far better than having a drink splashed on him, which had happened twice previously! The patient's new behavior enabled him to be more sympathetic. As a result, the patient saw that her fears were unfounded, and that she could act on her newfound emotional control and improved self-image with positive results for the relationship.

Not all behavioral experiments are this successful. Sometimes the behavioral tests have to be run numerous times before enough evidence can be gathered in order to evaluate the hypotheses adequately. Nevertheless, therapists should endeavor to help their patients formulate behavioral experiments that have high probabilities of success. The goal is to encourage patients to take growth-enhancing steps, not to engage in overly risky behaviors. By making small but steady advances in a BPD patient's adaptive behavioral repertoire, old schemas may gradually erode as self-esteem builds and the reactions of other people become more benign. Thus, a positive feedback loop of hope and change can be established.

SUMMARY

This chapter has reviewed the major techniques and strategies that are used in the advanced cognitive therapy of BPD. Four major components have been outlined:

1. Establishing a positive therapeutic relationship as a vehicle for change
2. Handling crises and pseudocrises in a consistent and calm manner
3. Using standard cognitive therapy techniques, such as DTRs, activity schedules, mastery and pleasure ratings, scaling techniques, assertiveness and communication skills, and antianxiety techniques such as relaxation and breathing control
4. Using schema-focused cognitive therapy techniques, such as imagery exercises, memory reconstruction, schema identification, and the use of physical cues to deal with "the cloud"

We have found all of the aforementioned strategies and techniques very useful in the treatment of this challenging population. Even so, the course of therapy is rarely smooth. Therapists must be prepared to deal with frustrating times of patients' resistance and regression. When this occurs, therapists can do the most good by modeling a calm, determined approach to facing such adversity. By continuing to demonstrate the central cognitive therapy qualities of collaboration, warmth, empathy, and genuine interest, and by continuing to engage in the important cognitive therapy activities of providing active feedback and making regular assessments of the patient's thoughts and feelings in session, the course of therapy can be kept on track.

Chapter 5

Pharmacotherapy and Associated Medical Issues in the Treatment of Borderline Personality Disorder

The primary focus of this book is an explication of the cognitive conceptualization and therapy of BPD. However, the implementation of cognitive therapy does not necessarily exclude pharmacotherapy as part of the overall treatment plan. A number of studies have investigated and demonstrated the utility of a *combination* of cognitive therapy and antidepressant medication in the treatment of unipolar depression (cf. Blackburn, Bishop, Glen, Whalley, & Christie, 1981; Hollon & Beck, 1978; Hollon, DeRubeis, Evans, Tuason, Wiemer, & Garvey, 1986). Although there is no commensurate literature on the combined pharmacotherapy and psychotherapy of BPD, a number of writers have noted the potential utility of research and practice in this area (Adelman, 1985; Cowdry & Gardner, 1988; Kroll, 1988; Soloff, 1987).

Pharmacotherapy and psychotherapy (such as cognitive therapy) need not represent competing ideologies (Bassuk, Schoonover, & Gelenberg, 1983). To suggest that psychiatric syndromes and their concomitant treatment plans are *either* biological *or* psychological is to engage in erroneous dichotomous thinking. The multidimensional characteristics of most mental disorders in general, and of BPD in particular, warrant consideration of the use of more than one therapy modality (Adelman, 1985). Bassuk et al. (1983) maintain that whereas psychotherapy may improve patients' interpersonal behaviors and relationships, psychotropic medication may improve mood and reduce somatic symptoms. They hold that the combined effects often appear greater than those produced by either treatment alone. Similarly, Soloff (1987) suggests that the acute stress reactions of many borderline patients can best be helped pharmacologically, as a *prelude* and/or *adjunct* to talk therapy. In this manner, the patients may be biochemically assisted into states of mind and body that are more conducive to the work of psychotherapy.

Likewise, Cowdry and Gardner (1988) view medical and psychological interventions as producing potential positive feedback loops, whereby the establishment of a working therapeutic alliance facilitates the patient's acceptance of medication, which then may reduce the borderline patient's extreme symptoms (e.g., self-mutilation, dissociative states). This bolsters the therapeutic relationship, facilitates the progress of psychotherapy, and further encourages medication compliance.

This chapter focuses on the pharmacological modality of treatment for BPD. Research on medication trials for this disorder is reviewed, and related medical issues are discussed. Also underscored are the difficulties that researchers and clinicians encounter in this area, as well as promising directions for future study and application.

THE RELIABILITY AND VALIDITY OF BORDERLINE PERSONALITY DISORDER: IMPLICATIONS FOR PHARMACOTHERAPY RESEARCH

It is well known that a psychological disorder is amenable to empirical study and systematic treatment only to the extent that the disorder is reliably diagnosable (i.e., consistently identifiable by independent observers) and valid (i.e., allowing researchers and clinicians to infer a common etiology, course, and outcome, given certain conditions).

A significant advance in the reliability of the borderline diagnosis was made in 1980 with the publication of the *Diagnostic and Statistical Manual of Mental Disorders,* third edition (DSM-III). Here, an attempt was made to define more clearly the core symptoms that make up the disorder. This refinement of diagnostic classification has allowed for more rigorous empirical evaluation of the disorder and its treatment (Waldinger & Frank, 1989). Accordingly, the bulk of the literature on controlled studies and case trials in the pharmacotherapy of BPD has been produced since 1980 (Ellison & Adler, 1984).

Unfortunately, there are still significant difficulties even with the DSM-III (APA, 1980) and DSM-III-R (APA, 1987) diagnoses that impinge on the degree of rigor that is possible in studying this disorder. Kroll (1988) notes that the reliability and validity of the diagnosis are compromised by the way the criteria are structured. Eight primary symptoms are presented, the existence of *any five* of which is sufficient for the diagnosis. As a result, two patients who may both be classified as suffering from BPD may actually look quite different in terms of clinical presentation. Furthermore, they may exhibit marked differential responses to various treatment approaches, including differing classes of pharmacologic agents.

Some researchers maintain that while there is no single miracle drug for the borderline disorder, careful analyses of symptom clusters *within* the disorder may suggest specific pharmacological treatments (e.g., Cowdry & Gardner, 1988). One approach that has been suggested is to target medications toward the most severe symptoms that each patient manifests (e.g., Ellison & Adler, 1984; Soloff, 1987; Soloff, George, Nathan, Schulz, Ulrich, & Perel, 1986; Waldinger & Frank, 1989). For example, neuroleptic medication might be chosen to treat the disorder when thought disturbance and dissociative symptoms are most prominent, whereas antidepressants and/or lithium might be the initial treatment of choice when depression and mood swings are the dominant features.

In the following section, the current data on the range of pharmacologic agents that have been used in the treatment of the borderline syndrome will be reviewed. Emphasis is placed on work that suggests a matching of subcategories of symptoms to different classes of medication, as per the philosophy mentioned above.

RECENT RESEARCH ON SPECIFIC PHARMACOLOGICAL APPROACHES

Although there is a growing body of literature on the pharmacotherapy of the borderline patient (Links, Steiner, Boiago, & Irwin, 1990; Soloff, 1987), there is a striking lack of rigorously controlled studies in this area relative to other domains, such as pharmacotherapy for depression, bipolar disorder, anxiety disorders, and psychotic disorders (Cowdry & Gardner, 1988; Kroll, 1988; Soloff et al., 1986). It is nearly impossible to draw conclusions on the basis of a cumulative review of studies conducted prior to the advent of the DSM-III in 1980, because there was such a wide variety of clinical syndromes that were subsumed under the rubric of "borderline" disorder. These included such diagnostic categories as "pseudoneurotic schizophrenia," "emotionally unstable personality," "phobic-anxiety depersonalization," "hysteroid dysphoria," and others (Kroll, 1988). Therefore, in order to bring some semblance of clarity to a metareview of the field, one must look at more recent studies, few though they may be. Aside from the fact that a small number of controlled studies prevents the formulation of general conclusions, the relative infancy of this area of study means that maintenance and generalization data are lacking as well (Soloff, 1987). Therefore, the *long-term* efficacy of drug treatments for BPD has not been adequately assessed at this time.

A review of the state-of-the-art studies in this area (e.g., Cole, Salomon, Gunderson, Sunderland, & Simmonds, 1984; Cowdry & Gardner, 1988; Gardner & Cowdry, 1985; Goldberg, Schulz, Schulz, Resnick, Mameer, & Friedel, 1986; Liebowitz et al., 1988; Links et al., 1990; Soloff, 1987; Soloff et al., 1986) provides some clues to why this research is lacking in sheer quantity. It is, quite simply, a most formidable task to execute (Snyder & Pitts, 1986). Consider the difficulties:

1. Finding a group of borderline patients with relatively homogeneous symptoms requires rigorous screening, access to a large sample, and ample treatment facilities to treat the many patients who do not meet inclusion criteria but who nonetheless need clinical attention.

2. Administering medications on a double-blind basis presents major logistical problems for an inpatient staff that continually must be on guard for crisis management.
3. The high rate of acting-out behaviors often necessitates emergency measures that require the patient's removal from the study; thus, attrition rates tend to be higher than rigorous research would dictate.
4. Patients' compliance with medication, even on an inpatient basis, is nearly impossible to ensure, thus presenting researchers with yet another possible confound.
5. Statistical artifacts are more likely to be a factor in the data analyses when the course of a disorder is as erratic as it is with the borderline patient.

These problems are the most obvious, but they do not represent an exhaustive list.

Furthermore, many of these studies are conducted in inpatient settings. Even in the best controlled studies, there is the question of whether findings are generalizable to outpatient borderline populations. In order to study outpatient populations directly, the problems of medication noncompliance and lack of safe controls over abuse, dependence, or polydrug interactions (e.g., if the patient uses alcohol to excess in addition to medication that acts in synergy with alcohol) become even more of an obstacle to the researcher. Additionally, attrition rates are less likely to be as manageable as they might be within the confines of inpatient settings.

The upshot of these lamentations is that the recent increase in interest in BPD does not necessarily translate immediately into an information boom. However, concerted efforts are now being made to shed light on pharmacotherapy for the borderline syndrome, with the result being that some general principles now can be outlined. The remainder of this section will present some of these principles of drug treatment of the borderline patient.

ANTIDEPRESSANTS

Conservative figures estimate that as many as 50 percent of all patients diagnosed as having BPD also suffer from an affective disorder, most commonly unipolar depression (Kroll, 1988). Given that tricyclic antidepressants are the standard pharmacological treatment of choice for patients who suffer from depression, they also merit serious consideration for application in cases of dual diagnosis of borderline and depressive syndromes (Ellison & Adler, 1984; Kroll, 1988; Millon, 1981), especially when endogenous features dominate the mood disturbance (Kroll, 1986). This is not to imply that the tricyclics should be prescribed in a cavalier fashion; on the contrary, there is evidence that some borderline patients evince exacerbated symptoms in reaction to these drugs (Gardner & Cowdry, 1985; Links et al., 1990; Perse & Griest, 1984; Soloff, George, Nathan, Schulz, & Perel, 1986; Soloff, George, Nathan, Schulz, Cornelius, Herring, & Perel, 1989). Such symptoms have included increased severity of anxiety, hostility, agitation, self-injurious behaviors, and dissociative experiences. Additionally, borderline patients, as a group, do not respond as favorably to these medications as do patients who suffer from major depression in the absence of BPD (Kroll, 1988).

Soloff (1987) writes that the atypical nature of depression in borderline patients, along with the unfavorable reactions that some patients show in response to tricyclics such as amitriptyline (Elavil), suggests that the monoamine oxidase inhibitors (MAO-I) class of antidepressants may be more appropriate. He contends that MAO-Is offer many of the same benefits that occur with the use of tricyclics, but *without* the untoward effects of disinhibition that are sometimes seen in borderline patients who take tricyclic medication. Tranylcypromine (Parnate) is described as having main effects in improving borderline patients' depressed mood, anhedonia, suicidality, impulsivity, anger, and sensitivity to interpersonal rejection. Phenelzine (Nardil) is noted to have improved borderline patients' mood reactivity, hypersomnia, hyperphagia, rejection sensitivity, behavioral impulsivity, and problems of emptiness, boredom, and loneliness. Ellison & Adler (1984) have also evaluated MAO-Is in a favorable light, citing their efficacy in dampening down extreme emotional responses to interpersonal events. Kroll (1986) echoes these sentiments, writing that there is preliminary evidence to suggest that the MAO-Is are useful in the treatment of borderline patients who evidence a preponderance of situationally triggered dysphorias.

Though cautious not to make grandiose claims, Kroll (1988) enthusiastically endorses further study of the efficacy of the MAO-Is. He reports anecdotal evidence from his own clinical experience that supports the notion that the MAO-Is can be very helpful to some borderline patients. Kroll (1988) especially recommends the use of drugs such as tranylcypromine and phenelzine in severe cases, where self-mutilation is an ongoing major concern. Here, he reasons, the potential benefits of the medication far outweigh the dangers involved in the use of this class of antidepressants. The contraindications alluded to here will be discussed in detail in the following section.

Cowdry & Gardner (1988) have also found beneficial effects of tranylcypromine, but caution that the seeming improvements that have been found in borderline symptoms (such as in self-injurious behavior) may be due primarily to improvement in mood. In other words, it may be premature to conclude that MAO-Is are an effective treatment for the borderline disorder per se. Rather, they may achieve indirect positive results in the behavioral realm as a function of the degree to which they produce results in the affective domain.

At present, a new wave of antidepressant medications, including fluoxetine (Prozac), bupropion (Welbutrin), and sertraline HCL (Zoloft), has received a great deal of positive attention. These medications may prove to be successful additions to the pharmacotherapy armamentarium in the treatment of BPD, although the data are not in at this time. Anecdotally, a combination of fluoxetine and low-dose neuroleptics has shown some promise with a very limited number of patients (Heller, 1991). The next area of pharmacological exploration may be here.

LITHIUM

Lithium carbonate is a well-documented efficacious pharmacologic treatment for bipolar disorder. Given that affective instability is also one of the core features of the borderline syndrome (Kroll, 1988), it seems logical that lithium might be an appropriate element of the treatment regimen for BPD as well. Although clinical experience supports this notion (e.g., Soloff, 1987), there are few empirical studies on the utility of lithium in the treatment of BPD, as defined by modern DSM-III or DSM-III-R criteria (e.g., Links et al., 1990). Pre-DSM-III studies on "emotionally unstable character disorder" (EUCD) have demonstrated that lithium facilitates mood stability and reduces aggressive behavior in hospitalized adolescent girls (Rifkin, Quitkin, Carillo, Blumberg, & Klein, 1972), and in impulsive criminal subjects (Shader, Jackson, & Dodes, 1974). To the extent that one may infer an overlap between EUCD and the modern-day borderline diagnosis, these studies offer some support for the use of lithium in treating BPD.

More recently, Links et al. (1990) performed an ambitious double-blind, random-order, placebo control, crossover trial of lithium carbonate and desipramine (an antidepressant) in the treatment of BPD. The authors found lithium significantly superior to both placebo and desipramine, especially in reducing the patients' troublesome impulsivity, irritability, anger, and suicidal symptoms. Despite these apparently encouraging findings, the authors note that their substantial dropout rate limits the generalizability of these data to all borderline patients. Although this was a model research design for the study of pharmacotherapy for BPD, the problems encountered in the Links et al. (1990) study exemplify the difficulties entailed in performing controlled treatment trials with this population. Many more such studies will be necessary in order to clarify the clinical picture.

Soloff (1987) notes a clinical phenomenon relevant to lithium treatment for borderline patients that has interesting implications for cognitive therapy. This phenomenon is described as a "reflective delay," whereby patients on lithium are on enough of an emotional even keel that they are able to think before acting impulsively. When ideation is frightening and/or bizarre, as often it is in borderline patients under stress, it is imperative that the patients' resultant emotional lability be controlled by whatever sensible and ethical means are possible. In this way, cognitive restructuring techniques have a chance to be utilized to greater advantage.

"Ms. J" had been diagnosed as having both bipolar and borderline disorders. Prior to reaching a therapeutic blood lithium level, the patient would go into a highly agitated depressive state when she experienced irrationally jealous ideation. At such times, she was practically incapable of using cognitive self-help techniques to pull herself out of this emotional abyss. Once she attained an appropriate blood lithium level, however, the same kinds of ideation did *not* lead to such extreme affect. Instead, she was quite capable of applying cognitive therapy skills in combatting her jealous thoughts. The combination of lithium and cognitive therapy helped the patient to control her irrational thoughts, hostile emotions, and impulsively destructive behaviors. Of course, in this case, the patient did have an actual diagnosis of bipolar disorder in addition to the borderline syndrome. It is unclear whether such an anecdotal finding would apply to those borderline patients who experience labile affect in the *absence* of a formal diagnosis of bipolar disorder. Kroll (1988) advocates looking into this matter and recommends consideration of the use of lithium when affective instability is the prominent symptom.

ANXIOLYTICS

Most of the leading researchers reviewed herein agree that the use of anxiolytics (e.g., benzodiazepines) in treating borderline patients is risky business and is best minimized or avoided altogether (Cowdry & Gardner, 1988; Ellison & Adler, 1984; Gardner & Cowdry, 1985; Kroll, 1986, 1988; Soloff et al., 1986; Waldinger, 1986). Although Soloff et al. (1986) report that two studies have supported the use of alprozolam (Xanax) with this population (Reus & Markrow, 1984; Faltus, 1984) as a way of ameliorating such symptoms as irritability, paranoia, and sleep disturbance, they note that there is considerable evidence suggesting that anxiolytics have little demonstrable value overall.

Kroll (1986, 1988) concurs with the foregoing, noting that although borderline patients may favor taking medications that reduce subjective anxiety, the result may be a dangerous lowering of inhibitions and impulse control. This is especially serious in a population where disinhibition and acting out often are part of the presenting problems in the first place. Although Kroll acknowledges that there may be some legitimate applications for antianxiety medication in cases where borderline patients also suffer from panic disorder and/or agoraphobia, he adds that these concomitant disorders are relatively uncommon. The cognitive therapy approach takes a dim view of the reliance on anxiolytic medications alone, arguing that this discourages patients from using their own cognitive-behavioral-affective resources in dealing with their problems. Furthermore, it encourages dependence on chemicals in order to terminate uncomfortable states—an unfavorable outcome for a population whose risk for substance abuse is relatively high.

Further support for these warnings against the use of antianxiety medication comes from the work of Gardner & Cowdry (1985) and Cowdry & Gardner (1988), who find that alprazolam and other anxiolytic medications often precipitate serious behavioral dyscontrol. Manifestations of this disinhibition include increased physical aggression, angry outbursts, self-damaging acts, and suicidal behaviors. Although these findings may result in part from the large dosages of alprazolam that were administered (e.g., average daily dosage of 4.7 mg in the Gardner & Cowdry, 1985, study), it would seem prudent to avert the risk by simply excluding this class of medication from the treatment regimen for this population until more promising data are produced.

Related to this area of study is Adelman's (1985) description of the therapeutic use of p.r.n. sedatives for borderline patients. Although he provides few details regarding specific medications and dosages, his rationale for the general use of sedatives is that these drugs have produced clinical success in overcoming resistances to other medications (e.g., antidepressants, lithium, and neuroleptics). He admits that this is an unorthodox use of medication—indeed, it may be quite controversial, given the contraindications to the use of anxiolytics (which similarly reduce subjective stress). According to Adelman (1985), it may be fruitful to examine empirically whether sedatives and/or anxiolytics can play a useful role in the treatment of the borderline syndrome when compliance with more potent medications is low.

NEUROLEPTICS

Antipsychotic medication, of proven utility in the treatment of schizophrenia, has also been found to be moderately efficacious in the treatment of BPD (Waldinger & Frank, 1989). Ellison & Adler (1984) state that antipsychotic medications serve a clear role in the treatment of this disorder when patients briefly regress to psychotic levels of functioning. They recommend low dosages for short periods of time, especially when the patient has not previously displayed a long-term thinking disorder. Brinkley, Breitman, & Friedel (1979) advocate the general use of low-dose neuroleptic medications in order to improve borderline patients' reality testing, attention span, and to reduce pervasive anxiety.

Neuroleptic medication also has been found to be efficacious in counteracting the tendency for borderline patients to act out aggressively and impulsively (Goldberg et al., 1986; Soloff et al., 1986). Furthermore, symptoms of derealization and depersonalization are ameliorated with relatively low dosages (Leone, 1982; Serban & Siegel, 1984).

An examination of the effects of specific antipsychotic agents reveals that haloperidol (Haldol) has been found to be superior to the antidepressant amitriptyline (Elavil) and a placebo in reducing overall BPD symptoms (Soloff et al., 1986). In this study, haloperidol was found to have broad therapeutic effects, inducing significant improvement in mood, anxiety, hostility, paranoid ideation, and psychoticism. Double-blind outpatient studies by Leone (1982) and Serban and Siegel (1984) demonstrated positive effects on both cognitive and affective dimensions with the use of chlorpromazine (Thorazine), loxapine (Daxolin), haloperidol (Haldol), and thiothixine (Navane). Goldberg et al. (1986) found that low doses of thiothixine (Navane) combatted depersonalization, phobic anxiety, anger, and hostility, in addition to cognitive disturbances that are typically more the province of psychotic disorders than the borderline domain.

Cowdry and Gardner (1988) found that trifluoperazine (Stelazine) produced favorable results for borderline outpatients when the medication was taken faithfully for at least three weeks. Those patients who were able to tolerate the side effects (e.g., muscle stiffness, jumpiness, weight gain) evidenced reductions in anxiety, dysphoria, suicidality, and sensitivity to rejection.

As a caveat to the findings mentioned earlier, it is important to note that the *magnitude* of the reported therapeutic changes tends to be modest. Therefore, although they may produce statistically significant results, their clinical benefits may at times be less readily apparent (Soloff, 1987). In addition, Links and Steiner (1988) hypothesize that neuroleptic medications "work" by inducing a nonspecific tranquilizing effect on patients. If true, this notion would lead us to conclude that the specific borderline symptoms are insufficiently targeted by this class of medications.

Kroll (1988) concurs that the antipsychotic medications have demonstrated some degree of effectiveness with certain borderline populations, but contends that the therapeutic benefits are not as dramatic as with the MAO-Is. He states that there are borderline patients who derive little or no benefit from antipsychotic medications, but agrees with Soloff et al. (1986) that borderline patients who fit the following profile do in fact respond well to neuroleptics: those patients who have severe cognitive disorganization and concomitant poor global adaptational functioning (GAF: Axis V of the DSM-III-R diagnostic system) under stress, and who are prone to hostile and aggressive impulsivity. Soloff et al. (1986) warn that the positive therapeutic effects mentioned previously may not be generalizable to less disturbed populations. Such a qualification leads us to hypothesize that significant results in the research may have been unduly influenced by statistical factors such as regression to the mean.

ANTICONVULSANT MEDICATIONS

At times, the angry episodic states of the borderline patient may appear to be seizurelike (Ellison & Adler, 1984). Sudden violent reactions, along with feelings of rage, identity confusion, and depersonalization, bear strong resemblance to the neurobehavioral sequelae of disorders such as head trauma and epilepsy (Soloff, 1987). Preliminary evidence suggests that in these instances the anticonvulsant medication carbamazepine (Tegretol) may be highly effective in controlling such outbursts (Cowdry & Gardner, 1988; Ellison & Adler, 1984; Gardner & Cowdry, 1986b; Soloff et al., 1986).

The Gardner and Cowdry (1986b) study is particularly compelling. Their double-blind study examined a group of borderline outpatients, all of whom had extensive histories of behavioral dyscontrol, including overdoses, self-slashing and burning, and rageful violence. During the six-week medication trial, the group that received placebo continued to show a high rate of acting out, and one patient attempted suicide. Of the 14 patients receiving carbamazepine, only one person had a major episode of dyscontrol, and no suicide attempts took place. In addition, patients in the latter group demonstrated an overall decrease in anxiety and an increase in global functioning. Cowdry and Gardner (1988) add that carbamazepine seems to have its therapeutic effects in the limbic areas of the brain, where abnormalities have been associated with the kinds of psychosensory and behavioral symptoms that are seen in many borderline patients.

A drawback to the use of carbamazepine seems to be its lack of therapeutic effect in improving patients' subjective mood (Cowdry & Gardner, 1988; Gardner & Cowdry, 1986a; Soloff, 1987). In fact, for those patients with histories of depression, carbamazepine may actually *precipitate* depressive episodes (Soloff, 1987). This finding is somewhat discouraging, given the promise that this drug holds for controlling the serious behavioral elements of BPD. However, it is possible that in the future we will witness studies that examine the *combined* efficacy of carbamazepine and antidepressants such as the MAO-Is, Prozac, Welbutrin, and Zoloft. Success in this area would be a much welcomed development.

SPECIAL ISSUES IN THE PHARMACOTHERAPY OF THE BORDERLINE PATIENT

Establishing a Pharmacotherapeutic Alliance

It is widely held that a good therapeutic alliance between clinician and patient is necessary in order for pharmacotherapy to proceed as planned (Bassuk et al., 1983). Even the most efficacious and least aversive medications stand little chance of attaining success if the patient is unwilling to follow the prescribed treatment regimen. In working with any psychiatric population it is important that a modicum of trust be established between therapist and patient before medications are prescribed. Ideally, the therapist should also educate the patient about the various properties of the prescribed agent, including clinical action, side effects, appropriate dosages over time, length of time before therapeutic effects are to be noticed, and cost (Bassuk et al., 1983). All of the above are *especially* salient with regard to borderline patients. Their acute sensitivity to physical and emotional discomfort and to interpersonal disharmony may lead them to abandon the medication altogether if the drug is not a cure-all. When medication is prescribed in a dictatorial manner, without an adequate rationale and/or concomitant emotional support, an untimely termination (or other form of acting out) may occur (Adelman, 1985).

Unfortunately, it is extremely difficult to foster the requisite trusting relationship with the borderline patient. Thus, the introduction of medication becomes a very touchy issue. Although it may be easiest to avoid a discussion of medication altogether, common sense and ethical standards demand that clinicians make patients aware of the complete range of treatment modalities that are available.

The following points are general guidelines that may serve to facilitate this process with the borderline patient (these suggestions apply both to psychiatrists and to nonpsychiatric therapists who are coordinating their treatment with a prescribing physician).

1. When possible, wait until some rapport has developed before suggesting pharmacotherapy. Similarly, it might be best to discuss this matter following a therapeutic success experience.
2. Maintain a positive attitude toward medication, without implying that it is a panacea (Cowdry & Gardner, 1988). Pessimistic expectations on the part of the therapist will be ascertained by the patient and will likely undermine the treatment (Bassuk et al., 1983).
3. Do not overtly or covertly introduce medication as a way of expressing exasperation and frustration with the course of cognitive therapy. Similarly, do not use medication as a "pacifier" for the patient (Waldinger & Frank, 1989). This will only serve to devalue the cognitive coping skills that the patient is trying to learn, and will foster a sense of rejection and/or hopelessness. Be alert to the possibility that the patient may be making these interpretations even in the *absence* of therapist negativity.
4. Be prepared to tolerate angry, critical reactions upon suggesting medication treatment, and further be prepared to deal rationally and promptly with noncompliance and adverse symptom responses.
5. When presenting the idea of medication as an adjunct to cognitive therapy, do so in the spirit of exploring and understanding this approach together (Adelman, 1985). Elicit and work to resolve the patient's automatic thoughts, beliefs, and schemas pertinent to the initiation of drug treatment (or making changes in dosages).
6. Combat your own negative expectations (as therapist) by looking at the patient's reactions to pharmacotherapy (at the very least) as a potential provocateur of a rich source of useful clinical material.
7. Calmly and respectfully clarify the roles and responsibilities of both therapist and patient (and the medication consultant, if a third party is involved in the process).
8. Openly discuss with the patient the potential risks and benefits of the medication. In choosing whether or not to proceed with pharmacotherapy, make the final decision as collaboratively as possible.

Establishing a pharmacotherapeutic alliance "requires a combination of knowledge, practice, positive attitude, humility, and persistence" (Bassuk et al., 1983).

Noncompliance with Medication

A patient's noncompliance with medication treatment recommendations can manifest itself in a number of ways. One form that noncompliance can take is in the patient's underuse of the drug. This is the most common form of noncompliance seen in clinical practice (Bassuk et al., 1983). Typical reasons for underuse include:

1. Fear of side effects
2. Concern about loss of control over one's own body
3. Inconvenience of the medication regimen
4. Misunderstandings about the medication itself and/or distrust of the therapist's intentions
5. Negative attitudes toward medication that are communicated to the patient by significant others

Another form of noncompliance is overuse. Borderline patients are at risk for this particular manifestation of the problem when they use their medications impulsively, underestimate the risks involved, and/or take other drugs (licit and illicit) that interact with the prescribed medication.

An additional abuse of medication, described by Bassuk et al. (1983), is simply dubbed "inappropriate use." This describes deliberate attempts by the patient to use medication intake so as to exert control in the therapeutic relationship, manipulate those around him or her, or unilaterally to self-medicate or self-destruct.

The issue of noncompliance is intimately tied to the importance of establishing a healthy therapeutic alliance, as described previously. The risk of noncompliance increases to the extent that the therapist has failed to appreciate the patient's apprehension and lack of clear understanding (Newman & Beck, 1992). A positive working alliance provides patient and therapist with the opportunity to assess and deal with distortions and/or deficits in cognition that might otherwise portend pharmacotherapeutic failure.

First, the therapist needs to gain the evidence that the patient clearly understands the prescribed instructions. In order to do this, the therapist must not merely explain things verbally and then assume that all is understood. Instead, the borderline patient can be encouraged to reflect on what he or she has heard and to reiterate the instructions verbally and on paper. Stimulus control techniques can be used to ensure that the patient will respond to daily cues that will facilitate taking the correct amount of medication at the appropriate times. For example, the use of a daily calibrated pillbox, and an instruction sheet taped to the inside of the medicine cabinet, are consistent with this approach.

Even if patients *understand* what they're supposed to do, they may not *want* to follow through. Automatic thoughts and beliefs that inhibit the patient from following instructions must be assessed and combatted for pharmacotherapy to have a chance to be effective. Meichenbaum and Turk (1987) present a list of automatic thoughts that they have encountered in patients who resist taking medication. These include the following (roughly adapted):

- "I don't have to take medication when I'm feeling good, just when I'm feeling bad."
- "I resent being controlled by the drugs."

- "The medication is so powerful that it should only be used for brief periods of time."
- "These drugs are poisoning me."
- "If you take medicines too often you may become immune to them and when you really need them, they won't work any more."
- "When I take medicine I feel like a pill-popper. I will become dependent on the medicine."

Similarly, Wright and Schrodt (1989) have observed patients avoid proper use of medication because of beliefs such as these:

- "I should get better on my own. Medications are a crutch."
- "If I get better, my family will credit the medication."
- "Doctors don't know what they're doing with all these drugs. I'm just a guinea pig."
- "How can drugs help me when I have a real life problem?" (pp. 274–275).

Wright and Schrodt (1989) present an excellent summary of the ways in which cognitive therapists can help patients to test these beliefs.

Figure 5.1 presents the Daily Thought Record of "Ms. J." This patient, mentioned earlier in this chapter, had a dual diagnosis of bipolar disorder and BPD. When the patient was noncompliant in taking her lithium, she would experience frighteningly bizarre ideation and intensely negative emotions when issues of therapeutic significance were brought up in the course of cognitive therapy. After two crisis-filled sessions, it became clear that lithium was a much-needed part of the treatment program. This was borne out by the fact that, once she reached an optimal blood lithium level, Ms. J responded well to her course of cognitive therapy, even when threatening core schema issues were discussed. Even so, her behavior indicated that she was not inclined to be vigilant in following the instructions according to her prescription. Recognizing the potential seriousness of another medication lapse, the therapist assigned Ms. J the task of completing a Daily Thought Record whenever she was reluctant to take her medication. The results are highlighted in Figure 5.1.

In doing this standard cognitive therapy self-help exercise, Ms. J came to the realization that her rationalizations for not taking her lithium put her at risk for relapse. Furthermore, she gained insight into the fact that she associated pharmacotherapy with insanity and feared that she would be ostracized and stigmatized by others who might see her taking her medication. By rationally responding to these automatic thoughts, Ms. J. achieved a significant therapeutic breakthrough, as evidenced by her subsequent compliance with both lithium and cognitive therapy, and by therapeutic changes in her cognitive, emotional, and interpersonal functioning.

	SITUATION Actual event leading to unpleasant emotion.	EMOTION (S) 1. Specify sad/ anxious/ angry, etc. 2. Rate degree of emotion from 0 to 100%	AUTOMATIC THOUGHT(S) 1. Write automatic thought(s) that preceded emotion(s). 2. Rate belief in automatic thoughts(s) from 0 to 100%.	RATIONAL RESPONSE 1. Write rational response to automatic thought(s). 2. Rate belief in rational response from 0 to 100%.	OUTCOME 1. Rerate belief in automatic thought(s) from 0 to 100%. 2. Specify and rate subsequent emotions from 0 to 100%.
DATE	It's early Sunday morning and I realize I forgot to take my midday and nightly dosage of Lithium the day before.	annoyed (85) apathetic (50)	1. Oh, well. It isn't going to kill me if I miss a few times. (100) 2. I probably don't need Lithium anyway. (90) 3. I don't want people to think I'm a freak or psychotic or something. I want to be regarded as a normal person!!!!	1. Well, should you suddenly plummet into a depression you might very well feel suicidal again. So it might actually kill me if I skip a few times. (90) 2. Most signs show that you do need Lithium. It's to your advantage to take the medication. It isn't painful and you have few side effects. And it isn't worth going off the medication and taking the risk of going through all that pain and craziness again. (90) 3. I'm not crazy. I have a treatable disorder that many successful and creative and important people have had. If someone does, by chance, regard you as abnormal, it's not worth your time to have them as friends. People who really care about you won't stop being your friend because you take Lithium. (100)	1. annoyed (20) 2. apathetic (0)

FIGURE 5.1. Daily Thought Record, "Ms. J"

Additionally, there are some practical considerations involved in aiding patients' compliance with medication. For example, Bassuk et al. (1983) recommend that the practitioner administer the lowest dose of medication for the shortest period of time, so as to minimize the risk of long-term side effects. They also suggest that medication regimens be structured as simply as possible. For example, drugs with a long half-life can be prescribed in once-a-day dosages (e.g., at bedtime), so that the patient can take the medication conveniently without much danger of forgetting or being side-tracked by daily responsibilities. Also, the authors suggest a "one drug at a time when possible" approach. Except in cases where it is clear that a combination of drugs will be more beneficial to the patient than one or no drugs at all, clinicians are encouraged to test the therapeutic effects of one medication at a time, so as to minimize side effects and facilitate compliance.

CONTRAINDICATIONS AND DANGERS OF PHARMACOTHERAPY WITH THE BORDERLINE PATIENT

The introduction of medication into the treatment plan poses risks as well as benefits. Risks include side effects, potential for overdose; interaction with other medications, alcohol, or illicit drugs; and addiction. Although these potential drawbacks to pharmacotherapy exist with any clinical population, they are particularly salient with borderline patients. This is so because the borderline patient is prone to impulsive self-destructive behavior, including drug abuse and suicide attempts via overdose. Additionally, as already discussed, there are some medications (e.g., benzodiazepines such as alprazolam, antidepressants such as amitriptyline, etc.) that have been shown to exacerbate inadvertently the borderline patient's undercontrolled behaviors, thus indirectly putting the patient at risk for harm, even when the medication is taken faithfully as prescribed.

Yet another reason that there is potential danger in prescribing medication to borderline patients concerns their cognitive style of inattention to details, such as instructions about proper use of their prescriptions (Kroll, 1988). For example, although Kroll (1988) expresses optimism about the therapeutic benefits of MAO-Is for this population, he also warns that these patients are ill equipped to follow the details of the diet that must go along with these medications. Maintaining a low-tyramine diet requires careful, methodical planning in the preparation of meals, including beverages, in order to avert a potentially life-threatening increase in blood pressure. Such cautious and sensible vigilance contrasts sharply with the typical borderline behavioral style of reckless acting out. Indeed, borderline patients may intentionally disregard their diet in order to harm themselves and/or precipitate dramatic crises for their therapists and/or loved ones.

The borderline patient's propensity for addictive behavior is also of concern. Alcohol and other drugs, in addition to their own dangers, often potentiate prescribed medications and therefore heighten the chances for accidental overdose. It is imperative that, at intake, therapists obtain a thorough drug and alcohol history as well as an assessment of the patient's attitudes toward licit and illicit drugs (Courtois, 1988).

Additionally, the borderline patient may consciously decide to use prescription medication (in combination with other drugs and alcohol, or alone) in order to attempt suicide. Although there may be obvious benefits to the prescribed medication when properly used, they may alternatively serve as convenient lethal weapons in the hands of a desperate, impulsive patient.

Not all of the contraindications to pharmacotherapy are directly related to patient misunderstanding, negligence, or dyscontrol. Each medication reviewed in this chapter carries idiosyncratic risks in its own right. For example, the antianxiety drugs are potentially habit-forming, the MAO-I antidepressants require a tyramine-free diet in order to avert serious side effects, the neuroleptic class of medications poses the long-term risk of tardive dyskinesia, lithium can be toxic to thyroid and kidneys when therapeutic levels are only moderately exceeded, and carbamazepine must be monitored closely in order to prevent liver and bone marrow complications (Kroll, 1988).

In order to militate against the kinds of harmful effects described here, the following points need to be observed scrupulously (Note: These items overlap and are congruent with those previously discussed regarding medication compliance and the therapeutic alliance):

1. Carefully build rapport and understanding by acknowledging patients' concerns about medication, educating patients about the pros and cons of the specific drug being proposed, reviewing patients' expectations about pharmacotherapy (and distinguishing the realistic from the unrealistic), and collaboratively instituting safety controls.

2. As a general rule, endeavor to prescribe (or work with your psychiatric consultant to prescribe) the smallest therapeutic dose for the shortest period of time (Waldinger & Frank, 1989).

3. When treating the borderline patient, *institute pharmacotherapy only when there is a clear and present need for a biochemical adjunct to cognitive therapy.* Do not take the extreme view that medication is always a necessary treatment, nor the opposite extreme stance that says that medication is superfluous in the context of cognitive therapy. For example, when a patient is posing a threat to self and others via angry, violent outbursts, medications that may decrease this dangerous behavior (e.g., neuroleptics, MAO-Is, and carbamazepine) are indicated and may facilitate the course of cognitive therapy as well. When dangerous behaviors can be controlled via cognitive controls alone, pharmacotherapy may be put on hold temporarily or permanently.

4. Give high priority to teaching the borderline patient self-monitoring and self-instruction skills. Continue to work on these areas until it is clear that the patient is capable of faithfully following the prescription. As a corollary to this point, build on these skills as a way of increasing the patient's capacity for concentra-

tion and attention to rules. In addition to facilitating safe, compliant use of the prescribed drug, this approach may teach the patient to control social, academic, and vocational behaviors more successfully.

5. At the first sign of noncompliance or abuse of medication, immediately assess the patient's automatic thoughts, beliefs, emotions, and intentions regarding the behavior in question. To ignore or give low priority to such actions is to invite further, more serious trouble.

6. Be careful not to associate medication with punitive measures or, conversely, to give the message that pharmacotherapy is a magic *substitute* for cognitive therapy and responsible living.

7. Allow the patient as much decision-making power as possible in deciding whether to begin or end drug treatment, or to change dosages or medications, but be firm about the need to conform to safe limits.

8. Maintain vigilance in monitoring the patient's daily medication use. Be alert to inappropriate use, "forgetfulness," and stockpiling of drugs for possible suicide attempts. When appropriate, keep close tabs on blood levels (especially with lithium and anticonvulsants).

HOSPITALIZATION

The borderline patient's wide range of symptoms poses a great challenge to his or her therapist. The clinician needs to pay attention to a number of ongoing risks, including self-mutilation, suicidality, and misuse of medication. As a result, the therapist may be faced with decisions regarding the hospitalization of the patient on a frequent basis. Aside from the practical and ethical questions involved in involuntary commitment, there is the problem of the resultant effects on the therapeutic relationship with which to contend.

There are no easy answers to the question of "when to commit?" It is always wise to be prepared to contact colleagues, crisis centers, hospitals, and the patient's relatives when urgent situations arise. Well-rehearsed knowledge of commitment procedures is advisable as well. It is probably a good idea to inform patients at the first indication of destructive behavior (or earlier) that certain actions, such as slashing or burning oneself, abuse of licit or illicit drugs, reckless sexual behavior, or dangerous eating abnormalities (anorexia, bulimia) will be met with a strong advisement to hospitalize. Along with this declaration should come the explanation that the patient will not be abandoned by the therapist, and that outpatient therapy can resume at the patient's request when he or she is discharged. A good therapeutic relationship may be of great assistance in convincing the patient to seek inpatient care voluntarily under these conditions.

Whenever other mental health professionals are involved in the care of your borderline patient, it is imperative that the lines of communication be open. Coordinated care is necessary to prevent "doctor-shopping" and abuse of medications that are being prescribed by multiple psychiatric sources (Waldinger, 1986). It is also important to endeavor to maintain a united front with other professionals on the case, so as to minimize the risk of the patient's playing one therapist against the other (Waldinger & Frank, 1989).

SUMMARY

In reviewing what is known about the pharmacotherapy of borderline personality disorder, the number of questions far outweighs the number of answers. Although there is some preliminary evidence suggesting that particular classes of medications may be effective in treating circumscribed symptom clusters, the rapidly shifting and fluctuating nature of the disorder often makes it difficult to know what the most salient symptoms are in a given patient (Ellison & Adler, 1984). It also hinders the researcher's ability to perform group-design studies with supposedly homogeneous subjects in each group. The potential importance and utility of carrying out controlled n = 1 case studies (Kazdin, 1976) with borderline patients is obvious in this respect.

Although there is no conclusive evidence that any single medication is consistently effective in treating this disorder (Soloff et al., 1986; Waldinger, 1986), a number of hypotheses are beginning to take shape. For example, if an identifiable Axis I disorder exists in the borderline patient, an emerging general rule is to treat the symptoms of this disorder pharmacologically if the therapeutic relationship is relatively well developed and if the patient can be trusted to take the medication safely (Kroll, 1988). This is especially true when the Axis I disorder is an affective disorder, where MAO-I antidepressants have had some success with dysphoria (Kroll, 1988) and lithium has shown some promise in curbing mood lability and aggressiveness (Links et al., 1990; Soloff et al., 1986). Tricyclic antidepressants have demonstrated some limited success as well but also have been associated with adverse reactions such as increased suicidality. Relatively new medications such as Prozac, Welbutrin, and Zoloft may represent promising additions to the armamentarium of treatment for BPD, although studies are lacking at this time.

Standard anxiolytics such as the benzodiazepines should probably be avoided because of both their propensity for reducing the inhibitions that are already dangerously low in this population, and the dangers of addiction (Kroll, 1988). Chronic anxiety states have been shown to be treatable by other means, including low-level neuroleptics and anticonvulsants.

Other concomitant Axis I disorders that typically require treatment in their own right include substance abuse, eating disorders, and organic brain disorders, among others. When thought disorder is present along with anxiety, MAO-Is have had some success. When the thought disorder is combined with eccentric, bizarre behaviors and with dissociative states, low-dose neuroleptics are the drugs of choice (Ellison & Adler, 1984). With regard to self-mutilation and other aggressive acting-out behaviors, MAO-Is again seem to be somewhat helpful, especially when dysphoria is a part of the clinical picture. Severely impulsive and aggressive patients may be helped best by anticonvulsant medications such as carbamazepine, especially when there are angry episodes that resemble seizure states. These benefits must be weighed against the drawback of an increase in dysphoria that has been seen in some trials of carbamazepine.

Hazards that are commonly associated with the medications discussed here are magnified and multiplied when the patient suffers from BPD. The patient's extreme reluctance to trust the therapist heightens suspicions about medication and thereby increases the risk of noncompliance. Impulsivity and a tendency toward self-destructiveness increase the dangers of accidental and intentional overdose. When habit-forming medications are prescribed, the borderline patient is more likely than most other patients to have a problem with abuse and dependence. "These dangers need not rule out the use of medications, but do call for judicious evaluation of the [therapist]/patient relationship and the risks involved" (Kroll, 1986, p. 104).

Cognitive therapy and pharmacotherapy can complement each other. Empathic attention to the patient's emotional pain and core schematic issues can build the trust that is necessary for pharmacotherapy to proceed in a systematic fashion. In addition, cognitive techniques can be used to improve compliance via disputation of fears, improvement in concentration, increased self-control, self-instruction, and attention span. Likewise, pharmacological interventions may help ameliorate the disruptive, impulsive, aggressive symptoms that would otherwise greatly interfere with a psychotherapeutic approach such as cognitive therapy. In this manner, cognitive therapy and well-designed medication programs can synergize to present borderline patients with potent treatments. Furthermore, the patient's idiosyncratic responses to the implementation of pharmacotherapy (e.g., hot cognitions) may contribute to the successful formulation of a cognitive case conceptualization.

Chapter 6
Countertransference, Cognitive Therapy, and the Borderline Patient

To be the therapist of a patient suffering from BPD is to be acutely reminded that one is a human being. Any myths that the therapist may hold suggesting that he or she is a paragon of cool, rational, scientific impartiality are unceremoniously shattered when dealing with patients whose feelings, beliefs, and actions are as intense, conflicted, and provocative as the borderline patient's. This chapter highlights how a cognitive approach may assist therapists in making sense out of their own reactions to such patients and to use this information to facilitate the patient's progress in cognitive therapy. Additionally, this chapter reinforces the premise that cognitive therapy self-help skills may readily be used by therapists themselves, not only to deal with the stresses inherent in treating patients with this disorder, but to serve as coping models for their patients to emulate.

DEFINING *COUNTERTRANSFERENCE*

The concept of *countertransference* as applied to cognitive therapy is far broader than the original, classical definition. The classic analytic view holds that counter-transference represents the therapist's *unconscious* reactions to the patient's trans-ference, and further posits that the basis for countertransference is the therapist's unresolved neurotic conflicts (Kernberg, 1975). Within this theoretical framework, countertransference has been viewed primarily as a hindrance to therapy. Further-more, the fact that therapists who were "discovered" to have such reactions to patients were often implicitly or explicitly denigrated has led to denial and neglect in studying this phenomenon (Mendelsohn, 1987).

Cognitive therapy's view of countertransference, however, is more in line with the current climate in the field, which views countertransference as a valuable means by which to gain a deeper appreciation and understanding of the therapeutic process (Eber, 1990; Mendelsohn, 1987). In cognitive therapy, countertransference represents the totality of the therapist's responses to the patient, including automatic thoughts, elicited beliefs or schemas, emotions, actions, intentions, and so on. These may be readily observable and accessible via reflection and observation, or may require greater self-exploration in order to ascertain and reevaluate rationally.

From this viewpoint, countertransference is seen as something that is not necessarily always a problem that must be resolved, but a *cue* that can be used to examine more closely the idiosyncracies of the therapeutic relationship. Given that the area of interpersonal relationships is typically a major trouble zone for the borderline patient, such a theoretical and technical approach is advantageous. This is clearly the case when the patient's interpersonal style of relating is chaotic and is based on many deep, troubling, and dysfunctional beliefs about the self, others, and the world, thus eliciting reactions in the therapist that may be analogous to those elicited from significant others in the patient's life. By rationally and objectively examining their own anger, dismay, fear, and attraction toward these patients, cognitive therapists have a golden opportunity to uncover the core issues that are at the source of so much of the patient's suffering in his or her personal life.

ISSUES OF THE BORDERLINE PATIENT THAT IMPINGE ON THE THERAPEUTIC RELATIONSHIP

Borderline patients tend to hold extreme and unrealistic expectations and beliefs in interpersonal relationships, and often are torn between two or more opposing or incompatible desires and/or fears. For example, a patient who was sexually victimized in childhood by someone she originally trusted and depended on learned that it was extremely dangerous to trust anyone. As a result, the patient cognitively and emotionally associated fear, humiliation, and loss of control with what could otherwise (in adulthood) be construed as an act of love and intimacy. At the same time, the patient learned that the only way to attain love was to allow herself to be violated in some way. In therapy, this patient craved affection and acceptance from the therapist, yet recoiled with horror, distrust, and outrage when she perceived that the therapist was showing the signs of caring that the patient associated with risk of exploitation. When the therapist responded by respectfully acting in a more reserved fashion toward the patient, she then jumped to the opposite extreme and perceived cruel abandonment and neglect. These responses indicated signs of great distress on the part of the patient. At the same time, the therapist became locked into a "damned if I do, damned if I don't" scenario, and then felt frustrated, dismayed, angry, and helpless. It is just such feelings that typify the countertransference that this chapter addresses.

The emotional and interpersonal problems that plague the borderline patient are often reproduced in the therapeutic relationship. In order for the therapist to deal effectively with his or her own role in the interaction, it is imperative that he or she have an intellectual and an empathic understanding of the cognitive and emotional baggage that the patient brings to session. Many clinicians and researchers have noted strikingly similar themes of which to be aware when working with these patients. Two of these themes include the schemas of unlovability and abandonment (Masterson, 1976; Millon, 1981; Pretzer, 1983; Young, 1990), whereby the patient is excruciatingly sensitive to rejection and separation. For example, a one-week break from therapy due to the therapist's vacation may precipitate a suicidal crisis, as the patient may interpret this relatively minor separation as stark proof that the therapist doesn't care and can't be counted on to be there. The patient's perceptions of deprivation and abandonment cause so much pain that he is rendered unable to make a rational distinction between a benign, temporary separation and malicious, permanent neglect. Similarly, the therapist's benevolent efforts to encourage the patient to assume more autonomy and self-sufficiency may be seen by the borderline patient as a patent wish to be rid of him. Patient reactions of disappointment, dejection, and rage are not uncommon in such instances (Millon, 1981).

Related to this issue are the borderline patient's fear of intimacy and reluctance to trust (Pretzer, 1983; Young, 1990). In examining the developmental histories of borderline patients, it is often found that they have experienced betrayal in their most significant relationships (e.g., incest; cf. Courtois, 1988; Goodwin et al., 1990; Stone et al., 1988; Zanarini et al., 1989). As a result, they have extraordinary difficulty in learning to trust others. This deficit seriously hinders such patients from building healthy, intimate relationships, which further exacerbates and perpetuates their profound sense of aloneness and unlovability. Although this perceived state of isolation contributes to the borderline patients' craving for acceptance and affection, they are at the same time acutely frightened by close relationships, which heighten their feelings of vulnerability and threaten their fragile sense of autonomy (Kroll, 1988; Pretzer, 1983; Young, 1990).

Because the borderline patient brings all of the above into the therapeutic relationship, it makes the establishment and maintenance of a working alliance difficult, and often taxes the therapist's intellectual and emotional resources. For example, a borderline patient casts his therapist in the role of savior and showers him or her with accolades. However, this positive regard is born of desperation and unrealistic expectations. When the patient finds that the therapist is fallible, the idealized image may turn to one in which the patient sees the therapist as uncaring, even sadistic (Waldinger, 1986). The therapist, dismayed and angered by this turn of events, may subtly or not-so-subtly look to end the therapeutic association, thus confirming the patient's views that nobody can be trusted and that abandonment is inevitable.

Standard cognitive therapy (e.g., Beck et al., 1979) suggests that the establishment of a collaborative therapeutic relationship is a necessary *precondition* to treatment. With many patients, especially those who do not suffer from moderate or severe personality disorders, this is readily accomplished, and the therapeutic relationship serves as a boon to the course of therapy, with relatively few complications. In treating borderline patients, however, cognitive therapists must bear in mind that the majority of these patients' problems generally are manifested in the interpersonal realm (Dawson, 1988; Young, 1990). Therefore, cognitive therapy for BPD is modified so as to treat the therapeutic relationship as one of the central issues of therapy. The patient's most problematic schemas, beliefs, and associated emotional and behavioral concomitants then are ascertained and reality-tested in the interactions between patient and therapist. As treatment progresses, the therapist endeavors to teach the patient to generalize corrective experiences in relating to the therapist and to other relationships.

In order to achieve this important goal, the cognitive therapist must learn to recognize his or her own dysfunctional thoughts and emotions in interacting with BPD patients, and must be undaunted by the prospect of addressing such problems directly as a routine part of therapy. If therapists understand their emotional reactions, if they examine these feelings with a critical eye and adequately control their behavioral and verbal impulses, therapeutic progress will be facilitated (Pretzer, 1983).

WAYS IN WHICH THE BPD PATIENT "PUSHES THE THERAPIST'S BUTTONS"

Therapeutic relationships with borderline patients are characterized by a high degree of emotional intensity. Masterson (1976) writes, "The borderline patient projects so much and is so provocative and manipulative, particularly in the beginning of therapy, that he can place a great emotional stress on the therapist" (p. 105). In cognitive terms, the patients see themselves as perpetual victims and are therefore hypervigilant to even the slightest sign that the therapist is being untruthful or exploitative. They will frequently jump to negative conclusions in interpreting therapists' behaviors, and they will be prone to seeing therapists in highly overgeneralized, black-and-white terms (e.g., "I *thought* my therapist could be trusted. Now I see that she's a self-serving liar like everybody else!"). Furthermore, any actual mistake that the therapist makes, or any angry or sexual feelings that the therapist truly has at any given moment will be tremendously magnified. The borderline patient's resultant response (also highly magnified) puts therapists at risk for feeling victimized themselves. As Sherby (1989) wryly yet insightfully notes, "the work with borderlines is a constant struggle around issues of love and hate, the patient's and the therapist's" (p. 574).

The patients' reluctance to trust their therapists paradoxically induces them to behave in ways that severely test the therapists' actual willingness to help. Dawson (1988) presents the following examples of such behaviors:

1. Patient pulls up her sleeve to reveal new self-inflicted cuts, then refuses to discuss the matter.
2. Patient waits until the end of a session to mention severe suicidal intentions.

3. Patient says to therapist, "You don't really care about me. You just want to get paid for seeing me."
4. Patient calls therapist at home, hints strongly that suicide is imminent, and cancels the next day's therapy appointment.

As a result, therapists often find themselves having to deal with unexpected and highly urgent crises, frequently at considerable personal inconvenience (e.g., repeated phone calls in the middle of the night), and typically without signs of patient appreciation. In fact, although therapists may have to go the extra mile for these patients, therapists are nonetheless subject to vilification if the patients detect exasperation or other signs of nonomnipotence in their helpers. This may either encourage therapists to discontinue the alliance (thus "proving" to these patients that nobody can be trusted or counted on, and that they themselves are unlovable and utterly alone), or compel therapists to become overinvolved and saviorlike (thus threatening patients with a sense of loss of autonomy, individuation, and control, and reinforcing a sense of dire dependency).

Another source of potential consternation for therapists is the borderline patients' propensity for recognizing and calling attention to vulnerabilites in their therapists (Kroll, 1988; Masterson, 1976; Nielsen, 1983; Strean, 1985). Examples include patients commenting on a therapist's overweight condition or progressive balding. This may be particularly disturbing if therapists have bought into the borderline patients' original views of the therapist as all-powerful.

Several authors have described the borderline patient as having a metaphorical "radar" when it comes to reading or misreading significant others in their lives (Kroll, 1988; Nielsen, 1983). They are extremely sensitive and aware of affective shifts in the therapist, as evinced by tone of voice, body posture, and other nonverbal cues, all of which tap into "the cloud." Strean (1985) suggests that these patients are especially adept at detecting subtle signs that the therapist is harboring either hostile or sexual feelings toward the patient. Even when these are accurate perceptions, they are generally magnified so that the patient feels seriously threatened even when no threat actually exists. As a defense, the patient may act out toward the therapist in a number of ways, the most direct of which is to confront the therapist on these feelings, thus exposing and scrutinizing real or imagined personal idiosyncracies on the part of the therapist (Masterson, 1976). Here, the therapist is at risk for responding defensively as well, which serves as more grist for the borderline patient's transference mill.

It is important that therapists not dismiss the borderline patient's accusations as merely being the product of gross distortions (Koerner & Linehan, 1992). First of all, it is wise to demonstrate that the patient will be taken seriously. Second, it is potentially beneficial for the patient that the therapist models a nonthreatened, nondefensive stance in response to interpersonal strife. Additionally, the patient's extreme viewpoints about the therapist's less-than-therapeutic intentions usually contain a kernel of truth that the therapist would do well to acknowledge. Therapists generally do not enjoy seeing themselves as persons with less than noble intentions. However, *by automatically denying all patient accusations, without first taking a dispassionate self-critical look, therapists run the risk not only of missing out on important interpersonal issues in therapy, but also of validating the patients' mistrust.*

As an illustration, one of the authors was seeing a borderline patient who was particularly loath to the idea of becoming dependent on someone else, especially a male. As a result, the most positively therapeutic sessions were often followed by a desire on the patient's part either to discontinue therapy or, at least, to cut back on the frequency of sessions. As she once said to the therapist over the phone (as she was cancelling an appointment), "It scares me how much I'm starting to trust you. I'm telling you things I don't even tell my closest girlfriends." In response, the therapist decided to end each session by allowing the patient to decide unilaterally (or so it seemed) when the next session would be held, so as to foster a heightened sense of patient autonomy. Ironically (or predictably, depending on one's point of view), the patient began to choose "voluntarily" to come in for sessions every week without fail.

One day, however, the patient confronted the therapist, saying in effect, "I figured out that you've been trying to control me by giving me the illusion that I have a choice about when to see you. I've been coming in every week since you started doing that, and that's exactly what you wanted me to do! Well, I don't think I'm going to come in for sessions as often any more!" The therapist's response was one of dismay and some indignation. His automatic thoughts were, "So this is how I get rewarded for respecting her autonomy! She not only accuses me of devious motives, but now she's going to interrupt therapy just as important issues finally are being addressed!" The therapist managed to keep his frustration in check enough to state that he could understand how the patient might come to such a conclusion, but not enough to convince the patient that she wasn't on target. The next session was scheduled for three weeks hence.

It was not until the therapist consulted with a colleague on the matter that it became apparent to him that the patient had accurately ascertained a *part* of the therapist's actual intentions. Yes, the therapist had the patient's best interests at heart, and yes, he felt that she could truly benefit from regular sessions. However, the therapist *had* used a counterintuitive procedure in order to achieve the goal of weekly sessions, in a sense using covert control under the guise of giving the patient absolute free will. The patient had selectively abstracted this facet of the truth out of the bigger picture.

As a result of this revelation, the therapist chose neither to drop the matter nor to continue to fume about it. Instead, he raised it as an agenda topic for the next session, owned up to his use of "reverse psychology," but further engaged the patient in an exploration of the larger issues of control and countercontrol in important relationships, and their relation to the patient's fears of losing her individuality if she got too close to others. From this point forward, the decision to schedule further appointments became more collaborative, both the patient and therapist were able to have a good-natured laugh about the interpersonal "dance" involved in making the decision, and sessions were scheduled with more regular frequency (though not perfectly so). This example serves to highlight the therapeutic utility of acknowledging when the patient may have hit upon a blind spot on the part of the therapist.

DISTINGUISHING HEALTHY VERSUS UNHEALTHY COUNTERTRANSFERENCE

In examining the potential range of therapist responses to patients, it is obvious that there is a continuum of possibilities. On one extreme we see those responses that are too detached and self-protective. At the other pole we see behaviors that are far too overinvolved and emotionally invested (Kroll, 1988). With many patients, therapists are readily able to avoid the pitfalls of either of these extremes, and can successfully navigate the inner sanctum of the continuum, characterized by sedate caring, interest, supportiveness, and objective understanding. With borderline patients, however, this is not an easy task, as these patients frequently interact with the world in black-and-white terms. As a result, the therapist either may be seen as responding at one or the other end of the continuum, or may be provoked into actually acting out in ways that are consistent with the polar extremes. In either case, the vast range of responses that ordinarily would exist within the healthy inner sanctum of the continuum is reduced (with borderline patients) to a veritable tightrope. One false move, one gust of wind, and the healthy therapeutic relationship is in danger of losing its balance.

At the self-protective extreme we see therapists who respond to the patient's outbursts and irrational demands with an eagerness to limit or terminate the therapeutic relationship. This reflects a view that therapy with this patient is noxious, unrewarding, and unlikely to effect positive change even if great effort is put forth. Typical automatic thoughts and beliefs of the therapists in such instances include variations on the following:

- "There is nothing I can do to help this patient."
- "This is a career patient I'm dealing with. I'd only be needlessly banging my head against the wall to work with him."
- "This is the kind of patient who could bad-mouth me or sue me, so I'd better provide her with no ammunition to work with. In other words, I'd better be as passive and as uninvolved as possible."
- "This patient will not appreciate anything I do, so I might as well not tax myself too hard."
- "Working with this patient means I'm setting myself up to be abused."

- "Letting myself care about this patient means I'm a pushover. I must be tough and detached in order to prove that I cannot easily be manipulated."
- "To whom can I refer this patient?"

These hypothetical examples represent just the tip of the iceberg (so to speak). Kroll (1988) notes that therapists are at particular risk for taking this stance when the patient arouses their fears of criticism, of fallibility, or of being seduced. When these fears go unchecked on a consistent basis, the therapist will fail to engage the borderline patient in a meaningful way. The patient's self-destructiveness will not appropriately be addressed; time, energy, and money will be wasted, and the patient will be subject to yet another experience of failure with further demoralization (Kroll, 1988). Furthermore, the patient's abandonment schema will strengthen, thus potentially hindering progress in future therapeutic relationships.

At the opposite unhealthy extreme of the countertransference continuum we have the therapist who adopts the unrealistic certainty of being able to "rescue" the patient from his or her psychological affliction. In this case the therapist risks exploiting the patient by paying more attention to his or her own needs (e.g., for power, dominance, love, etc.) than to the patient's. At best, the therapist becomes overly directive, fosters increasing patient dependency, and brings the patient's growth and development to a halt (Masterson, 1976). At worst, the overinvolved therapist presents the patient with interpersonal deception—namely, that the patient can (and must) rely solely on the therapist in order to be healed, that such help is guaranteed and permanent, and that the patient need never learn to care for him- or herself. Since no human being is able to fulfill this promise, the patient inevitably will be disillusioned and feel betrayed, especially if the therapist has unwittingly or knowingly fostered patient fantasies of an ongoing personal relationship with the therapist. The potential for ethical breaches in such therapist–patient relationships is serious indeed.

Kroll (1988) notes that the following countertransferential issues are key in the development of this potentially exploitative therapist stance: the therapist's unacknowledged and overriding need to be flattered, to be a caretaker, to control, to be correct, and to be sexually desirable. Although it is important that therapists show positive regard for their patients, and that they come across as benign, professionally helpful persons, they must be ever mindful that they are operating primarily for the benefit *of the patient*. Kroll (1988) warns that "the therapist who works intensively with borderline patients must take extra precautions to avoid any semblance of sexual interest in the patient or to be aware of his own leanings in that direction" (p. 207). On the other hand, the therapist must neither fear nor ignore the patient's sexual attraction towards him or her. To do this would be to close off prematurely an area of therapeutic significance, and to foster an unexplained and unresolved sense of rejection in the patient.

Complicating matters even further is the propensity for the therapeutic relationship to be so unstable that the therapist bounces alternatively back and forth between the overdistanced and the overinvolved extremes explained above. This flip-flop (or "emotional ping-pong" as Nielsen, 1983, describes it) is especially ironic in that the therapist is mirroring the patient's pathology. For example, the therapist initially may be fascinated by the borderline patient, show him or her a great deal of attention, work especially intensively in therapy, and greatly enjoy the patient's glowing admiration. Then, just as the therapist is congratulating him- or herself on the wonderful job he or she is doing, the borderline patient acts out in a way that brings the therapist's ego crashing back down to earth. It is not unusual for the therapist to respond with exaggerated anger and/or vengeful coldness in such instances, thus completing the emotional flip-flop and presenting the patient with a less-than-ideal model for emotional stability. It is at this point that the therapist needs to understand the process of the therapeutic interaction (and his or her own emotional reactions), so as not to become locked in a subjective, nontherapeutic struggle that is harmful for patient and therapist alike (Kroll, 1988; Nielsen, 1983).

The prospects for a productive therapeutic relationship with the borderline patient, however, need not be so bleak. It is possible for the therapist to "walk the tightrope" and to maintain a stance of benign objectivity, while still showing genuine concern for the patient's well-being. A number of writers have explicated the qualities that therapists must possess (and actions that they can learn to take) in order to accomplish and maintain this worthy goal. Most fundamentally, Masterson (1976) states that the therapist must be a "real person" who acts in a consistently positive, supportive manner. The therapist maintains a firm grounding in reality, an even temperament, and an unthreatened willingness to address the patient's actings-out and distortions as they occur. The therapist demonstrates "healthy countertransference" by showing that he or she is secure, honest, and direct enough to admit it when he or she has made a mistake in either perception or response (Masterson, 1976).

Strean (1985) holds that therapists must be relatively free from hostility, overambitiousness, or unrecognized sexual fantasies, and should have their egos sufficiently intact to examine their own motives before implementing given interventions. To operationalize the foregoing, therapists can ask themselves the following questions before making suggestions or giving advice: "How will my patient benefit from this intervention?" "How will *I* benefit from this intervention?" If the answer to the latter is more apparent than the answer to the former, the intervention should be shelved, at least temporarily, until further self-exploration and/or consultation can take place. Willingness to consult openly with a colleague is a good indication of a healthy approach to countertransference (Kernberg, 1975).

Another strategy and/or quality of a constructive approach to dealing with the chaotic emotionality of the borderline patient may be called the conservation-of-energy approach (Nielsen, 1983). Here, the therapist maintains his or her cool (even as the patient loses his), and does not try to match the fevered pitch of the patient as a way to bring order to the therapy session. On the contrary, the therapist demonstrates that extreme situations can best be dealt with in a level-headed fashion, and that it is still possible to relate to another individual with care and rationality when the stress level is high.

Similarly, the therapist should resist the temptation to respond to each new symptom or presented crisis as a true emergency (Pretzer, 1983). Given that borderline patients tend indiscriminately to respond to each acute problem or emotional pain as if it were chronic and intractable, it is important that the therapist maintain proper perspective until there is clear evidence that the problem is more than transitory. By doing so, the therapist teaches the patient an important lesson— namely, that it is the *longevity* of a problem that dictates its seriousness, not necessarily its *intensity*.

In general, nonjudgmental self-awareness on the part of the therapist is an important asset. Harris and Watkins (1987) write, "Counselors who are aware of their feelings are less likely to give symbolic homage to them in slips of the tongue or through confusing, contradictory body language and tone of voice" (p. 43). Pretzer (1983) points out that the therapists' emotional reactions, whether they include anger, hopelessness, or attraction, do not occur randomly. They are more likely indicative that the patient has behaved in a way that needs to be examined and understood. If therapists are concerned that their emotional reactions will be impediments to therapy, they can apply cognitive therapy techniques to themselves so as to modify their extreme emotions and to gain a more rational footing. One frequently used and highly successful method is the Daily Thought Record (DTR), a technique that patients are commonly taught to use as a way to view themselves and their problems more objectively (for a detailed explanation of the use of the DTR, see Beck et al., 1979; Burns, 1980; Newman & Beck, 1990; Newman & Haaga, in press).

Figures 6.1 and 6.2 highlight hypothetical instances in which therapists made use of this cognitive self-help technique to modify their potentially detrimental feelings and intentions.

Another related technique involves cognitive rehearsal prior to a session with a borderline patient. In this procedure, therapists anticipate potential problems that may arise during the ensuing session; chart their own automatic thoughts and feelings; and attempt to rehearse constructive, objective, and genuinely concerned responses.

Given that the therapist cannot anticipate every potential therapeutic snag or crisis, it is sometimes helpful for therapists to rehearse a number of positive self-statements as part of their preparation for sessions with their borderline patients. Examples might include:

- "I must remember that my patient's anger stems from hurt, insecurity, and fear, and therefore I won't take it personally."
- "No matter what my patient may throw at me, I'm going to show that I care just by calmly being there for her."

	SITUATION Actual event leading to unpleasant emotion.	EMOTION (S) 1. Specify sad/anxious/angry, etc. 2. Rate degree of emotion from 0 to 100%.	AUTOMATIC THOUGHT(S) 1. Write automatic thought(s) that preceded emotion(s). 2. Rate belief in automatic thoughts(s) from 0 to 100%.	RATIONAL RESPONSE 1. Write rational response to automatic thought(s). 2. Rate belief in rational response from 0 to 100%.	OUTCOME 1. Rerate belief in automatic thought(s) from 0 to 100%. 2. Specify and rate subsequent emotions from 0 to 100%.
DATE	My patient, Ms. L, called me at home at 11:00 P.M., crying and saying that she feels all alone and that she's thinking of suicide. She said that her only wish is that someone would show her that he cared. Then she hung up. I called her back repeatedly but she would not answer the phone. Images of hugging her and telling her that things will be O.K.	1. fear (90) 2. excitement (60) 3. sexual attraction (60) 4. guilt (40)	1. I have to go to her place right now to see that she's all right. She needs me. If I can't come to her rescue in this time of need, I will be abandoning her. (80) 2. If she kills herself, it's all my fault. (60) 3. I have to prove to her that I care. (95)	1. I *don't* have to go to her place. She doesn't need *me* per se. What she needs *from me* is an appropriate therapeutic response. That would be to assess her degree of actual suicidal intent, and to set up an appointment ASAP. If she refuses to answer the phone, I can either stop right here, or call the rescue squad. (90) 2. It's unlikely that she'll kill herself. She's pulled this ploy before. I have nothing to prove, and I'm doing all that I can to help her within therapeutic bounds. (100)	1. fear (40) 2. excitement (10) 3. sexual attraction (10) 4. guilt (0) Rerated Automatic Thoughts #1 = 0% #2 = 0% #3 = 20%

FIGURE 6.1. Daily Thought Record

126

	SITUATION	EMOTION (S)	AUTOMATIC THOUGHT(S)	RATIONAL RESPONSE	OUTCOME
	Actual event leading to unpleasant emotion.	1. Specify sad/ anxious/angry, etc. 2. Rate degree of emotion from 0 to 100%.	1. Write automatic thought(s) that preceded emotion(s). 2. Rate belief in automatic thoughts(s) from 0 to 100%.	1. Write rational response to automatic thought(s). 2. Rate belief in rational response from 0 to 100%.	1. Rerate belief in automatic thought(s) from 0 to 100%. 2. Specify and rate subsequent emotions from 0 to 100%.
DATE					
	My patient, Mr. R, was verbally abusive toward me in our session today, ostensibly because I seemed doubtful when he told me that he hadn't used cocaine all week. (Note: Mr. R is in treatment with me as per the terms of his parole.)	anger (60) fear (80) aggravation (100)	1. I don't need this garbage! I don't deserve it! Find another therapist . . . you're on your own, buddy! (90) 2. Mr. R is a God-damned liar! (100) 3. He doesn't want help. He just wants to beat the system. Well, he won't do it at my expense! (100) 4. This jerk could wind up kill- ing me if I'm not careful. (70)	1. I will not abandon Mr. R. I'm a professional and dealing with this kind of behavior comes with the territory. I will maintain a quiet, dignified strength. (100) 2. Mr. R is probably lying, but I will not label him a liar. He *has* been honest at times. (60) 3. Whether he wants my help or not is up to him, but I will con- tinue to offer it just the same. (80) 4. I won't play hero with Mr. R, nor will I provoke him. I'll play it safe and smart. I'll be cautious but I won't run scared. (70)	1. anger (30) 2. fear (20) 3. aggravation (50) Rerated Automatic Thoughts #1 = 20% #2 = 50% #3 = 50% #4 = 10%

FIGURE 6.2. Daily Thought Record

- "Act professionally, and be a real person."
- "I'm a good therapist and a good person. I don't need to be lauded to the sky, nor do I need to panic if I'm undervalued. I don't need to prove anything. I need only apply my skills to try to help my patient."
- "I won't let myself get too enthusiastic or too demoralized. I'll do well to temper my optimism with caution, and my hopelessness with an unfailing spirit to keep on trying."
- "By setting limits (where called for) I will show my patient that I respect myself. But I will set these limits in a way that will show that I respect my patient as well."

Such self-statements can be generated ad infinitum, as the therapeutic situations dictate.

Therapists who are able to self-monitor and reevaluate rationally their own thoughts and feelings in the immediacy of the therapeutic interaction can serve as excellent coping models for their borderline patients. They do so by demonstrating that troublesome thoughts and disturbing feelings need not be overwhelmingly threatening, and that confusion and conflicts can be approached and resolved with reasonable equanimity (Millon, 1981). Furthermore, by processing their reactions, therapists can highlight the fact that thoughts and emotions are not black and white entities, nor are they uncontrollable. Additionally, this strategy reinforces the notion that the therapist is competent, while disabusing the patient of the notion that the therapist is omnipotent.

The following scenario highlights the aforementioned point: A borderline patient angrily assails her therapist, saying that she feels that she is being "lectured and preached to." Rather than defending herself, or merely examining the patient's distortions in the interaction, the therapist openly looks at her own contribution to the problem and says: "You know, my automatic thoughts just before I started giving you suggestions were that I was failing you in some way, and that I'd better make up for it by giving you as much helpful advice as I could, as soon as possible. The result was that I started to come on too strong, and I didn't give you enough space or ask you what you wanted. I also felt a bit guilty as well. Now that I'm looking at this objectively, my rational response is that I'm not failing you, but merely overreacting to my perception that you're in dire need of help because of my lack of perfect solutions. The point is that we must both work *collaboratively* to find solutions to your problems. While I feel concern for you, I need not feel guilt, as that just detracts from the process of therapy. We each need to give each other enough room to reflect and speak."

The cognitive therapist must exercise clinical judgment in deciding whether to self-disclose in this manner. Such personal openness increases the level of intimacy, and the patient may find this very threatening (Pretzer, 1983). At the same time, to bypass this sort of intervention may be to lose an important opportunity to foster trust-building and interpersonal problem solving (Harris & Watkins, 1987). In the end, therapists need to be aware of their own intentions. If they are primarily "dumping" on patients and/or using them as one would a counselor, self-disclosure is contraindicated. If, however, the goal is to present oneself as a benevolent human being who wishes to find a way to work things out interpersonally, then the technique presented here is quite helpful. Ultimately, however, regardless of the true nature of the therapist's intentions, the therapist must be prepared to handle the patient's continued misperceptions of the therapeutic relationship.

SETTING LIMITS

Therapists are particularly vulnerable to counterproductive thoughts and feelings when they believe that their patients are taking advantage of them (Newman, 1990). As borderline patients typically have an inadequate sense of appropriate interpersonal boundaries, they are often highly demanding and intrusive toward their therapists (Kroll, 1988). Examples include making frequent late-night calls to the therapist's home, attempting to prolong the therapy hour, asking the therapist highly personal questions, and precipitating crises just before the therapist's vacation.

At times, it is sufficient for therapists to respond to the above with standard cognitive therapy procedures, such as highlighting automatic thoughts, beliefs, schemas, and emotions, as they pertain to the patient's acting out. Many times, however, these measures are temporarily inadequate because the patient's maladaptive behavior provides him or her with too great a degree of gratifying release from emotional tension. Thus, the patient's characteristic behavior provides a *disincentive* to engage in therapeutic work, leaving the therapist with feelings of anxiety, inadequacy, frustration, and hopelessness (Green, Goldberg, Goldstein, & Leibenluft, 1988). "The only resolution to such a therapeutic impasse is consistent implementation of carefully drawn boundaries" (Green et al., 1988, p. 6).

Although an exhaustive and comprehensive review of the theoretical and technical principles of setting limits is beyond the scope of this chapter (see Goldberg, 1983; Green et al., 1988; Gunderson, 1984), a number of points should be noted. First, the *timing* of the therapist's setting of limits is an important variable. One school of thought (Gunderson, 1984) states that the work of therapy is least inhibited when the therapist sets boundary limits as a *precondition* to treatment. Here, therapists spell out for their patients the parameters of appropriate behavior and realistic expectations, before therapy begins. Similarly, Linehan (1987) explains to BPD patients what is expected of them during the course of treatment via an explicit contract that is discussed and agreed on at the start of therapy. For example, Linehan's borderline patients know that they are obliged to discuss their suicidal impulses and other forms of behavioral actings-out as a primary agenda item in session. Furthermore, the patients pledge to engage themselves in activities out of session that enhance psychological growth and quality of life—such as school, hobbies, employment, and socializing—so that treatment does not become the sole and central focus of the patients' lives (Swenson, 1989).

A second school of thought (Green et al., 1988) holds that it is best to wait to set limits until such time as the acting out actually occurs. The rationale here is that the therapist shows the greatest amount of respect and positive regard for the patient by *not presuming* that regressive behavior will take place but, rather, by delineating precise limits when the situation calls for it.

In each stance highlighted previously, it is important to explain to the patient the therapeutic rationale for the necessity of setting limits. For example, the therapist can use a guided discovery (or didactic) approach to illuminate the negative consequences of such acting out for both the patient and the therapist, and for the course of therapy itself. The therapeutic goal is the formation of a healthy alliance between a self-respecting adult therapist and the more mature aspects of the patient's self-schemas (Green et al., 1988).

A common problem in this area occurs when therapists notice that they have allowed their patients' behavior to get out of control. Furthermore, the therapists feel hesitant to set limits, as they realize that they will be acting in a manner inconsistent with their previous leniency. In such cases, it is vitally important that therapists examine their own thoughts, beliefs, and emotions that may be inhibiting them from confronting their patients. Themes involving lack of self-respect and fear of harming the patient are most important to discover and reevaluate if therapy is to proceed in a positive direction. Additionally, we believe strongly that it is fitting and proper to confront patients on their maladaptive behavior, even in the context of a collaborative therapy such as cognitive therapy (Newman, 1988). By setting standards for appropriate behavior, therapists show that they have positive expectations for their patients, and thus communicate respect.

Another variable of interest is the *tone* that therapists take in confronting their patients with the realities of the need for setting limits. Even when therapists are adept at overtly explaining the need for therapeutic boundaries, they may be insufficiently aware of their concomitant *nonverbal* behaviors, especially if they are experiencing unacknowledged anger toward their patients. Given the borderline patient's acute sensitivity to mixed messages (the likes of which may activate "the cloud"), therapists must take care to monitor their own verbal and nonverbal behaviors in these instances, and must be willing to process these reactions when appropriate. In any case, it is clear that a respectful, empathic, nonparental manner is indicated in the process of setting limits.

SUMMARY

This chapter has reviewed the concept of countertransference as it pertains to cognitive therapy and cognitive therapists in the treatment of borderline personality disorder. We have noted that borderline patients bring extreme and distorted interpersonal issues into therapy, and consequently into the therapeutic relationship. Cognitive therapists, who are trained to establish healthy therapeutic alliances with patients before the specifics of treatment begin, must shift gears to focus on their

relationships with these patients as a central focus of therapy. Furthermore, therapists must vigilantly be cognizant of their own automatic thoughts, beliefs, emotions, and interpersonal behaviors in relation to their borderline patients, so as to
prevent a deterioration of the therapeutic process that might otherwise result.

This chapter has highlighted some common ways in which borderline patients
strain the therapeutic relationship, and ways in which cognitive therapists react so as
unwittingly to exacerbate this problem. It has been demonstrated that a cognitive
conceptualization of countertransference provides therapists with an understandable, workable self-help model that enables them to diminish their own distress, and
facilitates patients' progress in therapy. Additionally, the therapists' use of cognitive
self-help techniques helps them to serve as appropriate coping models for their
patients.

PART THREE
Case Studies

Chapter 7
The Borderline Spectrum: Introduction to Case Illustrations

Although significant advances in the reliability of the borderline diagnosis have been achieved with the publications of DSM-III and DSM-III-R in 1980 and 1987, respectively, Kroll (1988) notes that the reliability and validity of the diagnosis is still somewhat compromised by the way the DSM-III-R criteria are structured. Eight primary symptoms are presented, the existence of *any five* of which is sufficient for the diagnosis to be made. It is therefore mathematically possible for 56 distinct configurations and permutations of symptoms to be present under this single diagnostic umbrella. As a result, two patients who both may be classified as suffering from BPD actually may look quite different in terms of clinical presentation. Furthermore, although there almost certainly will be some significant overlap, they may present with rather distinct cognitive belief sets and schemas. At the very least, each patient's schemas will account for different amounts of explanatory variance in their respective manifestations of the borderline disorder. With this in mind, it becomes clear that it is crucial to assess in fine detail the entire spectrum of symptoms in each patient who is diagnosed as having the borderline disorder.

To illustrate, two borderline patients may possess the same abandonment schema. One, however, may manifest this in the assumption that "I must never allow myself to get close to someone, as that person will eventually leave me." The behavioral result would be social and emotional avoidance. The other borderline patient may derive an alternative belief from this same abandonment schema, such as, "I must do everything I can to make someone love me, and I must continue to overwhelm that person with my presence and passion, for this is the only way to keep that person from leaving me." This approach might translate to overly seductive and histrionic behavior.

Understanding these distinctions has critical implications for treatment. In these examples, the therapist would want to help both patients to become aware of their abandonment schemas; to understand the schemas' development and maintenance in their lives; and to appreciate the magnitude of their maladaptive influences on the patients' thoughts, emotions, actions, and interpersonal relations. The strategy for *change*, however, would need to be individualized for each patient. The first patient would need to be encouraged to experiment gradually with behaviors that *facilitate* caring and closeness with others, whereas the second patient would need help in *diminishing* the intensity of emotional bonding with others. However, the basic goals would be the same—to lessen each patient's expectations about interpersonal abandonment; to moderate the extreme emotional and behavioral responses that maintain the schema; and to develop healthier, more stable interpersonal relationships. This example serves to highlight the importance of a thorough, individualized case conceptualization.

Aside from distinctions that can be made between BPD patients *within* the diagnostic category, there are differences that can be ascertained between BPD patients by virtue of their *concurrent* DSM-III-R diagnoses. Indeed, it is very rare for a patient classified as "borderline" to have only the one diagnosis. The instability that characterizes BPD is such that a wide range of symptoms exists (and at times, fluctuates wildly) in the patient, many of which correspond to other diagnostic categories. Some of these include the affective disorders, panic disorder, obsessive-compulsive disorder, eating disorders, brief psychotic reactions, dissociative states, and other personality disorders (e.g., dependent, histrionic, antisocial, etc.). In our clinical experience, the BPD diagnosis looms largest even when additional psychological disorders complicate the clinical picture. This is reflected by the tendency for therapists to refer to their patients as suffering from BPD, even when there is a laundry list of diagnoses that exist as well, any of which appropriately could be invoked to describe the patient's problems.

A review of the literature on differential diagnosis in this area suggests that the most clinically meaningful points of overlap occur with the affective disorders (e.g., Adelman, 1985; Akiskal, 1981; Cowdry & Gardner, 1988; Ellison & Adler, 1984; Gunderson & Elliott, 1985; Kroll, 1988; Soloff et al., 1986), and other personality disorders (Gunderson & Zanarini, 1987). With this in mind, we will aid the cause of a more precise cognitive understanding of the patient in the borderline spectrum by highlighting the typical cognitive beliefs and schemas *across three hypothesized subtypes of the disorder.* We will illustrate these different "shades" of borderline personality (and concomitant cognitive sets) via the presentation of case illustrations.

We focus on the following three borderline sub-types:

1. Borderline–avoidant/dependent personality
2. Borderline–histrionic/narcissistic personality
3. Borderline–antisocial/paranoid personality

These three subtypes of BPD patients represent those patients who meet full DSM-III-R criteria for the borderline disorder and who demonstrate at least substantial features of the concomitant personality disorder profiles.

We have chosen these areas based on our collective clinical experience that these are the most frequently encountered subdivisions of BPD. Although each of our BPD subtypes involves overlap with other personality disorders, we acknowledge that many BPD patients present with an affective disorder as well. Chronic and marked emotional distress, often diagnosed as a depressive disorder, commonly serves as the impetus for the BPD patient to seek treatment. Therefore, a breakdown of BPD subtypes across the affective disorders is heuristically less instructive than a division of the BPD spectrum by concomitant personality disorders.

Furthermore, some BPD patients meet criteria for personality disorders that are not represented within our three categories. For example, we have treated BPD patients who also demonstrate cognitive, affective, and behavioral features that indicate concurrent diagnoses of personality disorders such as passive-aggressive, obsessive-compulsive, and schizoid. However, we find these to be less prevalent in the BPD population as a whole than the three subtypes that we review in this section. In those very rare cases when we have found BPD patients to meet criteria for passive-aggressive, obsessive-compulsive, or schizoid personality disorders, they also qualified for one of the three subtypes listed here. In sum, the BPD–avoidant/dependent, BPD–histrionic/narcissistic, and BPD–antisocial/paranoid classifications have proved most useful in helping us zero in on specific symptoms and schemas.

As a prelude to the case presentations, we offer an overview of the cognitive (and other symptomological) distinctions between the groups listed. These are not absolute descriptions; rather, they serve as guidelines for identifying the general profiles.

BORDERLINE–AVOIDANT/DEPENDENT PERSONALITY

Borderline patients who also suffer from avoidant and dependent personality disorders are a highly anxious lot. They tend to believe that they are incapable in all major spheres of life (academic, vocational, interpersonal, psychological) and therefore evidence very low self-esteem. The incompetence schema typically is very compelling in this subtype of borderline patient, fueling both the avoidance and the dependency disorders. Specifically, their beliefs about being unable to cope with demanding situations cause them to shy away from problems and challenges alike. This strategy prevents such patients from engaging in growth-enhancing experiences such as mastering a new job or asserting oneself to a significant other, and therefore reinforces their beliefs that they are helpless and hopeless. Likewise, their sense of dependency—typified by such beliefs as, "I can't take care of myself," " I need others to make decisions for me," " I can't live without others"—compels these patients to search desperately for people on whom they can rely for almost everything. This dependency schema is so extreme that it places a tremendous interpersonal burden on those closest to the patients, and readily predisposes their relationships to crises.

The patients' avoidance also is a by-product of the mistrust and lack-of-individuation schemas. Such patients are extremely sensitive to critcism and rejection, not trusting that others will respect them, treat them fairly, or refrain from exploiting or abusing them. Additionally, the BPD–avoidant/dependent patients have such under-developed senses of themselves that they fear losing their identities and autonomy if they become emotionally involved with someone else. At times, such patients believe that they must withdraw from their most significant relationships in order to survive as individual entities. They fear that their interests, goals, and needs will be overwhelmed by the more powerful and definitive identities of others.

Complicating the clinical picture is the fact that these patients typically have suffered emotional deprivation earlier in life. Therefore, they often excessively crave acceptance, nurturance, and love from others, which they cannot obtain as long as they remain avoidant. Therefore, they change their strategies around 180 degrees, and seek constant support and companionship. Unfortunately, even when they succeed in forming close relationships, their low self-esteem ("I am bad") causes them to doubt that their significant others will stay with them. In short, their abandonment and unlovability schemas come to the fore, inducing a heightened sense of dependency. This, in turn, translates into an escalation of dysfunctional interpersonal behaviors that seek continual reassurance and "proof" of love from others.

When the patients' loved ones react with annoyance and distancing behaviors, the patients' mistrust schemas are reinforced. On the other hand, when the patients' significant others are able to tolerate the patients' dependency, it does little to quell the patients' fears of abandonment and loss of love. They simply cannot believe that anyone would find them lovable for very long. Furthermore, even when the signifi-cant others "prove" their love, loyalty, and commitment, the BPD–avoidant/depen-dent patients' lack-of-individuation schema often reappears, causing the patients to withdraw fearfully from their relationships—the very relationships that they had clung to previously with such tenacious neediness.

Once they withdraw, it doesn't take long before the patients' incompetency schemas become salient once again, convincing them that they cannot survive without the help of others. In sum, the schemas that feed into the oscillating cycle of avoidance and dependency cause these borderline patients to be in constant states of turmoil in the form of approach–avoidance conflicts, an extreme version of the "can't live with 'em, can't live without 'em" syndrome.

In therapy BPD–avoidant/dependent patients alternately will withdraw and make excessive demands for total support from the therapist. They will avoid thinking about upsetting clinical material, instead feeling physically sick or cognitively "blanking out" (Young, 1990). Further, they will be prone to misinterpreting the therapists' benevolent attempts to teach self-help skills as attempts to be rid of them. Therefore, these patients are especially likely to be noncompliant with homework, with fear as the main concomitant emotion. (Note: This is in contrast to the BPD–antisocial/paranoid patient, whose noncompliance with homework is linked to anger and alienation.)

These patients are more likely than other types of borderline patients to suffer from concomitant anxiety disorders. However, unlike standard Axis I anxious patients, they demonstrate few well-formulated worries about specific outcomes that could befall them. Instead, they tend to have a vague but powerful sense of unspecified impending doom.

Finally, these patients are at risk for terminating therapy prematurely as a strategy to preempt the therapist's abandoning *them*. On the other hand, they will clamor for the therapist's attention and assistance when the therapist sets boundaries or plans to leave for a vacation.

BORDERLINE–HISTRIONIC/NARCISSISTIC PERSONALITY

BPD patients who demonstrate significant histrionic and narcissistic features typically experience tremendous mood lability, stormy relationships, overwhelming needs for attention and affection, and extreme rage when they believe that their needs are not being met. These patients often alternate between idealizing and vilifying their therapists, and are the most likely of any of the BPD subtypes to make suicidal threats and gestures as cries for help, or as ploys to manipulate the therapist and significant others.

The abandonment and unlovability schemas are heavily weighted in this BPD subtype. In their desperate attempts to obtain and hold on to love and care, borderline–histrionic/narcissistic patients resort to exhibitionistic behaviors and emotional melodramatics. For example, such a patient may attempt to obtain a committed love relationship by seducing someone on a first date, only to be enraged (and to feel betrayed) later when it becomes apparent that the partner has no such long-term intentions for the "relationship." These BPD patients may be perplexed and vexed by the thought that the intended mates do not appreciate their "specialness," yet simultaneously panic at the thought that they (the patients) may actually be unlovable. As a result, these patients commonly catastrophize that they will always be alone in life. Therefore, they may give strong consideration to committing suicide.

Therapists who treat borderline–histrionic/narcissistic patients recognize them as people who have significant trouble in perceiving and understanding the meaning of appropriate interpersonal boundaries. In similar fashion to infants in the egocentric stage of cognitive development, these patients are prone to assume that their needs are readily apparent to others, require immediate attention, and are congruent with the needs of the nurturer. For example, it may be difficult for this type of patient to understand that a therapist may not be as eager to answer the phone in the middle of the night as the patient is to make the call. When this patient detects that the therapist is not going to engage in symbiosis, the patient may jump to the extreme conclusion that *nobody* can *ever* help, and may punish a therapist who is trying earnestly to muster up as much empathic and practical assistance as is reasonably possible in the situation.

Patients in the histrionic/narcissistic spectrum of BPD crave stimulation, excitement, and novelty *around* them, but are profoundly loath to generate changes *within* themselves. Accordingly, they strive to control their interpersonal environments in order to gain the support and love that they believe will solve all of their problems. They frequently will idealize someone, only to feel deeply disillusioned and betrayed at the slightest hint that this person will not be able to fulfill all of their needs. They desire continual approval and reassurrance in order to support a very fragile self-esteem.

Impulsivity, impatience, and low frustration tolerance are hallmarks of this borderline type. Anger is readily expressed, generally in the form of verbal tirades toward those they feel have wronged them, including their therapists. These patients put great stock and credence in their emotions, and strikingly little in rational, constructive, sensible thinking. Their investment in their intense emotions may be based in a sense that only through grandstanding can they prevent people from withholding love and abandoning them.

BORDERLINE–ANTISOCIAL/PARANOID PERSONALITY

The typical person who meets DSM-III-R criteria for antisocial personality disorder shows a marked disregard for the formal and informal rules that govern social behavior. Usually, the antisocial person breaks these rules in the service of the self—to gain wealth, power, and stimulation at the expense of others. There is often a strong sense of self-importance to go along with brash defiance. Clearly, the person with this personality profile takes care of himself or herself first, with other people's needs and feelings taking on little or no significance. A related personality disorder is the paranoid group. These patients have a chronic and pervasive distrust for the motives of others, and are continually vigilant to the threat (imagined or otherwise) of attack. Jealousy and anger are readily experienced to extremes, and perceived criticisms are met with great indignation and animosity. A grandiose presentation of self thinly disguises a profound sense of self-doubt.

It has been our clinical experience that some patients who demonstrate such lack of regard for others and for social norms show the same disdain for themselves as well. They engage in the same kinds of reckless, impulsive, hostile, and destructive behaviors as the "pure" antisocial and paranoid person, but not for the same purpose of self-service. Rather, in line with the BPD pattern, they seem to act out their emotional pain and hostility in ways that are geared to hurt themselves as well as others. The prevailing attitude of this type of patient seems to be, "I don't give a damn what happens to me anyway, so I might as well do what I damn well please." In such cases where the patient exhibits this kind of self-destructive low self-esteem to go along with a strong sense of distrust and anger toward the world, the patient often meets criteria for borderline, antisocial, and paranoid personality disorders.

Hostility, suspiciousness, and recklessness typify these borderline patients. They have a malevolent view of others, and a superficially maintained false sense of power. They are prone to using and abusing those that they purport to love, and therefore rarely have long-lasting or stable relationships. They may defiantly claim that they feel close to nobody, yet be tremendously possessive, demanding, and jealous in their relationships. Anger is their chief expressed emotion, usually in the form of self-harming strategies such as daredevil recklessness and/or physically lashing out at others (e.g., deliberately getting into fights at bars in order to distract themselves from the emotional pain that they won't acknowledge). Other people are viewed and treated as adversaries, thus provoking unsympathetic reactions that serve to "confirm" for the patient that nobody can be trusted. Although there are no substantive data on the matter, reseachers in the field have begun to hypothesize that the borderline–antisocial/paranoid person is typically male (Gunderson & Zanarini, 1987). Furthermore, it is our hypothesis that expressions of suicidality in this subpopulation suggest that the patients are potentially homicidal as well. For example, a suicidal borderline–antisocial/paranoid husband may be as likely to kill his wife before killing himself as he is to simply take his own life. Additionally, these patients are intolerant of boredom and therefore are at risk for substance abuse. They are already a highly violent and impulsive lot, and their use of drugs and alcohol magnifies the problem by further lowering self-controls. In spite of their aggressiveness, borderline–antisocial/paranoid patients are low in self-esteem (maintaining "badness" schemas) and often show contempt for themselves in the form of self-destructive behaviors.

ADDITIONAL FACTORS

The fact that we present only one BPD–antisocial/paranoid case as opposed to two cases each of the BPD–histrionic/narcissistic and BPD–avoidant/dependent reflects our perception that the former subtype is less frequently seen in psychotherapy settings and therefore should receive proportionally less descriptive attention in our case studies. We do not intend to state definitively that this type of borderline patient is less prevalent in the natural population, but certainly it is less represented in our patient files. Nevertheless, we have found such patients to be seriously disordered and highly difficult to manage. Therefore, it is important to highlight the treatment of one such patient.

Additionally, by sheer coincidence, the two male borderline patients we present have been treated by the male authors of this text, and the three female patients have been treated by the female authors. This is not intended to imply that borderline patients necessarily make better progress with same-gender therapists. The matter of patient–therapist matching is an empirical question that we have inadequate data to answer at this time. Anecdotally, we have seen some borderline patients make significant strides while working with opposite-gender therapists; likewise, we have witnessed some other patients make less than optimal progress with same-gender therapists. The issue seems not to be whether or not the therapist and patient are matched on the basis of gender per se, but, rather, whether the patient believes that the therapist is capable of being sensitive to his or her problems, some of which may entail issues of control and trust in dealing with members of the opposite sex.

Chapter 8

Borderline–Antisocial/Paranoid Case Study: The Case of "Walter"

PRESENTING PROBLEMS

Walter, an obese, bearded man with heavily muscled and tattooed arms, entered therapy at the age of 37, having just completed an 18-month prison term. The terms of his parole dictated that he attend regular outpatient therapy for substance abuse. Failure to do so would result in his being incarcerated again.

Walter, a longshoreman, had been convicted on multiple counts of grand larceny as a result of his having stolen a shipment of high-tech electronic equipment. He purportedly had stolen these goods in order to fence them for drug money to feed his expensive cocaine habit. The thievery, ill conceived and committed out of desperation, was easily traced to Walter and led to his arrest and eventual conviction.

Walter's intake evaluation at the Center for Cognitive Therapy elucidated numerous problematic areas in his life. The patient's anger toward "the system" that had jailed him and his ongoing struggle with the urge to abuse cocaine were just part of the clinical picture. In addition, he was involved in a mutually abusive relationship with his wife, he harbored hatred and homicidal wishes towards his ex-wife, he was dangerously noncompliant in taking his insulin shots for his diabetic condition, and he was prone to getting into drunken scuffles at a number of taverns that he frequented. A sample of the patient's automatic thoughts and beliefs assessed at intake and early in treatment are as follows:

- "I'm going to die young one way or the other, no matter what I do."
- "If you trust someone you're asking for big trouble."
- "The only people who give a shit about me are my uncle and grandmother, both of whom are dying. I'm really on my own."
- "I have to do things my way, or else I'm sure to get screwed."
- "Life has no point except to see how much misery it takes to kill you off."
- "I'm a loser."

These thoughts and beliefs clearly highlight Walter's distress, sense of aloneness, hopelessness, low self-esteem, cynicism, and low regard for others. The patient willingly expressed these beliefs to the therapist as a result of the therapist's sensitive yet probing approach to gathering historical information about Walter. For example, whenever Walter related the details of an unfortunate event in his life, the therapist would ask:

- What lessons did you learn from this experience?
- How did you feel about yourself when this happened?
- How did you feel toward the world when this happened?
- How did your experience affect how you felt about life?
- After this terrible experience, what did you promise yourself that you would do if you ever were confronted with this type of situation again? What did you vow that you would never let happen again, if you could help it?

These and other questions helped to elicit a number of critical thoughts, assumptions, and schemas that helped the therapist to understand Walter better as an individual.

Walter met DSM-III-R criteria for BPD by evidencing the following symptoms:

1. Affective instability
2. Intense, inappropriate displays of anger
3. A history of stormy, abusive relationships
4. Reckless acts of impulsivity (e.g., drugs, fistfights)
5. Chronic feelings of emptiness and boredom

He also met criteria for antisocial personality disorder (AsPD) and paranoid personality disorder (PPD), respectively, as per the following characteristics:

1. A childhood history of truancy, running away from home, and physical fights with others
2. Unstable work history
3. Incarceration, both in the military and as a civilian
4. Reckless behaviors that endangered others (e.g., drunk driving)
5. Frequent lying
6. Impulsivity, poor planning skills, and deficits in learning from past mistakes
7. Hair-trigger anger in response to perceived slights
8. A tendency to hold grudges over prolonged periods of time
9. A reluctance to confide in others, including the therapist
10. Constant vigilance for signs of disloyalty or exploitation at the hands of others

On the plus side, Walter did seem to be capable of feeling remorse for past misdeeds, and he demonstrated appropriate parental care for his adopted children at those times when he was abstinent from drugs.

Despite all of these problems, Walter and his parole officer did not view these BPD, AsPD, and PPD characteristics as the primary targets for cognitive therapy. In their concordant views, Walter's main problem was his tendency toward substance abuse, which ostensibly led to his illegal behavior. Therefore, the therapist geared the course of therapy to focus on this problem, all the while realizing that many other psychological issues placed this patient at risk for drug abuse in the first place. As treatment progressed, the beliefs that engendered Walter's low self-esteem and anger toward the world at large would become more of a central focus in cognitive therapy.

BACKGROUND INFORMATION AND CASE CONCEPTUALIZATION

A more complete understanding of the patient's idiosyncratic views about himself, his world, and his future requires a thorough assessment of his developmental history. A review of Walter's learning history provided the therapist with a window into the sources of the patient's dysfunctional points of view.

As the oldest of six children, Walter assumed a great deal of care-taking responsibilities. This was necessary given that his father, a police officer, was alcoholic, and his unhappy mother immersed herself in prayer and the Catholic Church. It was Walter's job to find his father at the bar late at night and bring him home. On more than one occasion, he literally carried his father over his shoulder. His reward for this job was to be abused verbally by his father, who saw Walter as a daily reminder of his ties to the family life that he had never wanted. Walter learned to hate his father, who drank and gambled away most of the family's money, and who was surly, unloving, and dictatorial when he wasn't unconscious. Walter also learned to hate all police officers and, in a classic instance of overgeneralization, learned to have disdain for all authority figures.

Although he viewed his mother as a victim, he harbored a great deal of anger toward her as well. He saw her retreat into religiosity as an escape from her responsibilities to the family. The more that the father would drink, the more the mother would engage in isolated prayer. The situation became so extreme that Walter often took charge of feeding and clothing the youngest of his brothers and sisters, while the other siblings ran wild and got into constant trouble at school and in the neighborhood. Walter grew to hate organized religion, seeing it as a "fool's way of coping with the real world." He also developed an intense ambivalence about care-taking, saying on the one hand that "everyone should just learn to survive on his own and leave everyone else the hell alone," while also demonstrating a strong but unfulfilled desire to be appreciated by those he had helped.

Walter quit high school and joined the Army when he was 18 years old as an obvious escape from his dysfunctional family. However, Walter did not fare well in a military environment, as he had become accustomed to shunning authority and living by his own rules. When he heard that his family was in danger of losing the house (because of his father's debts) he seized the "opportunity" to go AWOL so he could "rescue" his family, and ended up spending six months in the stockade. Later, in therapy, Walter would reflect upon this experience as the time he came to the realization that he "would always fuck up, no matter what the circumstances,"and that "it doesn't pay to help nobody, 'cause they don't give a shit about you anyway." As illustrated by these beliefs, it became apparent that a most compelling schema was that of mistrust. Furthermore, despite his outward bravura, Walter maintained a hidden schema of incompetence.

Walter seemed to be making strides in his creating a life for himself when he left the army and became a longshoreman. He enjoyed the physically rigorous work, as he was able to work off a lot of his frustration. Furthermore, he enjoyed the sensation of straining and hurting himself (in lifting tons of cargo each day) without letting others know how much pain he was feeling.

It was also at this time that he met his first wife. In retrospect, it was clear that he knew she had a drug problem, but he was attracted to her and desired to gain her love by rescuing her from her dangerous habit. In a sense, he was hoping that this would not be a repeat of his experience with his family of origin, where his role as family savior led only to his feeling used and abused. Unfortunately, Walter's first marriage set him up to be hurt even more seriously, thus reinforcing his views of his own unlovability, further intensifying his ambivalence about taking care of others, and generally exacerbating his cynicism, bitterness, and mistrust toward the world.

By the time that Walter was 31, he was struggling to earn enough money to support himself, his drug-addicted wife, and their 5-year-old son. Walter, who distrusted banks (as yet another symbol of the corporate mainstream system that "fucks the working man over"), kept his cash at home but soon found that his wife was stealing from their savings in order to support her habit.

At first, Walter's reaction was to drink heavily and use amphetamines, rationalizing that "I might as well get loaded too." Of course, this led to a further depletion of household money, caused Walter to miss time at work, and set the stage for his own growing polysubstance abuse problem. When the family savings were gone, Walter's wife resorted to more drastic measures. First, she pawned Walter's most prized possessions in the world—his bowling trophies. This was a cruel blow for Walter, as the trophies symbolized for him the one aspect of his life where he felt some pride, recognition, and competence. Then, Walter discovered that his wife was prostituting herself in exchange for drugs. Walter reacted by beating her severely and followed this by getting high on speed and crashing his car (deliberately, he reports) into a telephone pole. These events ultimately would result in marital separation, divorce, estrangement from his son, permanent facial scars and a limp, and constant preoccupation with the idea that he might have contracted AIDS from his ex-wife. Over the course of the next few years, Walter would come to use cocaine as his drug of choice. He was lonely, bitter, obsessed with getting revenge on his ex-wife, and often out of work. Furthermore, he made numerous suicidal gestures, went through episodes of bulimia, and allowed his diabetic condition to deteriorate seriously. Though he did remarry, he again chose a woman who had a drug abuse problem, but he loved her two sons as if they were his own.

Eventually, as mentioned before, he wound up in prison, and then in cognitive therapy.

TREATMENT AND OUTCOME

Walter entered therapy with a very clear agenda regarding what he *didn't* want to work on. For example, he wanted to make it clear to the therapist right from the start that if the therapy involved putting faith in a Higher Power, then "you all can just shove it." Apparently, part of Walter's prison experience involved going to AA meetings, where a 12-step approach was taken. Unfortunately, religious references of any sort tapped into his memories of his devout but neglectful mother, thus eliciting a great deal of cynicism and anger. The therapist responded by assuring Walter that religion did not need to play any role at all in his treatment. The therapist explained that cognitive therapy placed great value in "learning how to take care of oneself."

The therapist phrased it in this particular way in order to appeal to Walter's sense of autonomy, and to avoid initially getting into issues of trust between therapist and patient. This is but one small example of the *art* of therapy, which is an important factor whether one is operating from a cognitive model or from any other theoretical framework. We have found that a thorough assessment of the patient's automatic thoughts, beliefs, schemas, and their etiological and maintaining factors puts the therapist in the best position to make use of the art of cognitive therapy. Here, the cognitive therapist can offer interventions that are sensitive to the patient's idiosyncratic vulnerabilities. In addition, the therapist can actually make therapeutic use of an otherwise dysfunctional patient belief. This is especially helpful in the treatment of difficult personality disorders such as the borderline–antisocial/paranoid.

As an example, Walter strongly held that "the system" was out to "screw him over." Because the therapist was seen to be part of "the system," it followed that Walter expected the therapist to do him wrong. By ascertaining this belief in working with Walter, the therapist was able to find a way to confront the patient without automatically being seen as part of an oppressive system. Specifically, when Walter claimed that he had not been using cocaine, despite the fact that he'd been missing his urinalysis appointments, the therapist expressed his skepticism. Walter became angry at the therapist's implied accusation, as his belief that therapy was adversarial to his well-being was elicited. The therapist, however, reframed this entirely by saying, "Walter, if I believe everything you say without question, then you have a fool for a therapist. Walter, you deserve better than to have a fool for a therapist. You deserve to have someone who cares and is aware of all possible problems that could hurt you." This comment was quite effective in defusing Walter's anger, as it provided him with a completely new and helpful way to construe the therapist's actions. Instead of viewing the therapist's confrontive statement as an attempt to control or harm him, Walter was able to understand that the therapist cared enough to speak directly and honestly, and to "take the heat" in return.

Another item on Walter's "I don't want no part of it" agenda was his refusal to do any written assignments. Given that such homework typically is a vital part of cognitive therapy, the therapist tried to engage Walter in an exploration of the pros and cons of following through with written assignments. Walter's response was to maintain stubbornly that "I ain't gonna do it, so you might as well save your breath." The therapist hypothesized that Walter may have been self-conscious about his marginal writing and spelling skills, which triggered his incompetency schema. Therefore, the therapist did not attempt to press the issue, and tried to establish collaboration in self-help skills training and assignments in other ways. He made a mental note to initiate a discussion on the topic of Walter's schema of incompetency at a later date. This is but one small example of how cognitive therapy must be modified in order to establish a productive therapeutic alliance with a borderline spectrum patient.

The first few months of therapy focused primarily on the patient's substance abuse problem. Therapist and patient discussed the situations, emotions, and thoughts that were most often associated with a strong craving to get high (cf., Beck, Wright, Newman, & Liese, in press). Walter had been used to recognizing the situations and emotions that elicited drug urges, but the idea that specific *thoughts and perceptions* could be implicated as well was completely novel to him. For example, he knew that verbal arguments with his wife or with men at the bar as well as the concomitant feelings of anger and frustration were often followed by a desire to "get wasted." Walter would do this by mainlining cocaine with the needle and syringe that were given to him by his physician for his daily injections of insulin. However, it was a revelation when therapeutic questioning led him to consider the thoughts that precipitated and fueled these arguments and angry feelings. Thoughts such as "don't take no shit off him/her" and "time to show who's boss" often spurred him to lash out in anger. If the result was that Walter felt that he had gotten his way, he would still think that "I got nobody on my side," and "everything has to be a God-damned hassle all the time." These thoughts would get him down, and, combined with an adrenaline decline, would motivate him to use cocaine. He believed that using cocaine was his only surefire way to experience a cessation of his misery. If he believed that he had lost the argument or otherwise lost face, he would feel humiliated and his already low self-esteem would plummet further. This too led to drug use.

In order to decrease Walter's risk for drug abuse, the therapist spent many therapy hours attempting to teach Walter alternative ways to view and deal with his interpersonal confrontations. One technique involved reviewing one or more of such confrontations and asking Walter to imagine "what would happen if you said [adaptive self-statement] to yourself at that time? How would you have felt? What do you suppose you would have done differently?" The therapist provided Walter with a number of rational responses, in an effort to see if Walter would respond favorably. Again, this highlights a deviation from standard cognitive therapy. In standard cognitive therapy, the therapist tries to have the *patient* generate rational responses. In this case, however, Walter was so stubbornly opposed to doing active work in therapy that the therapist had to take a more flexible, facilitating stance. Further-more, the patient may not have been capable of applying formal cognitive operations at this early stage in treatment, and therefore was unprepared to formulate rational responses on his own. In any event, the goal was still the same—to teach Walter alternative and more benign ways to view his personal world. The therapist hoped that this approach would bring about some small success experiences that later might encourage Walter to take a more active role in the work of therapy.

Again, therapeutic roadblocks were encountered. Although the therapist gener-ated what he thought were excellent rational responses, the patient's underlying beliefs worked against acceptance of the therapist's ideas. For example, the therapist offered the following self-statement possibilities for Walter to use in order to quell anger and to defuse the conflicts that put him at great risk for drug use:

- "Don't waste your time with this jerk. He's not worth arguing with. You know you're right, and that's all that matters."

(Note: As the therapist was putting forth this rational response, he did not really believe that Walter was always in the right in his tavern scuffles. That was immate-rial. What *was* important was solidifying the therapeutic relationship by suggesting that the therapist was in agreement with Walter's point of view vis-à-vis the taproom adversary. The therapist's strategy was to help Walter to interrupt the cognitive-emotional-behavioral cycle that often led to cocaine abuse.)

- "Walter, you can rise above this scum by just ignoring him and walking away."
- "This situation is bad news for my recovery. I'd better drop it or leave now. It would be better to call my therapist and bitch and moan to him rather than to get into a fight and then get high."
- (With regard to cursing at his wife) "I can't do this to the kids. Even if she's a bitch she's still their mother and they love her and need her. They'll hate me if I treat her that way. I want my kids to respect me, not fear me and loathe me. I have to find another way to deal with her."

(Again, the therapist did *not* personally subscribe to the belief that Walter's wife was a "bitch." Such global labeling is anathema to standard cognitive therapy.

However, cognitive therapy with a borderline–antisocial/paranoid patient requires some relatively extreme measures in joining with the patient and helping him to save face while he's backing down from a confrontation. Later, the therapist worked with Walter to get him to modify his view of his wife as well as his language toward her. For now, the therapist believed it made more sense to utilize crisis management and rational responding *before* tackling the patient's mistrust schema.)

At first, these rational responses were *not* effective in helping Walter to diminish his anger and urges to fight and use drugs. Walter's explanations as to why he would not even *want* to have these thoughts shed light on some of his dysfunctional beliefs. He argued that the therapist's rational responses "might work in *your* neighborhood, but not in mine." He went on to suggest that if he convinced himself to walk away from a confrontation, he would be giving a message to the other bar patrons (many of whom were current or former motorcycle gang members) that he was weak and that he could "be fucked with without retribution." Furthermore, his own personal "code of honor" led him to believe that if he avoided fights he was "not a man." In addition, he viewed barroom brawls as an opportunity to throw around some muscle, while at the same time experiencing the physical pain that he liked. This physical pain distracted him somewhat from his emotional pain. (Remember that he enjoyed his job as a longshoreman in part because the work strained his body.) Finally, getting into fights was a way to harm himself, and to justify his "me against the world" belief system (indicative of a mistrust schema) and, by extension, his self-medicating drug abuse. With regard to his wife, he was not about to let cooler heads prevail, as he strongly held that he would never again allow a woman to take control over (and destroy) his life, as he perceived his first wife had done.

Here we see a network of beliefs that was rigid and highly dichotomized and overgeneralized. In effect, his marital behavior had turned 180 degrees from his behavior in the first marriage, and he acted in ways that would tend to make a rule out of what otherwise might be isolated negative incidents. It never occurred to him that he might be able to associate with new, less violent people, or that he could use his street smarts rather than his fists to solve a problem or save face. Part of this huge oversight on Walter's part was due to his incompetency schema, typified by the core belief, "I'm a loser." (Walter had admitted that he felt this way about himself in response to the therapist's asking why he always disparaged the therapist's encouragement and hopefulness.) With this self-view, it was impossible for Walter to consider that he might be able to establish and fit in with acquaintances and friends who were more law-abiding and personally successful. His self-destructive behavior in taverns and at home was also fueled by his sense that that was what he deserved anyway—that positive outcomes were just not fitting for someone as "bad" as himself. These beliefs, which the therapist spelled out for Walter as theories about his attitudes toward himself and life, became important targets for cognitive intervention.

However, as therapy progressed well beyond the first 16 to 20 sessions and the therapist and patient spent more time on these issues, there was always the need to focus on Walter's immediate survival needs. His continual problems in employment, family life, adherence to parole, and staying abstinent from drugs and alcohol required continual monitoring and problem solving. The scheduling of activities was an extremely important component of crisis intervention. Walter was encouraged to generate pleasurable and/or meaningful (legal) activities in which to engage. Examples of these included finding employment (and, once he found a new job, working overtime in order to stay out of trouble and to earn more money), going bowling with the money that he would normally use for alcohol and cocaine, lifting weights and doing other forms of enjoyable exercise, spending time with his children (whom he really did love, in spite of his less than ideal parenting behavior), or simply hibernating in his bedroom and watching cable TV, instead of roaming the streets looking for trouble.

During those times when his desperation and emotional pain would lead him to think, "I don't care anymore. I might as well go back to jail" (or, "I might as well die high"), he was taught to remind himself of the things in this world that he *had* cared about, including his children, his job, and his desire to bowl a perfect game at some time in his life.

When Walter experienced intense anger and frustration, and was tempted to engage in violence or drug use, he was taught to ask himself, "What's in it for me if I do this?" and "What's in it for me if I *hold off* from doing this?" In general, whenever Walter's maladaptive beliefs and schemas were discussed in session, the therapist entreated Walter to talk about the purpose these beliefs served (e.g., "How does this work for you?" "How does it work *against* you?" "What *would* work for you better?"). Again, this strategy met strong resistance from Walter's "I'm bad" schema, which dictated that he *deserved* to have things work against him. At these times, the therapist made Herculean efforts to find things in Walter that sincerely were praiseworthy, and to support him and compliment him for whatever efforts he had made in therapy to that point. The therapist often said a variation of the following to Walter: "Walter, I've admired the way that you've struggled and single-handedly fought all the odds to overcome all the shit that's gone on in your life. I've admired your strength and your grittiness and your courage. I've seen you work very, very hard to get to the point where you have a chance to get a life for yourself. Don't blow it now, Walter. You've worked too hard to get to this point to waste it all now because you feel angry [depressed, a craving for drugs]. Can we talk about how you can ride this out? Can we talk about how you're going to get through all this until you can see it in a different and better way again?"

As a last resort, the therapist implored Walter to call him on the phone if he felt that he was going to "bust out and do something." Walter rarely called, but when he did, he was verbally congratulated for doing so, and an appointment was set up as soon as possible.

During the latter part of the first year of therapy, Walter's grandmother finally succumbed after a long battle with cancer. At his next therapy session, Walter spoke poignantly about his loss. He was clearly distraught as he explained that his grandmother was the "person who practically raised me." He believed that the one person who truly loved him unconditionally was now gone. The therapist acknowledged his grief and offered sympathy and condolences. At the same time, he asked that Walter consider that there may be other people in his life who also cared about him. His response was that anyone who cared about him now did so because there was something in it for him or her. At this point, the therapist briefly touched upon the love of his children, and of his uncle. Unfortunately, this served only to remind Walter of his uncle's terminal illness, and how he would soon lose him too. The therapist sincerely felt sorry for Walter and spent the rest of the session providing emotional support.

In retrospect, this was an incomplete strategy. Walter's vulnerable emotional state put him at extremely high risk for drug relapse. So much work had been done in combatting anger, frustration, and low self-esteem as a means by which to avert drug urges that the emotion of grief did not automatically cue the therapist into the urgency of the moment. Unfortunately, before the next session could be held, Walter went on a cocaine binge. Days later, he called the therapist in an almost incoherent state (he called collect from a phone booth in a run-down part of town where he'd been living on the streets since he began the binge). It was clear that he was in need of immediate medical attention, as he had not taken his insulin in days. The only way of securing medical care for Walter was to contact the parole office and inform them of his location. Walter agreed that he needed to "come in," and the therapist continued to talk to him on one line while the parole officer was contacted on the other line.

Fortunately, Walter was found in the nick of time, as he had lapsed into unconsciousness by the time the police had arrived. While he was recuperating, it was learned that Walter matched the description of a man who had committed at least two burglaries during Walter's days doing drugs on the streets. In the end, Walter went back to prison for 15 months. At the time of the writing of this case description, he is due to be released in four months. Arrangements have been made for him to resume treatment at the Center for Cognitive Therapy when he regains his freedom. Walter has yet another chance, but also another powerful failure experience in his life to overcome. Again, it is expected that substance abuse will be only part of the clinical picture. Walter's maladaptive views of himself and his world will continue to pose major challenges to progress in cognitive therapy.

Chapter 9

Borderline–Histrionic/Narcissistic Case Study #1: The Case of "Evy"

The following case illustrates the treatment of a borderline–histrionic/narcissistic patient, and demonstrates the importance of working toward a realistic, stable therapeutic relationship as a model for other adult relationships in the patient's life. At the same time, the therapist helps the patient to believe in her lovability and potential for bonding with others, even in the absence of symbiosis.

PRESENTING PROBLEMS

Evy, a 34-year-old previously married woman who worked as a part-time clerk in a music store, presented with chronic depression, suicidal impulses, excessive use of tranquilizers and alcohol, and a great sense of loneliness following the breakup of her relationship with her married boyfriend.

Though quite dysphoric, Evy noted that her moods were variable, depending on such factors as the time of year and her level of involvement with other people. At first, the therapist wondered if the patient was suffering from a seasonal affective disorder, whereby winter darkness would exacerbate her depressed mood. Interestingly, Evy explained that her suicidality markedly worsened every *spring*, when she would witness a reemergence of young couples walking arm in arm in the park on warm, sunny days. This phenomenon alerted the therapist to the fact that the seasons themselves did not impact on Evy's mood as much as the concomitant stimuli that reminded her of her "unbearable loneliness."

The therapist assessed the following thoughts that Evy held about herself and her life:

- I get hyper but I'm still fundamentally depressed.
- I'm always the class clown, trying to make people happy to be with me, but it never works.
- If I commit suicide I want to be thin so I'll be a beautiful corpse.
- I'm the family psycho; they take me out for entertainment.
- I don't enjoy things anymore. Why am I still trying? It's all so useless.

These thoughts highlighted Evy's heavy investment in being noticed by others, even though it might be at her own expense. Her hopelessness was apparent as well and led the therapist immediately to discuss her intentions to harm herself. Realizing that Evy placed great importance in being appreciated and loved, the therapist enticed her into agreeing to a verbal antisuicide contract by saying, "Evy, I'm very, very sorry that you have been suffering so, and I'm worried that you might do something to hurt yourself *before I ever get the chance to really know you*. Will you work with me and agree to postpone any intentions of suicide for the foreseeable future?" This entreaty served as the "hook" that elicited Evy's initial cooperation with the therapeutic plan.

At the same time, the therapist was well aware that her demonstration of interest and caring toward Evy represented a double-edged sword—the therapist would now be at risk for severely disappointing Evy at the first sign of therapist fallibility. Recognizing this, the therapist regularly elicited feedback from Evy on her perceptions of the status of therapy and the therapeutic relationship.

Evy met DSM-III-R criteria for BPD based on the following symptoms:

1. A history of unstable and intense personal relationships
2. Affective lability
3. Recurrent suicidal threats
4. Ill-formed sense of self
5. Chronic boredom and emptiness
6. Exaggerated fears of abandonment

In addition, she qualified for a full diagnosis of histrionic personality disorder (HPD), and demonstrated features of narcissistic personality disorder (NPD), including (respectively) the following:

1. Constant need for approval, reassurance and praise
2. Excessive concern with her physical appearance
3. Exaggerated displays of emotionality
4. Discomfort in situations in which she was not the center of attention
5. Preoccupation with fantasies of unlimited success, beauty, fame, and ideal love
6. A strong sense of entitlement
7. A belief that her problems were so unique that only very special people could understand her

BACKGROUND INFORMATION AND
CASE CONCEPTUALIZATION

Evy hypothesized that her depressive episodes and low self-esteem were tied to her negative experiences with her family of origin and peers as she grew up. She described her father as evasive and distant, so busy with his career that she could get his attention only if "I got right in front of his face and entertained him." Her mother often accompanied the father on his frequent business trips, leaving Evy with a live-in nanny. These experiences set the stage for Evy's development of a hypersensitivity to the threat of abandonment by significant others.

The patient described her mother as "abusive, neurotic, out of control, unhappy, and unmotivated." A heavy drinker, Evy's mother was verbally abusive and at times physically abusive, lashing out at her for minor or imagined transgressions. The patient recalled her parents' marital relationship as having been characterized by miscommunication, vicious arguments, and the holding of grudges. Evy remembered her nanny explaining to her that her parents "satisfy each other in some sick way," a comment the patient had never come to understand fully but felt bad about nonetheless. Notably, Evy often tried to distract her parents from their arguments by trying to play the role of "court jester," a strategy that succeeded well enough to encourage her to continue responding in this way.

Perhaps the most harmful aspect of Evy's upbringing was her family's frequent moves resulting from her father's work. Evy estimated that she was uprooted more than a dozen times during her school years. As a result, the patient was forcibly separated from friends on a regular basis (thus reinforcing a powerful abandonment schema, even though it was the patient who left), and she always found herself as the outsider with each new peer group she tried to join. Evy recalled having a sense that nobody would ever really have the time or take the time to get to know her. In her frustration, loneliness, and desperation to be noticed and liked, Evy resorted to displays of clownish behavior that were intended to make friends but instead often made her the object of jokes. Nevertheless, she was convinced that such behaviors were necessary lest she "fade into obscurity."

Another strategy that Evy employed in order to gain acceptance was to subjugate her will completely to those of the most popular people in her successive and changing peer groups. As each move brought her into contact with classmates of varying interests and demographic characteristics, Evy would change her behaviors and attitudes in chameleon-like fashion in order to fit into each respective group. Looking back, Evy tearfully recounted that she never had a true sense of herself. Instead, she said, "I could be whoever you wanted me to be." The result of this strategy was the formation of a compelling and pervasive lack-of-individuation schema.

Evy's desire to earn a place among a steady group of friends led her to experiment with drugs when she entered high school. She hung out with the "burnouts" and regularly abused alcohol and marijuana. Although she eventually gave up her use of marijuana, she found a substitute in minor tranquilizers, which she continued to abuse along with alcohol up until the present.

Evy enrolled in a music conservatory after high school and majored in performing arts. She completed her B.A. degree but sabotaged her subsequent quest for a master's degree. Having been through a succession of intense, short-term involvements with a variety of men, Evy decided that she needed some stability in her life. Her impulsive and dysfunctional method to gain this stability was deliberately to become pregnant by the most successful man she knew at the time. She convinced him to marry her and take care of her, and she dropped out of her graduate program. The marriage lasted ten months, and she was left to raise a baby daughter on her own. Evy never returned to school.

Evy's psychiatric history consisted of two hospitalizations during her adolescence as the result of drug-related suicidal gestures, and a course of long-term outpatient therapy following her divorce. The patient noted with some disdain that the latter therapy was harmful to her; she explained that she fell in love with her psychiatrist but that he was "cold and aloof and simply used me up and tossed me away." The present therapist obtained Evy's permission to contact her former doctor, who proceeded to explain that he had treated her for eight years without significant improvement, that the patient was far too dependent on him for therapy to continue, and that Evy was miffed at his refusal to continue to prescribe antianxiety medications.

All of the aforementioned historical and developmental information was used to formulate a conceptualization of Evy's problems, including dysfunctional patterns of behavior, emotionality, interpersonal functioning, and cognitive assumptions and schemas. What emerged was a portrait of a woman who felt she had never experienced a secure home base, a stable meaningful relationship, or a positive sense of self. Her parents were physically and emotionally absent, giving her positive attention only when she distracted her mother and father from their preoccupations by acting as the household comedienne. In addition to parental abandonment, Evy continually suffered significant episodes of loss and separation from friends each time her family moved. As a result, the patient adopted extreme measures to become liked and accepted, including subjugating her wishes to those of others, and joining a drug-abusing crowd. Even so, Evy never believed that anyone who liked her truly knew her; instead, she posited that she was fundamentally unlovable. Her short-lived marriage seemed to confirm this notion, and her discontinuation of graduate school further lowered her self-esteem by feeding into her incompetency schema.

Evy's strategies for coping with emotional pain and loneliness were narrow, rigid, and highly dysfunctional. Her self-medicating abuses of alcohol and antianxiety medications kept her isolated from others, reduced her potential for finding a better job, and hindered her parenting skills, all of which further increased her self-hatred.

Likewise, Evy's histrionic, seductive, self-aggrandizing, life-of-the-party behavior was self-defeating in that she succeeded in attracting men, but only for a short time. For example, at social gatherings she would try to pick up the most attractive men by dressing provocatively, sprinkling clever sexual innuendoes and double entendres into her conversations, and casually touching the men while they conversed together. As a result, Evy often achieved intense encounters with men, thus raising her hopes that she would find someone to love her and care for her. Unfortunately, her neediness, demands for constant attention (apparently in order to make up for the attention she didn't get when she was a youngster), and inability to moderate her affect quickly overwhelmed and turned off men. As a result, Evy's compelling and pervasive unlovability and abandonment schemas were reinforced time and time again, and her hopelessness and depressed mood worsened.

It was evident to the therapist that she would need to give Evy an appropriate amount of attention and care, and would have to demonstrate that she wanted to get to know and to appreciate the "real" Evy, not just the social jokester. At the same time, the therapist would have to work to build Evy's reliance and trust in *herself*, without giving the patient the sense that she was being prepared for abandonment. No small task indeed.

TREATMENT AND OUTCOME

Evy's beliefs about needing to entertain and impress people in order to obtain their positive regard showed themselves in the therapeutic relationship. Instead of thoughtfully discussing her problems and attentively listening to the therapist's questions and feedback (as most nonpersonality disordered patients do), Evy launched into comedic monologues about her misfortunes and the unfairness of life in a style reminiscent of Woody Allen or Rodney Dangerfield. The therapist knew that she would have to help the patient to structure the therapy session so that the focus would be clearer and the work more productive. At the same, the therapist's awareness of the patient's belief system cued her in to the possiblity that Evy might misinterpret the therapist's attempts to structure the session as indicative of her lack of interest in the patient. Such perceptions on the part of the patient could activate her abandonment and unlovability schemas, leading to depressive crises and/or a premature flight from therapy.

The therapist carefully explained the rationales for setting agendas, remaining focused on one issue at a time, allowing time for equitable give and take between patient and therapist, and setting specific goals. The therapist stated that she was indeed entertained by Evy's humorous diatribes, but that she believed she could be of more help if she didn't allow herself to become an "audience" to the patient's "routine." The therapist had to remind Evy of this point of view time and time again throughout the course of therapy, as the patient's habit of comic self-denigration was well ingrained and served to deflect attention away from dealing with heartfelt emotions and solvable problems.

The therapist watched Evy for signs of affective shifts that might indicate that her feelings were hurt by the therapist's comments. Even when no such signs were apparent, the therapist would check by saying, "I hope that you understand that I really do care about you and about what you're saying. You don't have to entertain me to keep me interested in you. I *am* interested in you, plain and simple, and I'll do all I can to help you. At the same time, there will be occasions, such as right now, when I'll have to remind you to work with me *as a team* so we can be productive in session. Does that make sense to you? Is that okay with you? What do you think about what I just said?"

Such therapist statements were very difficult for Evy to understand, as it was a novel notion for her to consider that somebody might like her even when she was sad, crying, slow to speak, and discussing "heavy" topics. Later in treatment, the therapist would plan carefully to help Evy take small, calculated risks in everyday life to see who else might also accept her as a whole person, not just for her song-and-dance act.

The first cognitive skill that the therapist introduced to Evy was the standard monitoring of automatic thoughts. This was a difficult task. Evy had spent most of her life vigilantly scanning her interpersonal environment for signs of rejection or acceptance from others. She had very little awareness of her own emotional reactions and even less insight into her own patterns of thinking. The therapist steadfastly tried to teach this skill to Evy, as she knew that it was important to ascertain the thoughts that preceded the patient's emotional outbursts and suicidal gestures. Furthermore, if she could teach Evy the skill of cognitive self-monitoring, she then could instruct the patient in the skill of rational responding, which would help Evy to modulate her behaviors and high expressed emotions.

Initially, Evy was not interested in practicing the skill of cognitive self-monitoring. She found it "boring" and a "waste of time." The therapist responded by using the patient's personal language and experiences in order to make the task seem more familiar and congenial to her personality. Knowing that Evy had an interest in meditation and yoga, the therapist noted that Evy could "heighten her consciousness" if she became more skilled at detecting the thinking process underlying her emotional and behavioral reactions. This tactic underscores the importance of the therapist's: (1) not giving up on teaching cognitive techniques in spite of the patient's resistance, (2) using the case conceptualization as a tool for understanding ways to make the work of therapy more attractive, and (3) being flexible in the means by which skills are explained and taught.

In order to facilitate the patient's learning to use her own emotional and behavioral reactions as *cues* to ask herself what she was thinking, the therapist alerted Evy to her thinking at times when she would escalate her humor or otherwise try to entertain the therapist. There were occasions when Evy ignored the therapist's questions and continued to speak in a highly animated fashion with no therapeutic focus. The therapist responded by placing her outstretched hand in the patient's line of vision and asking directly, "What is going through your mind right now?" After a number of repetitions over the course of months of therapy, Evy learned to attend to her thoughts at these critical moments. As a result, she was able to understand that her exhibitionistic behaviors were in response to an activated belief that she was becoming boring, unlovable, and on the brink of being abandoned.

This set the stage for an in-depth evaluation of her self-worth on more objective terms. Therapist and patient explored Evy's personal charateristics, her achievements, and her impact on other people, both past and present. A great deal of evidence from Evy's life was rehashed and reevaluated, and the technique of continua ratings was used to help Evy to break the deleterious cognitive habit of all-or-none self-observations (e.g., to cease saying, "I am bad. I am wrong. I am hopeless," in favor of statements such as "I was partially wrong in that instance, but I was motivated by good intentions; therefore, I was 50 percent right and 50 percent wrong").

Another important therapeutic goal involved Evy's acquiring the skill to distinguish between *schema-driven* and *data-driven* reactions. In the past, when Evy would begin to worry that someone did not care for her, she would assume that this assumption was based on factual evidence in the here and now. In therapy, the patient was taught to compare her current cognitive, emotional, and behavioral responses with those of upsetting periods earlier in her life. When she noticed similarities, Evy was encouraged to reflect on whether or not her unlovability and abandonment schemas (formed long ago) had been activated. If she hypothesized that this was indeed the case, she immediately felt a sense of relief in that she was able to make sense out of her seemingly extreme (schema-driven) reactions. First, this helped to prevent her from blaming herself for her "craziness." Second, this technique gave Evy the impetus to examine her current life situation more objectively, on the basis of its own (data-driven) merits and deficits, rather than making gross overgeneralizations related to the past.

Evy's problems with tranquilizers and alcohol were addressed regularly throughout the first year of therapy. Luckily, she had never stockpiled her anxiolytics; thus, when her previous psychiatrist chose not to renew the patient's prescription, she was unable to continue abusing these medications. On the other hand, Evy tended to compensate for her rebound anxiety by increasing her alcohol intake. (Note: Given the problematic impulsivity of the BPD patient, the wisdom of the previous doctor in prescribing disinhibitory drugs alone is questionable. In general, it is far wiser to teach BPD patients to use active coping skills in dealing with the anxiety that invariably arises when schemas are activated; see Beck et al., 1985).

In order to elicit Evy's cooperation in decreasing her drinking, the therapist was careful not to moralize about the problem. Instead, the therapist expressed empathy for Evy's condition by acknowledging the deleterious effects of modeling a parent's (the mother's) alcohol abuse and by stating that the patient's use of anxiety-reducing substances in social situations was understandable (albeit unhealthy) given her fears of rejection.

Evy's motivation to be different from her mother was an important factor in her cooperation with an alcohol-reduction program. Further, when Evy came to realize the drawbacks of clowning around in public, she was more inclined to stay sober. In this way, her undampened social anxiety served as an active reminder to behave in a more mature, reserved fashion toward others. Although she feared that she would become a dull, lifeless person, Evy was willing to experiment with social interactions when she was alcohol-free. As a result, her exhibitionistic behaviors decreased in frequency and intensity, and the positive reactions she received from others seemed to be more "real." Furthermore, the "pressure to perform" lessened, thus lowering the patient's anxiety even more, which led to a decrease in her need for the antianxiety effects of alcohol. Evy had successfully established a positive feedback loop (in sharp contrast to her more typical vicious cycles) in her overall functioning.

After two years of therapy, Evy had made significant strides. Her depression had partially remitted, she was more gainfully employed (as the full-time assistant manager of the music store), she was feeling better about her performance as a mother, and she was enjoying new relationships with two female friends. One important goal that remained was to gain the self-confidence and emotional security to begin dating men again. In order to facilitate the process toward this end, the therapist decided to walk Evy through some imagery exercises, as a low-level graded task. Ultimately, the therapist planned to help Evy to engage in some in vivo experiments with real life potential dating partners.

During one imagery exercise, the therapist asked Evy to imagine that a man was showing romantic interest in her. As the therapist proceeded to ask the patient what she was thinking and feeling, Evy began to sob and to rock back and forth in her chair. A memory had emerged that took both the therapist and the patient completely by surprise. Evy recalled a scene from early adolescence, when her father entered her room late one night. Through her tears, she recounted something that she had long forgotten—how her father massaged her, fondled her, and forced her to kiss his penis. The therapist was very sympathetic and attentive, and asked Evy if she felt able to continue describing the memory. Evy proceeded to express tremendous rage toward her father, who had been indifferent to her in every other way, yet demanded adult "love" from her against her will. She further stated that she felt "dirty" and "disgusted" with herself, and that she wanted to die.

For the next few weeks, Evy experienced a renewed depressive episode with urges to hurt herself. The therapist explicitly told Evy that she would be available for additional sessions and phone contacts, and convinced her to agree to a verbal antisuicide contract. Later, Evy noted that this was a positive turning point in therapy. The therapist had proved that she "really cared" because she did not abandon her as expected (quite the contrary) and because Evy felt that she finally could speak freely about the "worst" aspects of herself and her life. A comedic song and dance was not forthcoming at this critical time in treatment, and none was required. This was a major corrective experience for Evy. As is common for the BPD patient, *the most therapeutically meaningful changes in schemas took place under conditions of intense patient affect that were well managed by the therapist.*

When the patient telephoned the therapist, telling her that she wanted to cut her arms, the therapist adopted a technique from Linehan (1987), instructing her to use a red felt-tip pen instead of a razor or knife. By doing this, the therapist validated the patient's feelings of emotional devastation while simultaneously showing that she valued Evy's life and health. The therapist appealed to Evy's disdain for her abandonment schema by adding, "Evy, you've felt so much pain in your life as a result of people abandoning you; please do not add to this injustice by abandoning *yourself* in your time of greatest need. Be your own best friend, don't hurt yourself, and I pledge my support to help you work through these memories and feelings."

The acute crisis lessened, and therapist and patient resumed their work in a more deliberate, structured fashion. Now the focus was on helping Evy to take the blame for the sexual abuse away from herself. Further, Evy's newly strengthened belief that "I am bad" was challenged through a repeat of the technique of objectively looking at her "worthiness," using continua ratings to adjudge her strengths and weaknesses across the span of her lifetime. In order to restructure the "I am bad" schema even more effectively, the therapist employed guided imagery exercises that increased affect and therefore dealt more directly with the memories. The most successful imagery intervention involved the therapist's asking Evy to remember the room where she was abused, but this time to imagine (and to speak out loud) that she was telling the father to get out of the room. Then, the "adult" Evy in the image was instructed to console the frightened "child" Evy by telling her that she was a good person, that she could have a happy life, and that she could one day find real, mature, meaningful love with others if she could learn to appreciate herself. This process was repeated for a variety of upsetting childhood images, with positive results.

The final phase of active treatment focused on separating the effects of the incest from her current feelings, beliefs, and behaviors regarding romantic relationships with men. Evy came to realize that she had learned from her father the destructive belief that she was unlovable except if she allowed herself to be vulnerable and used. As a result, she craved love but always believed that she had to make an odious forced choice between (1) being alone, (2) being with someone who really didn't love her for herself and therefore would be likely to abandon her (hence the exhibitionistic, self-aggrandizing behavior), or (3) being with someone who really knew her and therefore would abuse her because she was "bad."

The therapist assisted Evy in taking small, gradual steps toward reestablishing a social life with men. For a number of months this entailed talking to men at work and reestablishing contact with a former friend (male) from graduate school. As she gained greater confidence and trust, Evy began to go out on casual dates. She proudly told her therapist that she was cutting back significantly on her "clowning around" and, as a result, found that she was more relaxed socially. Further, she engaged in less catastrophizing about the possibility of being disliked, abandoned, or abused. After a number of months of stability in this social realm, along with a continued abatement of her depressed affect, Evy agreed to begin the process of tapering off the number of therapy sessions. At this time, she no longer meets the criteria for BPD or HPD, and she is fairly satisfied with herself and her life situation.

Chapter 10

Borderline–Histrionic/Narcissistic Case Study #2: The Case of "Edward"

PRESENTING PROBLEMS

When Edward came in for his initial evaluation at the Center for Cognitive Therapy, he wore an English-tailored three-piece suit and carried an attaché case. At the beginning of the intake process, he handed the intake interviewer a folder filled with reports from three previous therapists, along with Edward's commentary on the reports. He also gave the interviewer several articles from his hometown newspaper that mentioned his name, along with old clippings of reports of the separate suicides of his father, mother, and brother.

The interviewer reported that it was very difficult to conduct the intake and collect the pretreatment data because Edward kept interrupting to add to the interviewer's questions, rephrase the questions, or ignore the inquiries entirely by choosing to answer questions of his own. The intake evaluation, normally a two-and-a-half-hour process, became a four-hour session that was, in the interviewer's own words, "an ordeal." When asked to complete the Beck Depression Inventory (BDI) along with other forms, the patient altered the items, writing in question #3 that "None of these multiple choices truly fit, so I've amended them for greater accuracy." His overall BDI score was 42, indicting severe dysphoria. When the interviewer ended the intake session, Edward was reluctant to leave; he kept wanting to add "just one thing further." Finally, he was escorted out of the office.

Edward is a 45-year-old divorced white male. He has a son, aged 14, whom he has not seen for seven years since a bitter divorce from the boy's mother. Edward, an attorney, has held several jobs during his 19 years in the legal profession. In the private sector he worked for four firms but was asked to leave without being made partner in any of them. In the patient's view, this was due to jealousy on the part of less bright, less talented, and less well educated attorneys who were in positions of power. Later, Edward attempted to establish a solo private law practice but was unable to develop a referral base. Most recently he had been employed by the state government but had been let go in a budgetary shake-up. Edward planned to file a discrimination suit against the state for firing him while other "less talented" lawyers were still employed. In the meantime, he supported himself with the savings he had amassed from the termination settlements given to him by various firms.

Edward was not at all clear about his reasons for coming into therapy. Although he had made a point of showing the intake evaluator the news clippings of the suicides of three members of his immediate family, he did not admit to feelings of unresolved grief or other emotional aftershocks, nor did he wish to speak about the loss of these people as part of therapy. When the therapist also pointed to the loss of his wife and son as a potential source of depression, loneliness, and regret, Edward stated that he did not miss his son anymore. He proceeded to tell the therapist about his former wife's "low breeding," her impoverished childhood, and her completion of a "second-rate" medical school.

Initially, Edward's only straightforward explanation for his presence at the Center for Cognitive Therapy was that he had been referred by the psychoanalyst with whom he had worked for a number of years. The analyst had reasoned that Edward would have more therapeutic success starting fresh with a new therapist whose focus in treatment would be directed cognitive and behavioral change. (Later, when the cognitive therapist telephoned the analyst, the latter described Edward as "demanding and obnoxious," and admitted that he had reached the end of his tolerance for the patient's interpersonally aversive style.)

After a number of sessions of questioning, the therapist was able to ascertain some areas of Edward's life that he agreed would represent fruitful areas of focus in therapy. These included Edward's employment difficulties, his heavy smoking, his lack of friends, and his sexually unsatisfying relationship with his girlfriend. It had been quite a difficult task to delineate these points of intervention, as Edward had been hell-bent on spending all his time in session regaling the therapist with his feats of accomplishment and colorful tales of confrontations and injustices at the hands of others. A review of some of these stories provides a flavor of Edward's interpersonal style and resultant life crises, issues that would become central to therapy.

1. Inasmuch as Edward had been laid off from his state position, he was entitled to unemployment compensation. The office to which he reported was located in a predominantly poor area of Philadelphia. Edward would dress in his usual work dress of three-piece suit, regimental tie, and wing-tip shoes to go to the unemployment office. On several occasions he got into verbal altercations with other clients at the office. The most flagrant of these confrontations resulted in the patient's being arrested. As Edward related the situation, he had been in one or more interminable lines behind "these nether people." Having reached the counter, he was told that he had filled out the wrong form and was instructed to get the correct form, complete it,

and go to the back of the line. Edward, miffed, demanded to see the supervisor, whereupon he was told that there was no supervisor and that he had better just "go along." In his attempt to deal with the "rude and inefficient clerk," he sought the supervisor by going through a door marked "Restricted Access/Employees Only." This action set off an alarm, and Edward was stopped by a uniformed guard. Asserting his right of free access and speech, he tried to force his way into the restricted area. The guard then threw Edward against a wall, knocking the wind out of him, handcuffed him, and had him arrested. Edward claimed police brutality and infringements of his constitutional rights. Although the police sergeant suggested that each party drop charges and forget the whole matter, Edward persisted and filed a brutality suit.

2. Edward was displeased that his girlfriend Mary Elizabeth, a devout Catholic, disapproved of sex outside of marriage. He was dissatisfied that she would allow only tongue kissing and breast touching on top of her clothes, but no bare-skin intimate contact. Playing out his role as attorney to the hilt, Edward tried to argue, debate, convince, cajole, and challenge Mary Elizabeth's reluctance, but she stayed true to her religious convictions. Edward's response was to telephone the office of the Cardinal of the Archdiocese of Philadelphia and try to arrange an audience with the Cardinal. The patient's idea was that the Cardinal, an educated and sophisticated man, would see that Edward's arguments were reasonable and would give his girlfriend the go-ahead to have sexual intercourse. Edward was able to make an appointment with a Monsignor attached to the Archdiocesan office. After meeting with Edward and Mary Elizabeth and ascertaining that they were neither married nor planning to marry, and that Edward simply wanted his blessing for sex, the Monsignor forbade any sexual contact, under the clothes or on top. Further, he questioned the appropriateness of tongue kissing. The result of the meeting was that Edward's situation became even less tolerable for him. He had defeated his own purpose, a phenomenon quite common in Edward's life.

3. Edward came into the therapist's office with a black eye and a swollen cheek. He reported that he had been assaulted by a homeless man. The man had said to the patient, "Hey buddy, could you spare a smoke?" Even though Edward was smoking a cigarette at the time, he refused and began to lecture the man about the way he was dressed, how he looked, and the fact that Edward certainly was *not* his buddy. The man hit Edward in the face and walked away.

4. Recently, with the help of a former law school colleague, Edward was hired on a per diem basis to work in a large law firm to clear away a backlog of files. This was a job more typically taken by very junior attorneys or advanced law students. Edward was quite excited about the prospect of working in such a prestigious firm and was sure that when they saw the quality of his work, they would want to keep him on and

possibly make him a partner. The job lasted three weeks before he was asked to leave. On his first day at work, Edward sent memos to the managing partner with copies to all of the senior partners about the inadequacy of his office. In his view, it was too small, too far away from the more senior and experienced people with whom he belonged, and too close to the men's room. He also spent his time generating memos suggesting more effective ways to run the office, based on his observations of the present office protocol. The final straw for the firm appeared to come when he demanded to speak with the managing partner. Edward believed that he and the partner had a constructive dialogue about positive changes that Edward could bring to the firm if he were promoted. But by the end of the work day, Edward was fired.

Although Edward did not enter therapy specifically to deal with interpersonal problems, it was apparent from the examples cited here that he had great difficulty in relating adaptively to others at work, in intimate relationships, and in casual interactions. His poor impulse control was based, in part, on the following sequence of beliefs:

- If I have an urge to do or say something, I must act on it regardless of the immediate or long-range consequences.
- To do otherwise would be extremely uncomfortable, so that anyone who gets in the way of my satisfaction must be pushed aside.
- I must continue this process until my goal is achieved.

Edward met DSM-III-R criteria for borderline, histrionic, and narcissistic personality disorders, and demonstrated obsessive-compulsive and paranoid features as well. He also was diagnosed as having a severe major depressive episode.

BACKGROUND INFORMATION AND CASE CONCEPTUALIZATION

Edward, born and raised in Chicago, was the middle of three brothers. His father was a businessman, and his mother was a homemaker. Edward attended a liberal arts college in Chicago from which he graduated with highest honors; later, he was accepted to Harvard Law School. His three years in Boston were important and noticeable in that they left him with the long *a* of Harvard Yard. After graduation, he spent a year studying at Oxford University, which added a vaguely British pronunciation to his Bostonian accent. Edward was proud of his speaking voice, played up his affected upperclass diction, and succeeded in sounding highly pretentious.

Edward's younger brother committed suicide by freezing to death on the shore of Lake Michigan in winter. He was found nude and encrusted in ice one February morning. The patient's older brother became a physician in Denver. Edward described this sibling as "unkind and ungiving . . . just interested in himself . . . I have little to do with him." Their most acrimonious interactions centered on Edward's asking the brother for money and being turned down repeatedly.

Both of Edward's parents also took their own lives. His father committed suicide (while Edward was in law school) by cutting his throat while hiding in a closet of the family home. Five years later Edward's mother killed herself by lethal overdose of a prescribed tricyclic antidepressant medication. Edward explained to the therapist that, given the family history, his deep depressions obviously were inherited traits. He stopped short of saying that the tragic deaths were stressors in and of themselves. What was obvious was the histrionic style of the family (indeed, of the suicides), a style that was well developed in the patient.

Shortly after his mother's suicide, Edward married a physician. They had a child, but the marriage quickly deteriorated and ended in a bitter divorce. Later, the former wife obtained a restraining order against Edward that prevented him from seeing his son. This was the result of Edward's demanding and intolerant manner of dealing with his son's occasional enuresis. Edward screamed at his son for hours, threatened him, and on one occasion shook him violently. The son became frightened to be alone with Edward, and visitation rights were ended by the mother's legal action.

At intake, Edward met all eight DSM-III-R criteria for BPD. His pattern of intense and unstable interpersonal relationships was clear throughout the course of therapy. He was highly impulsive in ways that damaged his relationships, his career, his health, and his work in therapy. He demonstrated marked affective instability, inappropriate loss of control of his temper, frequent threats of suicide, uncertainty about his values and direction in life, and chronic emptiness that led to constant efforts to avoid the threat of abandonment by people whose respect and admiration he felt he needed.

He also met five of the criteria for histrionic personality disorder (HPD). He constantly sought approval and praise, was overly concerned with his physical attractiveness, expressed emotions in an exaggerated manner, was uncomfortable in situations in which he was not the center of attention, and was unwilling to delay gratification. Edward also met all nine DSM-III-R criteria for narcissistic personality disorder (NPD). For example, he reacted to criticism with rage, took advantage of others, was grandiose, believed that only special kinds of people could understand him, was preoccupied with fantasies of unlimited success, had a marked sense of entitlement, required constant attention, lacked empathy for others, and was excessively jealous and envious.

Edward met criteria for all three personality disorders (BPD, HPD, and NPD) that subsume the "erratic and dramatic" cluster of Axis II, according to the DSM-III-R. These diagnostic groups have in common the general characteristics of poor impulse control; pervasive all-or-none thinking, feeling, and behavior (e.g., grandiosity, extreme rage when rejected, provoking confrontations); and difficulties in relating to other people in a stable, congenial manner. The most compelling schemas for such patients appear to be those of unlovability, abandonment, and incompetence. (Note: In Edward's case, the abandonment schema was less evident at first. Although he denied that he felt abandoned by the family members who had killed themselves, and by his ex-wife and son, the therapist hypothesized that Edward's abandonment schema would be activated at some point during treatment, a prediction that later proved to be accurate.) Unlike BPD–avoidant/dependent patients, who consistently believe they are unloved and incapable, BPD–histrionic-narcissistic patients like Edward alternate between feeling unlovable and, conversely, believing that they are worthy of everyone's undying affection, and between feeling like failures and conversely believing that they are special, gifted, and misunderstood by the "common people" who ploddingly run the world.

It was difficult for the therapist to conceptualize the genesis and development of Edward's maladaptive personality style because of Edward's evasiveness in providing historical information. For example, he refused to discuss the circumstances of the suicides in his family, and he denied emotional investment in the people who had been important to him in his past. When the therapist obtained records from Edward's former analyst, his notes similarly contained a dearth of information on these subjects (most of the notes centered on hypothesized, unconscious, psychosexual conflicts, rather than on actual events or conscious memories).

The therapist posited that Edward resisted discussing his past and his personal losses, as these might provoke his schemas of unlovability, incompetence, and abandonment. Young (1990) has dubbed this phenomenon "schema avoidance," which, he hypothesizes, occurs regularly in all personality-disordered patients. Edward was very invested in presenting himself as a *superior* person and did not want to disturb this fragile persona by delving into his most painful memories and feelings. Nevertheless, his presence in treatment signaled that Edward was in some distress. Unfortunately, Edward externalized this distress, blaming his troubles on the jealousy, stupidity, and fickleness of others. He did not admit to playing a role in these concerns. The therapist recognized that this would have to be a major focus in therapy but that he would have to proceed very cautiously, lest Edward view him malevolently as well.

Despite Edward's reticence about his past, it was possible for the therapist to make several inferences that might guide his approach to treatment. First, as one of just two survivors from his family of origin, it was conceivable that Edward might have "survivor guilt," whereby he blamed himself in some way for the suicides of his family members. The therapist planned to try to obtain a more exact chronology of the family tragedies. For example, Edward's father had killed himself while the patient was away at law school. Was Edward having some difficulties at the time that may have added to the father's distress, especially if the father was overinvested in the success of his sons? Did Edward blame himself for not being at home at the time? With regard to the brother's suicide, was his fatal despair due in part to a sense of being a failure? After all, achievement needs seemed to be very pronounced in this family. Likewise, would the patient's ongoing lack of vocational success give Edward sufficient reason to want to end his own life, given the unwritten rules of the family that implied "succeed or die"? Was the mother's suicide, which coincided approximately with the time of Edward's engagement, due to her feeling abandoned by yet another male in her immediate family? Had he gone ahead with plans for the wedding in spite of her disapproval? What effect did the mother's suicide have on his marriage, his view of women, and his willingness to become intimate with a woman? The answers to all of these questions were expected to serve as clues to the conceptualization of Edward's case. Unfortunately, the answers were never to be clearly ascertained.

Other inferences that the therapist drew about Edward and his family may be summarized by the following set of hypothesized, implicit rules:

1. Suicide is an acceptable method of dealing with emotional pain.
2. Emotional suffering must be broadcast to others in the most dramatic fashion possible.
3. People close to you cannot be depended on for emotional support, so the best you can do is to retaliate by letting them know just how badly they have treated you.
4. Achievement and success are the main routes to love and acceptance.

On the basis of this preliminary case formulation, the therapist expected that Edward would have suicidal crises precipitated by experiences of thwarted success, underappreciation by others, and perceptions that the therapist was not fully invested in the patient's life. These expectations were realized in treatment.

TREATMENT AND OUTCOME

During the first two sessions, several goals were formulated. One was to educate Edward regarding the format and content of cognitive therapy, especially in light of his previous experience with a contrasting model of therapy. Instead of being assigned the homework of reading *Feeling Good* (Burns, 1980), which is the standard self-help source that the Center for Cognitive Therapy recommends to new patients, the therapist assigned Edward the task of reading *The Cognitive Therapy of Depression* (Beck et al., 1979). The therapist's strategy was to facilitate rapport by appealing to Edward's need to be seen as special. Therefore, he instructed Edward to read the book that was "written for professional psychotherapists" and not simply the book that was geared for "lay people." Edward was pleased.

A second goal was to engage Edward in the process of gathering more information about his life, using the intake report and the analyst's records as the basis of questioning. Here, Edward was a bit less forthcoming, arguing that "cognitive therapy is supposed to deal with the here and now." The therapist agreed that that was so but added that cognitive therapy posits that an exploration of the past facilitates the process of "understanding the cognitive and emotional *obstacles* to solving problems in the present." He drove home his point further by explaining that "beliefs learned in childhood that are still maintained today are very much in the here and now."

A third goal involved allowing Edward to voice his concerns, anger, and resentment over his perceived rejection by the previous therapist. Rather than simply encouraging a cathartic experience, the therapist taught the patient the cognitive therapy approach. The therapist noted that the foregoing issue gave rise to many automatic thoughts that could be evaluated for accuracy and functionality. The aforementioned approach held great appeal for this attorney.

Another goal was the establishment of limits. Therapist and patient discussed the times, length, and scheduling of sessions; the handling of payment of fees; and the rules about telephone contact. This last rule stated that a ten-minute call was acceptable but that longer calls would become billable therapy time.

The first ten sessions were held on a weekly basis, with Edward attending all sessions on time. He was cooperative with his homework assignments, which focused on scheduling activities that kept him focused on finding new employment. Edward voiced great pleasure at these early sessions. He liked this new, more interactive, structured therapy, and he believed that his therapist cared about and understood him.

As predicted earlier, the initial crises in treatment involved Edward's feeling neglected by the therapist and feeling like a failure in public. The first crisis of this sort occurred in session 11, when Edward informed the therapist that he would need "lots more time that day than usual." The therapist informed Edward that there was another patient scheduled shortly after Edward and that there would not be lots more time available, but that they could try to make optimal use of the upcoming hour. Edward's agenda for the session included one item—a "mortifying" experience that he simply had to get off his chest at some length.

Edward reported that he had been to a singles bar the night before and that he had put on his best Oxfordian accent. Having regaled two women with a story of his having recently come from England, where he was doing important work at Oxford, one of the women said loudly enough for all to hear, "What bullshit! You're an unemployed lawyer from Chicago! I met you at another bar two weeks ago without that bullshit accent!" Edward's British persona was destroyed, and his incompetence schema was activated in grand style. He felt embarrassed, unsuccessful, and unappreciated, and his suicidal ideation increased.

Each attempt by the therapist to ask questions and to structure the focus of the session was met by Edward's anger. At one point he loudly stated, "Your job is just to listen. Now shut up and listen!"

With three minutes left in the session, the therapist informed Edward that the session was about to conclude and that it would be useful for Edward to review the main points of the session. The patient ignored the comment and continued to talk. The therapist tried a number of other tactful ways to end the session, with no success. Finally, ten minutes later, the therapist said, "We really do have to stop now," walked to the door, and motioned for Edward to exit with him. Edward got out of his seat, walked to the door, and said melodramatically, "I will most likely go home now and kill myself. Now, will we discuss that or not?"

The therapist agreed that this was a very serious issue and that, inasmuch as time did not permit a discussion now, Edward had several options. He could go immediately to the university hospital's emergency room and sign himself into the psychiatric unit, he could use the cognitive therapy techniques he had learned to date to deal with his thoughts and feelings, he could schedule another appointment for later that same day, he could write down his thoughts about the session to understand better the process of his interactions with the therapist, or some combination of the above.

As may be inferred from this interchange, the therapist chose to deal with the suicidal threat primarily as Edward's maladaptive attempt to cope with his activated schemas of unlovability, incompetence, and abandonment. It was essential that the therapist demonstrate that he took Edward seriously while simultaneously setting clear limits. Later that day Edward called the office and apologized for his actions. The therapist reaffirmed his commitment to help Edward and added that this experience provided useful information about how Edward inadvertently strained his relationships with important others—namely, by escalating his interpersonal demands, losing sight of the needs of the other person, and using his sincere suicidal feelings in an insincere manner (manipulation) so that they provoke anger and not sympathy.

Through the next 25 sessions, Edward made progress in therapy. During this time, the patient's BDI scores were in the range of 15–17, significantly lower than at intake, and in the mild to moderate range of clinical depression. The DTR format found favor with Edward's highly intellectualized style, and he completed many of these records as homework. The result was that he learned to modulate his extreme and labile emotions with sound, rational thinking.

Another important focus of therapy was to help Edward gain greater self-control. Several specific impulsive behaviors were targeted for intervention: (1) smoking, (2) saying things to others that "might come back to haunt" him, and (3) spontaneously telephoning others to express his displeasure. Several techniques were successful. These included examining alternative methods for "making his statement to the world," structuring his time by scheduling activities, relaxation training, and self-monitoring for schema activation (e.g., recognizing when his anger was the result of the arousal of his feelings of inadequacy, unlovability, or abandonment). These techniques did not eliminate his dysfunctional interpersonal behaviors altogether, but they did buy him some time between his intended actions and the actions themselves, thus increasing his chances of applying other self-control techniques.

Given the fact that Edward's impulsivity was a central issue in therapy, a number of other techniques were employed in order to deal with this problem. A six-step problem-solving model (Freeman, Pretzer, Fleming, & Simon, 1989) was employed:

1. Edward was to identify a particular "automatic response" (as opposed to the term "impulsive response") that he wanted to control—for example, his hostile arguing or unsolicited self-aggrandizement. The therapist then explored with Edward the advantages and disadvantages of controlling the response. By using a

double column of the pros and cons of delaying or controlling these reactions, and composing a second list of the pros and cons of not controlling his responses, the therapist often reached agreement with Edward on whether or not to try to exercise restraint.

2. This step involved generating a list of thoughts and actions to employ in place of the problematic "automatic responses." For example, rather than scream at Mary Elizabeth for not allowing him to touch her breasts, he was either to back off respectfully, tell her that he was frustrated but that he loved her and would respect her wishes, ask her to give *him* a massage, or suggest that they go out and do something entertaining or recreational. Furthermore, Edward was helped to recognize that his initial anger was not merely the result of sexual frustration but also the product of an aroused unlovability schema. Instead of viewing Mary Elizabeth's brushoffs as being indicative of her lack of attraction to him, Edward was asked to focus on the religious significance of her sexual decision making. The goal was to make this interaction less personally damaging than it was when he was unaware of the pernicious influence of his maladaptive schema.

3. This step focused on weighing the potential costs and benefits of each alternative solution. Edward was instructed to focus on how the chosen behavior would be constructive *in the long run*. It was important that Edward learn that he had options other than the ones that would bring instant gratification.

4. Here, Edward chose a response from the list (from point 2).

5. In step 5, Edward was to implement the response. To prepare for this, patient and therapist role-played the proposed interaction in session. The therapist provided coaching and corrective feedback, and assisted Edward in imaginally rehearsing possible outcomes. For example, in dealing with someone who annoyed him by arguing with his point of view, Edward was taught to envision two images. The first involved Edward's being able to walk away successfully and calmly without a fight. The second involved Edward's accepting what the other person said while saying, "I don't agree with you." Additionally, the therapist taught Edward that his apparent "need" to prove his point was a reflection of an activated incompetency schema. By deliberately *not* getting into an argument, it was reasoned, Edward would be showing himself and others alike that he had nothing at all to prove and that he was competent indeed.

6. This final step entailed a self-evaluation of the result of the attempted change. If at least somewhat successful, step 1 would be used to identify another target for intervention. If the attempt was unsuccessful, therapist and patient would return to step 2 and continue through the sequence anew.

The process of therapy took a negative turn when Edward became ill with a chronic cough, respiratory infection, and general flu-like symptoms. His cough was exacerbated by his smoking, and he refused to see a physician. Edward finally sought medical attention after three weeks of suffering, including difficulty in breathing. During this time a number of the patient's schemas were activated, causing him significant difficulties with other people in his life as well as in therapy. These schemas included unlovability ("I'm practically dying and nobody cares about me. I could drop dead today and nobody would miss me"), abandonment ("Without someone to nurse me back to health, I cannot survive"), and incompetency ("I could die at any moment, and what have I accomplished in life? I have nothing to show for my promise and brilliance"). These schemas triggered a great deal of hopelessness as well as an escalation of his demanding, entitled behaviors.

During this time of increased vulnerability, Edward began to telephone the therapist incessantly, including calls late at night (e.g., at midnight) and early in the morning (e.g., at 6:00 A.M.). Even after the therapist set limits, the patient continued to call. Even worse, he demanded that the calls last as long as he "needed." The only way that the therapist could end the phone calls was to tell Edward that he (the therapist) was going to hang up. Edward's response was, "You don't care about me. All you want is my money." He added that the therapist's "obvious" lack of caring had induced him to smoke three packs of cigarettes that day. He went on to say that he held his therapist responsible for his worsening medical condition and, therefore, would send him his future hospital bills.

In retrospect, the therapist could have focused solely on the schematic meaning of Edward's demanding behaviors. For example, he could have noted that Edward's desperation for love and nurturance in a time of need was maladaptively translating into outbursts of anger and vilification of the therapist. The therapist then would have told Edward that he could give him much more of the sympathy that he deserved if the conversation were briefer and more collaborative.

Unfortunately, Edward terminated therapy abruptly at this point, and the suggested dialogue between therapist and patient never took place. In an ironic turnabout, Edward did not return the therapist's calls. He did send a letter a month later, however, stating that he was now seeing the "finest therapist in the East" and that he was "starting to recover." Edward had left therapy on his own terms, abandoning the therapist in an impulsive overreaction to the perception that he was uncared for and abandoned by the therapist. Given Edward's schemas of unlovability and abandonment, learned through the powerful experiences of his family of origin's life-style and death-style, this may have been the easiest way for the patient to leave therapy.

Edward had alternately overidealized and condemned the therapist, a phenomenon that is quite common in borderline patients, especially those in the histrionic/narcissistic spectrum. Dealing with the stress of working with Edward required the therapist to talk over the case with colleagues on a regular basis. This had allowed

Chapter 11

Borderline–Avoidant/Dependent
Case Study #1: The Case of "Helen"

PRESENTING PROBLEMS

Helen, a 33-year-old single woman who works as a bank teller, presented with vague global complaints about dissatisfaction in her personal life and employment situation. Aside from her borderline diagnosis (with significant avoidant and dependent personality features), she met criteria only for an atypical anxiety disorder (anxiety disorder, not otherwise specified). This latter diagnosis was reflected by her daily sense of "dread" at work, her social timidity, her night terrors (accompanied by numerous physiological symptoms and subclinical features of panic disorder), and general worries about "how I will survive in the future."

In her work life, Helen was distressed by her chronic fear of being found to be incompetent. Although she performed her job as teller well by all objective reports (e.g., biannual supervisory evaluations), Helen was convinced that she was on the brink of failure. She would have a near panic attack if she made a mistake, received any constructive criticism, or was asked to learn a new job skill. She avoided taking on new challenges, such as filling in for the head teller when the latter was on two weeks' vacation, and thereby lost opportunities to advance in her career. Although the branch manager told her that she believed Helen to be capable of taking on new responsibilities, Helen was certain that she would be unable to perform and that she would be fired. Despite her fear of losing her job, Helen's fears of incompetence actually would *cause* her to risk the wrath of her superiors, as when she called in "sick" when she knew that the bank would be short-staffed. By avoiding work on such days, she escaped from having to handle extra demands, but she simultaneously shirked an important responsibility and let down her co-workers.

On the other hand, Helen would comply with inappropriate demands to perform menial tasks. For example, she became the designated "go-fer" when her co-workers wanted coffee or a snack. Helen willingly performed these tasks because they were easy (no risk of failure) and because she believed that these actions would make everyone like her. Even when she felt a certain degree of resentment at the belief that the others were taking her for granted, she said nothing out of fear that they would reject her. She fully realized that she had put herself in this position in the first place, but she was angry about it and felt unable to rectify the situation. Her sense of helplessness and inferiority grew along with her resentment.

Helen reported that her love life was a "confusing mess." One relationship was with an older man, Frank, who wanted to nurture and care for Helen. This suited Helen well in the beginning, as she wanted a man in her life who would provide for her financially, run errands for her, make important and trivial everyday decisions alike for her (e.g., how she would vote and where she would eat lunch, respectively), and be at her social beck and call at a moment's notice. Unfortunately, when Frank complied with all of these conditions, Helen began to feel as if she were going to "suffocate and disappear." Nevertheless, she further immersed herself in Frank's life by neglecting to see her own friends, opting instead to join her lover's circle of acquaintances and involving herself solely in his activities. Complicating matters were Helen's beliefs that she had to agree to any sexual demands that Frank might make, even if she found them repulsive, and that her refusal to comply would lead to his leaving her immediately.

Helen's feelings of fear, stagnation, and resentment at work, coupled with her intense ambivalence about her relationship with Frank, served as the prime motivators for her to seek therapy. The common threads through these problems were her dreadfully low self-esteem, her fears of failure and rejection, and her strong needs for and concomitant discomfort with a dominant love partner in her life.

Helen specifically met criteria for the DSM-III-R diagnosis of BPD by evidencing the following:

1. A history of unstable and intense interpersonal relationships
2. Affective lability
3. A poorly formed personal identity
4. Recurrent suicide threats
5. Marked fears of abandonment

Her most salient features of avoidant personality disorder (AvPD) and dependent personality disorder (DPD), respectively, included the following:

1. Excessive vulnerability to criticism or disapproval
2. An unwillingness to initiate social contact without a guarantee that she would be liked
3. Feeling intimidated by tasks outside her normal routine, and difficulties coping with the responsibilities and discomforts of everyday life
4. An inability to make everyday decisions without an excessive amount of advice or reassurance from others

5. A tendency to volunteer to do menial or unpleasant tasks in order to elicit approval from others
6. Great difficulty in initiating activities or projects
7. Significant discomfort when alone

BACKGROUND INFORMATION AND CASE CONCEPTUALIZATION

Helen's early childhood history was characterized by inadequate parenting on a daily basis. Her parents' ideas regarding discipline were harsh and cruel, and their understanding of the psychology of the child was minimal at best. Although Helen's parents made the kinds of mistakes that competent parents also make, they made no attempt to rectify those errors. When effective parents mistreat their children, they do so typically in momentary lapses or flashes of anger. Thus, in a fit of pique a benign parent might say to a child, "Go away and don't come back." However, the parents recover from this sentiment rapidly and reassure their children that they are loved and wanted. By contrast, when Helen's parents made these kinds of rejecting statements, they were long drawn-out accounts that were never recanted. Helen's parents made these kinds of rejecting comments almost on a daily basis, by the patient's report. Moreover, there were no influential, caring adults in Helen's environment to act as buffers.

The genesis of Helen's abandonment schema was traceable to ineffective methods of discipline that the mother used when Helen was a youngster. As the patient recounted, if she misbehaved, her mother threatened to call "Mrs. Smith" to come and take Helen away forever. The mother then played out the charade to the fullest extent. The mother would pretend to phone "Mrs. Smith," and then go and pack Helen's suitcase. The mother then would slip out the back door, come around to the front door, and ring the bell. Leading Helen to the door usually would bring on a torrent of tears and pleas from the child that she would be perfectly behaved from then on. This threat-of-abandonment ploy was carried out many times throughout the patient's early childhood years.

Helen remembered that she and her sister were called "ragamuffins" by their mother if they weren't well dressed and looking pretty. On one memorable occasion when the mother and daughters were in a store, the mother said her daughters looked so unattractive that she didn't want others to know that they belonged to her. She proceeded to leave the store, leaving the girls standing alone. Helen learned from these experiences that she would be abandoned and left helpless if she did something wrong or didn't look her best. These dysfunctional rules continued to dominate her psychological life into adulthood.

Helen's parents divorced when she was eight years old, with the father remarrying a woman who was younger and sexier than the mother. Helen felt uncomfortable visiting with her father and his new partner, and asked her father if she might see him alone. He reportedly refused angrily, telling Helen that if she didn't want to see them as a couple, she could not visit them at all. This event led Helen to feel both abandoned and unloved. It also spawned beliefs about men and love, such as "Men pick wives who are attractive and leave wives who aren't" and "Men favor their lovers over their daughters."

Helen's father taught her that love was conditional on one's appearance. He was quite vain about his looks and judged others on their physical attractiveness as well. When Helen dressed in a manner that pleased him, he would tell her that he "wouldn't sell her for a million dollars." When she dressed plainly or didn't have her hair fixed just right, he would tell her, "I'd sell you for a penny." Such statements served as evidence for Helen that the most important men in her life were likely to stop loving her and to leave her unless she looked and did things the way they wanted.

Helen grew up to believe that men would find her unlovable, hurt her, and ultimately abandon her. When she was 22 years old, her boyfriend convinced her to have plastic surgery on her nose. Helen didn't like the idea (photos taken before the surgery show a normal, attractive nose), but she agreed to the procedure in order to please him with an "improved" appearance. She expected that he would break up with her if she did not comply. After the surgery, he left her anyway.

As a teenager, Helen was told by her mother that men were incapable of sexual fidelity. Later in life, when Helen's boyfriends would go on business trips, she would become quite suspicious and jealous. Her accusations and recriminations served to alienate these dating partners, often precipitating rifts in the relationships. The boyfriends often told Helen that they found her to be demanding, possessive, and childish. Helen would translate these sentiments to mean that she was right all along—that her boyfriends were just waiting for lame excuses to dump her.

Helen avoided friendships with other women, as she was afraid that they would be competitive and judgmental. She continually compared herself to other women and usually found herself lacking. She assumed that other women were coming to the same negative conclusions about her.

Helen's incompetence schema emanated from her days as a student in grade school. As a youngster, she felt intimidated by her homework and shied away from tackling it out of fear of failure. Helen's mother, rather than giving her encouragement to face her schoolwork, accepted her daughter's unfavorable assessment of her poor intelligence at face value. As a result, the mother, along with the grandmother, took on the task of doing Helen's homework for her. As the grandmother was a professional writer, the book reports that Helen presented at school were of such high quality that she was placed in a gifted class at the age of seven. Now Helen was expected to contend with an even higher level of scholastic demands. This situation made Helen's mother happy, as she wanted others to see her daughter as being a positive reflection on her. She did not seem to consider the pressure that Helen would have to face, nor did it matter to her that Helen was not really learning or developing confidence as a student.

A crisis occurred one day when Helen was asked to write a book report in class. She feigned an illness and was excused from school for the day. This represented one of the first times that Helen used the strategy of avoidance in response to the arousal of the incompetence schema. Such behavior would be repeated and strengthened by negative reinforcement (a diminishing of anxiety) until it became Helen's automatic mode of operation in dealing with life's challenges.

As an adult, Helen's employment record was one of taking jobs that were below her level of skill and that required little responsibility. In addition, men at her workplaces sometimes harassed her, as happened the time that her boss demanded sexual favors. Believing that this was the only way she could please her boss and be valued in return, Helen had sexual relations with him after hours at the office. Later, she was passed over for a promotion that she had rightfully earned. Such incidents lowered Helen's self-esteem and accentuated her mistrust schema.

At the time she entered therapy, Helen was evidencing major problems in the areas of love and work. She had rushed into her relationship with Frank on the basis of the belief that she needed a strong man for emotional support. As the relationship strengthened, however, Helen was gripped by the fear that Frank would lose interest in her and would leave. The patient had been trying to compensate for this fear by acquiescing to his every desire and whim, thus subjugating her individuality to his. This, in turn, would activate Helen's lack-of-individuation schema, which produced fears of engulfment and loss of identity. The next step usually involved Helen's doing something to precipitate a crisis in the relationship, such as arranging a date with a younger man. Frank would then threaten to leave, stimulating her sense of unlovability, mistrust toward men, fear of abandonment, and expectations that she would be unable to take care of herself. Helen globally labeled herself as a "bad person" but did not have a well-formulated conceptualization of how her specific beliefs, emotions, and actions fed into her interpersonal turmoil.

At work, Helen tried to blend into the background, doing as little as possible to call attention to herself as a teller. Although she tried to gain favor by bringing coffee and snacks to her co-workers, she generally stayed aloof and revealed very little about herself. If she made a mistake on the job, Helen would become very anxious, and she would want to leave work for the day.

Time and time again, Helen was torn between her need to be nurtured and her fear of utter rejection, and between her hopes for success and her desire to eliminate all risk of failure. This constant push–pull between avoidance and dependence showed itself clearly in Helen's emotional lability, unformed sense of herself, unstable interpersonal relationships, low self-esteem, and extreme fears of emotional abandonment. Ironically and tragically, many of Helen's strategies for dealing with these problems inadvertently perpetuated her difficulties, and seemed to "confirm" her hopeless view of herself and her life. The therapist came to realize that an important part of treatment would involve Helen's recognition of these self-defeating phenomena and her willingness to experiment with frightening new modes of operation.

TREATMENT AND OUTCOME

Helen was motivated for therapy and readily warmed up to her female therapist. The therapist made a point of noting Helen's areas of strength and highlighting specific examples from Helen's life that were indicative of hope for change. Such behavior from the therapist was in marked contrast to Helen's view of "typical" female peers, who she believed were catty, judgmental, competitive, and fair-weather friends at best.

Helen's mistrust schema rarely was aroused in her interactions with the therapist. The therapist facilitated a trusting relationship through her active collaboration with the patient. For example, Helen had expected that her therapist would tell her what was wrong with her and then tell her exactly what she should do differently. Instead, the therapist shared and exchanged viewpoints with Helen, paid attention to Helen's agenda for each session, showed respect for the patient's points of view, regularly elicited feedback from her, and showed a commitment to working with Helen through times of progress, stagnation, and regression alike.

The following comment typified the kind of communication style that the therapist employed in order to build trust:

"Helen, I want you to know that I'll do whatever I can to help you. At times, *the best way that I can help you may be to encourage and teach you how to make changes for yourself.* I realize that at such times you may feel that I'm abandoning you in your time of need. Let me assure you that I have every intention of giving you support and guidance throughout your time in therapy. Ultimately, though, you're going to feel much better about yourself and about your life if we work on your learning how to take care of yourself. What do you think about what I just said? Do you have any concerns about it? I'm willing to listen to any questions or further ideas that you may have about this."

Helen would then respond, whereupon the therapist might add the following:

"Helen, I think it's vitally important that we work as a collaborative team. For example, you can expect that I will be very attentive to you and your concerns in session, and you will have the bulk of the responsibility to apply what you've learned in session to your everyday life. Then we'll get together again and compare notes on how you're doing, and what further changes you believe are reasonable to make. What are your thoughts about this?"

After eliciting more feedback from Helen, the therapist communicated another important fact about therapy (indeed, about all important relationships):

"Helen, neither of us is perfect, and neither of us *has* to be perfect in order for therapy to be helpful to you. If you do something that I think is not adaptive, I'll tell you about it, but I won't put you down in any way or force you to change without your permission. Likewise, it's very important that you let me know when you think *I've* made a mistake. I'm human, and it's inevitable that I'm going to say the wrong thing once in a while. I'm depending on you to let me know how you feel in such instances and to set me straight. My main goal is to work with you to change your life for the better, not to prove that I always know what's right."

Helen admitted that she felt a bit worried about the idea that the therapist was not a perfect person who would take absolute and flawless care of her. Nevertheless, the therapist helped the patient to understand that an imperfect, benevolent, collaborative relationship would be a good model for other relationships in Helen's life.

Over the course of months of therapy, Helen was able to recognize that her views of potential significant others were maladaptively dichotomized; they either were perfect and wonderful (at least temporarily so, until the first disappointment), or horrible, cruel, and depriving. Helen agreed that it would be more useful to begin to examine carefully the relative merits and drawbacks of a given relationship, without idealizing or condemning the other person. In order to succeed in changing the nature of her relationships, however, Helen would have to understand and change her own reactions as well.

The first change that Helen made was to become comfortable with accepting at least half the responsibility for setting the agenda for each therapy session. At first, Helen wanted the therapist to choose the topics and to do most of the talking. The therapist explained that therapy sessions would provide a safe and regular testing ground for new ways for the patient to think, feel, and act. One of these new patient actions would have to involve her playing a more active role in taking control of her life. What better way to begin to practice this than by taking control of the agenda for the session?

Helen did not feel comfortable with this idea at first. She worried that she would pick the "wrong" topics and that she would waste the hour. She also feared that she would look silly and stupid, and that the therapist would grow bored with her. The therapist responded by reviewing the patient's history of fearing failure and avoiding chances to learn and succeed. She explained that this led to an incompetency schema that silently and pervasively undermined Helen's self-esteem and caused her to depend too heavily on others for too many things in life. The therapist added, "The way that I'm going to show you that I care will *not* be to do everything for you but, rather, to find ways to help you develop confidence in yourself. Would you be willing to start on this project by choosing some topics for us to discuss in therapy?"

Helen began to take a more active role in therapy, and soon habituated to her anxiety and felt an increased sense of self-efficacy. Patient and therapist agreed that a long-term goal of treatment would be Helen's taking a more proactive stance to life across all important spheres, including vocational and interpersonal. "Carpe diem" ("Seize the day!") became their battle cry when Helen evidenced passivity and self-doubt. This little phrase became an important adaptive self-statement for the patient as therapy progressed, and solidified feelings of collaboration in the therapeutic relationship.

Most of the important work of therapy involved a combination of schema identification and behavioral experimentation. Schemas were identified by looking at themes in Helen's current emotional crises, and linking them to critical experiences earlier in life. By doing so, Helen was able to understand better her emotional reactions and, therefore, to feel less out of control and helpless. Also, such schema identification helped Helen to separate the "then" from the "now."

For example, when Helen received a bad haircut, she became distraught and asked for an emergency session. She believed that her boyfriend now would leave her for sure. The therapist sympathized with Helen, in light of the latter's childhood experience with a father who would "sell her for a penny" if she didn't look especially pretty. At the same time, she taught Helen to examine the *current* situation and the *current* relationship in question. Helen was asked to consider questions such as these:

- How is your boyfriend different from your father?
- What is the evidence that supports or refutes the idea that your boyfriend will leave you if you don't look your best?
- What are the personal qualities that you bring to a relationship that a man would find attractive, *aside* from your hair?
- How do you now have more power to control the course and destiny of your relationships than you had when you were a little girl?
- What can you do to test out your concerns about your boyfriend's reaction to your haircut?
- What are a *number* of ways that he might respond? What will you think of each of these potential reactions? What can you *do* in each of the hypothesized cases to maximize the chances that you will feel good about yourself and about the relationship?

Following discussion of these points, Helen and the therapist role-played a number of potential scenarios involving the boyfriend. In addition, Helen was asked to generate several self-affirming statements that she might say to herself in order to boost her confidence. Finally, the therapist helped Helen to design behavioral experiments to test her schema-based catastrophic expectations. For example, one experiment had Helen telephone her boyfriend (which was less threatening than seeing him in person) to tell him that she was displeased with her haircut. However, she was *not* to make global self-disparaging comments or tell her boyfriend that he would "hate it too." Then, Helen was instructed to note his reactions, both over the phone and later in person, and to compare these reactions to her previous predictions of abandonment. Invariably, Helen found that when she didn't avoid seeing the boyfriend and didn't go out of her way to make self-defeating comments, her problems could be solved fairly easily. These results were documented in Helen's "schema-busters" notebook, which was filled with behavioral examples of situations that disconfirmed her most entrenched, maladaptive beliefs.

Helen often asked, ". . . but what if my horrible predictions come true?" The therapist responded by saying that yes, there might be times when Helen's fears would be borne out. However, these situations would provide opportunities to increase her self-sufficiency, in that Helen would have to cope actively with real problems. The therapist explained that although this experience might not be very pleasant in the short run, it would boost Helen's sense of inner strength in the long run, thereby improving her quality of life. When Helen expressed fear about this process, the therapist reaffirmed her commitment to help Helen get through any crisis she might face. An important caveat was added, however—namely, that the therapist could help only to the extent that Helen was willing to help herself. She likened this phenomenon to the practice of "matching funds," whereby corporations contribute to charitable organizations in an amount that equals the combined gifts of individual donors. The therapist said, "The more that you put into your therapy, the more *I* can put into your therapy. Only in this way can I give you the optimal help you need while also helping you to trust and depend on yourself."

A breakthrough in therapy took place when Helen was able to muster the courage to attempt some behavioral, "schema-busting" experiments with her father. Helen's father had gone through a number of physical changes in his late years resulting from diabetes, alcohol, and natural deterioration. True to form, he was very self-critical about his reduced attractiveness. Helen was able to see the effect his maladaptive beliefs about appearances had had on him, as well as the problems those beliefs and rules had caused her. Helen, who was fearful of her father and his criticisms, typically avoided having contact with him. Now, however, she felt ready to attempt to establish a closer relationship with him, based on sympathy. She experimented with initiating contact with him, and with being attentive and compassionate toward him. In sum, she approached him with insight combined with affection and acceptance, and her long-standing anger and fear diminished.

The results of this experiment were tremendously positive and therapeutically instructive. Helen's relationship with her father became the best it had ever been. Most notably, the father spoke glowingly of Helen, both in the present and in regard to the past. For example, he told her that he regretted not spending enough time with her in the past, and that she deserved more attention than she actually got from him. He also commented that he believed that she would "make some lucky guy a wonderful wife," provided he had "the common sense to appreciate her." These words had a tremendous emotional impact on Helen. Yes, she shed tears of grief and regret regarding the years of needless self-derogation, avoidance, low self-esteem, and estrangement from her father, but she also felt rewarded for having the courage to face a difficult situation. Helen documented these events in her schema-busters notebook and referred to them whenever she needed to boost her confidence in tackling other interpersonal challenges.

There were many other fruitful examples of Helen's identifying situations that activated her various schemas, and then following up with well-rehearsed behavioral experiments. These included situations at work when she would have to assume greater responsibilities, and situations with her new boyfriend, Glen (who was younger than Frank and less oversolicitous than Frank had been). In fact, one of Helen's behavioral experiments was partly responsible for her meeting Glen in the first place, as she took a chance on accepting an invitation to come to a co-worker's Fourth of July barbecue. In braving her fears of feeling left out and disliked, she succeeded in attracting the attention of the man who was to become her new beau.

At work, she chose not to avoid special tasks and eventually performed outstandingly on a difficult project. She received a commendation and was the subject of an in-house newsletter. Her increased pride in her performance was evident and justified. Her incompetence fears were dealt a serious blow!

With Glen, Helen noticed that she was acting much more autonomously than she had with Frank. She was making more decisions for herself and was socializing with new friends that she had made on her own. This was good. However, her unlovability and abandonment schemas still were aroused by rather innocuous situations, as when Glen would give another woman on the street a passing glance. As therapy continued to progress, Helen worked diligently to develop a new, more functional behavioral rule. When the schemas were activated, she would tell Glen what she was thinking and feeling and would explain the reasons. She would name the schema and tell Glen that she might flee or rage at him if she acted on her impulse. They then would talk about the matter, consider alternative behaviors, and pledge to "work it out." In most cases, this strategy successfully defused the schema and its concomitant thoughts, emotions, and impulses. The result was a more intimate and warmer relationship with Glen.

After a little less than two years of weekly therapy sessions (on average), Helen was referred to another therapist, as the current therapist was about to take a one-year sabbatical abroad. The therapist at first feared that her leaving might reactivate Helen's abandonment schema, but Helen demonstrated that she had made significant gains in treatment by remaining relatively unfazed. Helen concluded that she was not really losing her therapist as much as she was gaining another support person who would conduct booster sessions. This was an excellent response, one that Helen could not have dreamed of making when she started cognitive therapy two years previously. In fact, Helen has continued to make progress, and now receives "checkup" sessions only on an occasional basis.

Chapter 12

Borderline–Avoidant/Dependent Case Study #2: The Case of "Gail"

PRESENTING PROBLEMS

Gail is a 35-year-old, single Jewish woman who came into treatment at the Center for Cognitive Therapy after being referred by a previous therapist who had moved to Boston. She had been working with the previous therapist for approximately three years, had been taking a steady dose of an MAO-I antidepressant medication, and was diagnosed as having a major depressive disorder superimposed on a primary, early-onset dysthymia, as well as an atypical eating disorder. Furthermore, she met DSM-III-R criteria for BPD, avoidant personality disorder, and dependent personality disorder, and she had features of histrionic personality disorder. Her specific BPD problem areas included the following:

1. A history of unstable and intense interpersonal relationships
2. Impulsivity in at least two areas that were potentially self-damaging (bingeing and purging, unsafe sex)
3. Inappropriate, intense anger
4. Recurrent suicidal threats
5. Poorly formed sense of self
6. Chronic feelings of emptiness and boredom
7. Excessive fears of abandonment

Gail's symptoms of AvPD, DPD, and features of HPD (respectively) included the following:

1. Excessive vulnerability to criticism or disapproval
2. Having only one close friend outside her immediate family

3. Avoidance of social or occupational activities that would involve significant interpersonal contact
4. Reticence in social situations out of fear of saying something foolish
5. Exaggerated fears of engaging in tasks that are outside her routine or in coping with the responsibilities and discomforts of everyday life
6. An inability to make everyday decisions without an excessive amount of advice or reassurance from others
7. Difficulty in initiating tasks or projects on her own
8. Feelings of helplessness and marked discomfort when alone
9. Emotional devastation in response to the dissolution of relationships
10. Excessive concern with her physical appearance
11. Constant demands for approval, reassurance, and praise
12. Low tolerance for frustration (difficulty in delaying gratification)

Her presenting problems included dissatisfaction with her work life, her relationships, and her body image. Gail had a difficult time succinctly describing the specific nature of her difficulties, even though she had been in treatment for three years with the referring psychologist. Therefore, in addition to working to establish a therapeutic alliance with the patient, the therapist set out to define Gail's complaints more clearly.

After four sessions of gentle, direct, open-ended questioning, the therapist was able to elucidate Gail's major areas of concern. Her problems with relationships were central. Gail was experiencing ongoing grief over her mother's death, even though she had passed away several years earlier. The patient explained that she believed that she could not fill the void that her mother had left. The therapist mentally noted that this was an ironic and conflicted sentiment, as Gail described her mother as always having been distant and emotionally depriving. This incongruence would be discussed later in treatment, as a prototype of her ambivalence in relationships typified by her alternately overidealizing and undervaluing her most significant others.

Gail also was having difficulty in dealing with the loss of her previous therapist. Throughout the first few months of her treatment at the Center for Cognitive Therapy, Gail continued to refer to the Boston psychologist as "my therapist," and expressed a desire to contact her. She explained that she wanted to tell the Boston therapist two important things about the way she felt about the therapist's leaving. The current therapist explored this area with Gail and discovered that the patient held two seemingly contradictory feelings and opinions about the former therapist. Furthermore, she noticed that Gail did not realize the contradictory nature of her sentiments. First, Gail wanted to tell the Boston therapist that she had kept Gail in therapy too long and had encouraged her to become too dependent. Second, Gail wished to tell the Boston therapist that she felt hurt that the therapist would not consent to continue contact with Gail now that she lived in another city. The current therapist was struck by Gail's angry expression of her need for individuation from the Boston psychologist, while concurrently demonstrating her feelings of ongoing dependency and sense of having been rejected. Gail's conflict between approach/ dependency and avoidance/rejection would be seen as a recurring pattern in the current treatment as well.

Gail also had difficulties in relationships with the men she was dating. The main focus at the outset of therapy was a man named David, who had made it clear to Gail that he wanted only a casual, uncommitted sexual relationship with her. She found him to be indifferent to her emotional needs, and she was confused and hurt by his behavior and intentions. Gail defined sexual relationships by their very nature as involving commitment and emotional intimacy. She expected that sexual inter- course with a man would lead automatically to emotional closeness and long-term companionship. When David did not meet these expectations, Gail became very angry and believed that she had been betrayed. At the same time, she dared not express this anger openly to David, lest she lose him. Instead, she would make her feelings known subtly by neglecting David when he would initiate contact with her (e.g., not returning his calls). In this sense, Gail, not David, was "controlling" the process of rejection. Nevertheless, Gail always found it upsetting when her renewed efforts to contact and to be with David were met by lukewarm responses.

The patient did not perceive her own avoidance as playing a role in this interpersonal dance with her lover. Instead, she immediately concluded that David's less than enthusiastic greetings were proof of his failure to meet her needs. Again, she felt used, and responded either with renewed, feigned uninterest in David, or an occasional escalation of her desire to be sexually intimate (typified by the implicit belief, "Maybe this time he'll change his mind and want to be with me as much as I need to be with him"). In neither case did Gail have insight into the process of her own reactions or into the mixed messages that she must have been sending her lover.

Gail's responses to her troubles with David are typical of the BPD–avoidant/ dependent patient. Unlike the purely avoidant patient, who is content to remain distant from the source of the anxiety, the BPD patient's poor sense of self leads to an inevitable increase in anxiety when alone. Unlike the purely dependent patient, who seeks nurturance and care from strong, benevolent others, the BPD patient searches for love in a much more ambivalent way. This is typified by the BPD patient's pursuit of poor caregivers who are destined to disappoint the patient, or by the patient's growing to fear those people who really are capable of having a mature, intimate relationship. In either situation, the BPD patient constantly feels torn, confused, anxious, and deprived.

Most of Gail's interactions with females were with relatives. She had an assort- ment of sisters, cousins, and aunts with whom she spent her free time. Many of these interactions were typified by Gail's talking about her problems and asking for advice and reassurance. Unfortunately, Gail often did not follow their recommendations. More commonly, she would find herself unable to take her relatives' directions to act in calm, thoughtful, nonimpulsive ways. Instead, she would act impulsively (e.g., calling David and pleading with him to see her right away), which would lead regularly to crises, which in turn would bring Gail back to her female relatives for more "discussion and advice." This pattern was irritating and disconcerting to Gail's relatives. Not surprisingly, the same pattern would come to exasperate the therapist as well.

In the area of work, Gail had been unemployed for long periods. When she entered treatment at the Center for Cognitive Therapy, she worked as a temporary secretary and continued to be out of work periodically. When she was working, she found her jobs emotionally difficult to tolerate. She was afraid of criticism and failure (both work-related and social) and found having to interact even in superficial ways with her colleagues to be highly anxiety-provoking. The current therapist found that Gail nearly met DSM-III-R criteria for social phobia.

Additionally, Gail exhibited what seemed to be an atypical eating disorder. She was below normal weight, greatly restricted her diet, and believed that if she allowed herself to eat freely she would binge continuously. She had an all-or-none view of eating, as she would call ingestion of normal-sized proportions of food "binges." When she ate more than she liked, Gail voluntarily would bring her food up her esophagus to her mouth, but then would swallow again. She did not lose any of the contents of what she ate, and she said that she did this to "relieve tension." Gail demonstrated her distorted body image when she commented that her habit of partially regurgitating and reswallowing her food was an apropos behavior, "given that I've always felt like a cow anyway." Gail complained that this practice caused her to experience ear pain, yet she persisted in this self-harming strategy. The therapist, believing Gail's pain might represent inflammation or damage to the eustachian tubes, recommended a medical consultation. In addition, a psychiatric consultation was called for as well, in order to monitor Gail's use of the MAO-I antidepressant medication. In fact, Gail's eating disorder led her therapist to hypothesize that a change in medication was called for, as someone who had such problematic eating habits probably would not be a good candidate to maintain a strict MAO-I diet.

BACKGROUND INFORMATION AND CASE CONCEPTUALIZATION

Gail's belief that she was unlovable was a strong theme in her childhood. The development of the patient's unlovability schema was aided and abetted by incidents in which Gail's mother was unresponsive to her needs. One particularly memorable event occurred when Gail was three or four years old. She had been traveling in a car with her family for a long period of time. When they arrived at their destination, Gail's legs were cramped and aching badly. She recalled being carried into her cousin's house and being placed in a bed. She cried to her mother, telling her that her legs hurt. Gail remembered an image of her mother's face that was both unresponsive and uncaring. She wanted her mother to rub her legs, but the mother did not. Later in therapy it was learned from an aunt that Gail's mother was clinically depressed during that period. In fact, the mother suffered from recurrent depressions throughout her entire adult life.

Gail noted that she had always tried to win her mother's love and affection but that the mother typically seemed preoccupied and distant. When Gail's mother died, the patient was distraught, not only because of the loss of a parent, but because she believed that she had never realized her goal of achieving her mother's love. Now, that goal was dead as well.

Gail's father was reported to have been controlling and overprotective. He always made decisions for Gail and treated her as if she could not take care of herself. Even when she became an adult, her father still tried to run her life, encouraging her to let him choose which car she should buy and which apartment she should rent. He still was supporting her financially when she was 35 years old; he expected her to call him every day, to accompany him to dinner several times a week, and to drive him to visits with relatives each weekend. The only area of Gail's life that her father did not try to control was her love life, as Gail was too embarrassed to tell him the details of her heterosexual relationships. She saved such discussion for her female relatives and her therapist.

Gail's perpetual overdependence on her father fostered her belief that she could not manage without the aid and advice of others. Nevertheless, she often failed to follow others' suggestions, and when she did do so, she held them responsible for the outcome. Gail focused her dependency needs on her father, female relatives, boy-friends, and therapist alike. Gail frequently called the therapist to get her definitive opinions about major decisions that invariably had to be made immediately. On one occasion she called about the advisability of renting a particular apartment on the day that the lease was to be signed. On another occasion she phoned from an automobile dealer's showroom about a car she was indecisive about buying. Each time the questions were the same: "Should I do this? Is this a good idea?" In both situations her father was financing the deals.

Gail's dependency also showed itself in her frequent in-session questions about whether or not she should end a particular heterosexual relationship. Her questions never focused on *how* to decide but, rather, on *what* to conclude. When the therapist attempted to discuss problem-solving and decision-making strategies so that Gail could decide for herself, the patient selectively ignored the therapist's statements and simply restated the request for the therapist's decision. For example, during one session the therapist gave Gail a detailed description of the step-by-step process of solving problems. In addition, the therapist alerted the patient to notice any thoughts or emotions that interfered with this process, so that they could understand better her difficulties in making autonomous choices. Gail seemed to listen attentively, nod-ded, and then asked, "So do you think I should see him again or break it off?" Her attentive nodding and waiting were more out of politeness than understanding. Her belief that "I can't make these decisions on my own" was very strong indeed. Gail explained that all her previous therapists had freely answered such questions for her. Although the current therapist considered the possibility that this might have been an inaccurate or otherwise distorted memory, it was equally plausible that Gail's previous therapists had indeed fallen prey to the patient's need for a strong figure to control her life, thus unwittingly reinforcing Gail's incompetency schema and concomitant overdependency. The current therapist would have to work very carefully so as not to fall into the same trap.

Gail had a patchy work history. She had been a schoolteacher for a number of years but had found the responsibilities involved physically difficult and emotionally overwhelming. She proceeded to be unemployed for an extended period of time, and then worked at temporary secretarial jobs. Gail had been unable to support herself financially with any of these jobs. This fed into her overreliance on her father.

In addition to Gail's incompetency schema, she suffered the effects of a strong unlovability schema as well. Inadequate nurturing in childhood had left Gail with an emotional void that seemed to her to be a bottomless pit. Now, even when someone sincerely wanted to offer love and support, it seemed to Gail never to be enough.

Gail's equating of sex with emotional intimacy worked to her disadvantage, as she often stated that she needed sex to live. She believed that she could not work on any of her other problems (e.g., employment, relationship with father, self-esteem) unless she was involved in an ongoing sexual relationship. She explained that she would have far fewer difficulties in life if she were having her sexual (i.e., emotional) needs met on a regular basis. She did not seem to notice that life did not magically improve during those times when she did have a steady sex partner.

Gail's belief that she could not handle life's decisions (incompetency schema), coupled with her exaggerated needs to fill the void left by emotional deprivation (unlovability schema), encouraged the advice seeking and emotional clinging that were so prominent in Gail's life. As much as these factors were pushing Gail toward people, however, there were also other factors pushing her away.

Although Gail craved love and affection, she also believed that anyone who got too close would realize that she truly was unlovable. Each time a relationship started to become exclusive and committed, with the *man* pursuing most of the contact, Gail would begin to withdraw. Gail tearfully recounted how five years earlier she had alienated a "wonderful" man named Carl who wanted to marry her. When she learned of his serious intentions, she became cold, distant, and indifferent. She assumed that by marrying Carl, she merely would be setting herself up for the worst rejection of all—divorce. Thus, she passively sabotaged the relationship. Predictably, when Carl left the scene, Gail felt bereft, abandoned, and helpless.

One of Gail's chief avoidance strategies was her frequent complaint that the man she was dating was not sufficiently attractive. A historical review of Gail's love life indicated that the men involved had seemed physically acceptable early in the relationship but became less acceptable as the relationship turned more serious.

Interestingly, when the therapist questioned Gail about her criteria for attractiveness, Gail came to the startling realization that the men's faces didn't look enough like her mother's! Gail had gone to extremes in attempting to fill the emotional void left by her mother by finding another face that looked similar, but with love expressed in it this time around. However, no man's face ever matched the template to which it was compared, and each one was rejected. This dysfunctional overdiscrimination became an important focus in treatment.

Gail's rapidly shifting reactions to the prospect of intimacy—excessive desire, exaggerated fear, and back to extreme neediness—often precipitated rifts with her current boyfriend, David. A typical scenario would find Gail upset about being alone on a given evening. She then would call David and beg him to come over. David, assuming that he was being seduced, would arrive and begin to kiss and undress Gail. Gail's response was to recoil, partly out of fear that David would find her body unattractive and reject her (a reflection of Gail's distorted body image, in which the slender woman saw herself as a "cow") or that he would quickly have sex and then leave (i.e., she would be used and then abandoned). Her subsequent rebuffs annoyed David. In turn, David's annoyance would be interpreted by Gail as a lack of caring, and she would ask him to leave. After he had left, Gail's need for love and intimacy would be reactivated and she would proceed to call him the same evening to try to convince him to come back. This pattern of schema vacillation was played out on a larger scale in the form of numerous breakups and reconciliations. One of Gail's sisters used to ask her sarcastically, "So, Gail, are you and David together or broken up today?" David's barbs were sharper, as he often told Gail that she was crazy. In relating these events to the therapist, Gail wondered aloud if indeed she was insane.

TREATMENT AND OUTCOME

The therapist worked with Gail to establish some goals for treatment. In the process, it soon became painfully obvious that Gail's goals were inappropriate and were guaranteed to perpetuate the chaotic status quo in her life. One of Gail's goals was to have the therapist help her to find a man who would take over her life so that she would be emotionally secure and would not have to make decisions or support herself financially. The therapist silently conceptualized a long list of reasons that this was a dysfunctional goal for therapy. Rather than simply telling this to Gail, which would risk reinforcing Gail's obedience to someone else'e commands, the therapist engaged the patient in Socratic questioning and dialogue in order to be collaborative and to stimulate Gail's thinking for herself. The following dialogue is a representative, condensed example of such an interchange:

T: Gail, you say that you want to find a man who will do everything for you, and that this will make your life better. Is that right?

G: Right. I need you to help me find the right man.

T: Gail, your description of the "right" man sounds a lot like your father. After all, you said he pretty much controls your life, makes your decisions for you, and supports you financially. Can you see the similarity?

G: I guess so, but that's different.

T: How so?

G: I don't want someone like my father, because he makes me feel like a child. He doesn't have any faith or respect for me. I want someone who will take care of me and love me and respect me.

T: If your goal is to find a man who will take complete care of you, what will be the basis for his respecting you?

G: What do you mean?

T: Here's what I'm trying to say, Gail. If your father takes care of you and makes all your decisions, and provides for you financially, but sees you as a child and doesn't respect you, then how will another man do all of those things for you but somehow treat you as an equal? Do you see my point?

G: So what you're saying is that no man will ever respect me, right?

T: No, no, no, Gail. I'm merely asking you to carefully consider the logic of your goals. That's one of the most important things that we do here in cognitive therapy. We have to examine your life as objectively as possible, and this requires that we look at both the benefits and the drawbacks of what you're saying. I'm very hopeful that you will be respected by a man. First, though, I'd like to enlist your cooperation in discussing how you're going to find some *self-respect*. This seems to me to be as important, if not more so, than immediately finding the man of your dreams.

G: I see what you mean. I see what you mean. (Pause) But what's so wrong about wanting to find a man to love me?

T: Nothing. Nothing at all. But I think that there may be some *prerequisites* to achieving that particular goal, and I see my job as primarily being to help you to achieve those prerequisites.

G: You mean self-esteem?

T: Exactly.

G: Well, you're right, I have no self-esteem at all. (Pause) But I think that having a man who loves me completely would give me self-esteem.

T: Well, let's look at the evidence. Have you ever been in a relationship with a man who you believed loved you?

G: (Becoming tearful.) Yes. Carl. I drove him away. (Sobs)

T: What happened? (Gives Gail a tissue) Take your time. I'm listening.

G: I was scared. I was too scared.

T: Gail, I don't mean to rub it in, but is that the kind of experience that's going to give you self-esteem and make you happy?

G: (Cries and shakes head "no")

T: Gail, I want you to be happy. Someday, when our work together is long finished, nobody will be happier than me to hear that you're happily married and content with your life. It's just that for now I think we have some other work to do first. Are you with me?

Interchanges like this one often seemed quite productive at the time they took place. Unfortunately, Gail's passive understanding of the therapist's important feedback did not readily translate to a change in the patient's behavior between sessions. This should not have been surprising, as one of the hallmarks of the personality-disordered patient is a chronic, inflexible, dysfunctional approach to coping. One or two gems of wisdom from the therapist scarcely would be sufficient to change deeply engrained, schema-driven response patterns. It soon became clear to the therapist that numerous repetitions of all noteworthy messages to the patient would be needed in order for change to be possible. To facilitate this process, the therapist assigned Gail the regular task of audiotaping the therapy sessions. Gail then was to take the tape home with her after each session, listen to the tape from start to finish at least once, and take notes on statements from the therapist that she had either forgotten (which were many) or otherwise deemed important to remember. Sometimes the therapist would facilitate this process during the session by flagging a noteworthy point. Typically, she would say, ". . . and this is important to note, so when you hear this again on the tape, make sure you write it down in your therapy notebook."

Therapy with Gail progressed very slowly. The therapist's attempts to teach Gail to think for herself or to take decisive action elicited great anxiety in the patient. This phenomenon was due to several factors. First, Gail had little confidence in her own judgment or coping skills, believing instead that all attempts to chart the course of her own life would meet with utter disaster. Second, the notion of helping herself was foreign to Gail. As is typical of the borderline patient, the prospect of change was quite threatening. Patients like Gail prefer to maintain all that is familiar in their lives, even when the status quo involves chronic pervasive unhappiness. Third, the therapist's attempts to foster autonomy often were interpreted by Gail as signs of imminent abandonment. She reasoned that if she were to improve in treatment, the therapist would ask her to leave therapy. Therefore, the patient had sufficient motivation to remain at least somewhat helpless and depressed.

The therapist addressed this problem by discussing it directly with Gail. Gail argued that her experience had taught her that self-sufficiency would lead only to being ignored, and that she could garner love and affection only through being "pathetic." Rather than take this statement at face value, the therapist engaged Gail in a historical review of her life in order to chronicle instances that would be representative of the phenomena that Gail alluded to. Part of this task was accomplished via a homework assignment, one of the few that Gail was willing to perform.

The outcome of the assignment came as a complete surprise to Gail. She learned through an objective reevaluation of her memories that she had often been ignored by significant others *despite the fact that she had been needy and "pathetic."* The memory of her mother's paying no attention to her cramped legs when Gail was four years old was a prime case in point. The problem was that Gail had formulated a *faulty belief*—namely, that she must not have been pathetic *enough*. Therefore, she reasoned erroneously, she would have to become even *more* helpless and agonized in order to expect the tender loving care she craved so much. This belief was congruent with her incompetency and unlovability schemas and therefore was well entrenched. Almost all of her interpersonal behaviors were predicated on the notion that wellness brings loneliness, and sickness brings care. Strikingly, this schema-driven strategy flew in the face of almost all the objective data of her life. For example, men such as David were repulsed by her neediness, whereas Carl ("the one who got away") was most attracted to Gail when she was cheerful, trusting, and comfortable with sex. Prior to this point in her treatment, Gail had never seen these most fundamental of contradictions in her life.

In order to provide ongoing interpersonal evidence in support of these findings, the therapist told Gail that she would continue to treat her and to care for her even as she would become well. She explained to the patient that she would neither punish nor reward her for being "pathetic," but that she would be attentive in any instance. The therapist added that she would be most pleased by any attempts on Gail's part to do the work of therapy, thus giving support to the idea that wellness could elicit nurturance and approval from others. The application of this principle in session was a precursor to Gail's experimenting with the approach in everyday life. The therapist did her utmost to live up to her promise, and was willing to speak frankly with Gail when there was any tension in the therapeutic relationship.

One such real-life application took place when Gail established a satisfying platonic friendship with a man. She was happy with this relationship, as it helped her to challenge her belief that sex was the essential element in relating to men. Another between-sessions application of her new insights involved Gail's taking more active steps in social activities. She even began going alone to social events, such as singles gatherings sponsored by her synagogue. She tried to establish friendships with women, and for the first time began to invite female cohorts to her apartment for lunch or dinner. Gail also increased her solitary recreational activities, including swimming and walking for pleasure and for good health.

Some progress was made in the area of Gail's employment as well, a reflection of some success in modifying her sense of incompetency. Signs of improvement included Gail's obtaining and holding a full-time job for over a year, and being able to work through a difficult relationship with a critical and demanding supervisor. In order to accomplish this feat, therapist and patient often performed role-plays that were pertinent to the conflict at work. When Gail would falter in the role-play (e.g., by bursting into tears or becoming withdrawn and morose), the therapist would help Gail address the thoughts and feelings that were emanating from her incompetency schema. Through many repetitions, Gail was able to recognize that her fear and sadness were not reflective of actual lack of self-worth but, rather, of an activated schema—a schema that was antiquated, self-defeating, and in need of change. The role-playing practice, combined with Gail's awareness of her schema-driven reactions, helped the patient to become desensitized to the in vitro conflict with the supervisor (as played by the therapist) and to think of self-statements that were self-affirming. Finally, she applied her newly developed assertiveness skills by asking for an actual meeting with her supervisor. This action, although it did not initially bring about a major change at work, did wonders for Gail's self-confidence. She had had very little previous experience in standing up for herself in an assertive way. She found this to be a welcome change from her usual modes of operation, such as avoidance, or begging and pleading.

On the negative side, the job was still below Gail's level of competence, and she was very slow to investigate more challenging employment opportunities. She continued to avoid reading the classified section of the newspaper, going to job services, and keeping interview appointments. Although Gail had learned to assert herself in her present job, she still believed she was not ready to find employment that would test her skills more appropriately. Her salary remained modest, and she continued to accept financial assistance from her father.

With regard to heterosexual relationships, Gail was no longer seeing David, and she felt quite lonely. In the past, it had been at times such as this that the patient impulsively began trying to establish a new intimate relationship. Now, with the therapist's support, Gail agreed to a temporary "moratorium on men." The goal was for Gail to take this opportunity to demonstrate to herself that she was capable of managing her life without a lover. Therapist and patient agreed in principle that it would be beneficial for Gail to gain experience in taking care of her own needs via friendships, hobbies, exercise, proper health habits, and other self-improvement activities. They concluded that Gail would gain a better sense of herself and of her worth if she undertook these tasks without the presence of a man in her life. Gail found this strategy difficult to follow, and she continued to date whenever she was asked out.

The therapist often encouraged Gail to talk about her mother. The rationales were to give the patient a chance to express her grief to a sympathetic person, to find some meaning and purpose to her past relationship with her mother, and to reframe experiences that Gail had had with her mother in such a way that she would feel more lovable. The therapist assisted Gail through numerous highly evocative imagery sessions, wherein Gail was given the opportunity to reenact covertly crucial events with her mother. On some occasions during these exercises Gail's mind would go completely blank, as painful memories would lead to cognitive avoidance. It was at such times that the therapist believed that some of the most important material had been tapped. In order to facilitate the memory process when Gail's thinking would go blank, the therapist sometimes spoke as if she were the mother, instructing Gail to tell her what she was thinking and feeling. Then, the therapist, in the role of the mother, would offer sober apologies and words of solace and support. These sessions were among the most emotionally significant and draining of all.

Significantly, after a number of trials of imagery and months of grief work, Gail reported that she noticed that she was no longer looking for a man who "has my mother's facial expressions."

Some progress was achieved in the area of Gail's eating disorder. She followed through on the therapist's advice to undergo a thorough medical exam and to see a psychiatric consultant with regard to psychotropic medication. The results were not alarming, but Gail learned that her weight was significantly below normal and that she had some inflammation in the throat. In relation to these findings, the psychiatric consultant recommended that Gail taper off her MAO-I medications. The consultant and the therapist concluded that Gail's eating habits should be a major focus of therapy, that she should wean off of all medications until her body weight normalized, and that she should continue with cognitive therapy alone barring worsening of her condition.

Gail was compliant in monitoring her eating habits, and she learned to eat a more healthful diet with the assistance of her physician. Therapy helped her to cease dichotomizing her views of eating as consisting of either starvation or binges. One particularly helpful skill involved Gail's use of a continuum rating system to distinguish normal eating from harmful extremes in eating. For example, Gail was asked to compose three lists (representing breakfast, lunch, and dinner) of potential meals, and to assign them a number from 0 to 100, where zero signified starvation and 100 meant that she was bingeing. Once completed, Gail was encouraged to eat regularly those meals that made up the range from 20 to 80. Gail also monitored her incidents of partial regurgitation and learned to assess the source of the "tension" that led her to engage in this behavior. As she learned to normalize her eating, to assert herself more in some of her relationships, and to feel better about herself in general, the regurgitation diminished in frequency, but it did not cease altogether. Accordingly, she was not given a new trial of medications.

Gail continues to attend cognitive therapy sessions regularly at this time. She no longer meets criteria for a diagnosis of major depression, but her dysthymic condition persists. Her eating disorder is in partial remission, and her borderline disorder has lessened in its severity, although technically she still evidences enough symptoms to maintain the diagnosis. Work continues in the areas of taking on greater work responsibilities and of taking care of herself without depending on a man. Gail is showing progress in the areas of schema recognition, assertiveness, rational responding, affect modulation, diminished avoidance, and lessened dependency on her father and female relatives for reassurance and advice.

Epilogue

Cognitive therapy, renowned for its efficacy in treating affective disorders and anxiety disorders, also is successfully applied to the treatment of personality disorders. We have focused our attention on the borderline personality, one of the most difficult disorders for psychotherapists to treat. Written for clinicians who already have a basic understanding of standard cognitive therapy (Beck et al., 1979), this book has expounded on the recent work of writers such as Aaron T. Beck, Arthur Freeman, and Jeffrey Young in focusing on new advances in the conceptualization and treatment of this most chronic and troublesome disorder.

We have highlighted the use of traditional cognitive therapy methods such as the daily thought record (DTR), the activity schedule, and mastery and pleasure ratings, and have described more advanced techniques such as guided imagery, schema identification, and a sensitive use of the therapeutic relationship. Further, we have noted the utility of teaching patients to assess and modify their dysfunctional thinking patterns in the here and now, while stressing the critical importance of gaining a developmental perspective on the patients' problems in thinking, feeling, and action. We have focused on the core maladaptive schemas that appear to plague borderline patients from childhood and adolescence into their adult lives, and how these schemas manifest themselves in patients' responses to everyday life that perpetuate their misery.

We continue to emphasize the merits of key ingredients of cognitive therapy: collaboration between therapist and patient, active and regular exchanges of feedback between therapist and patient, the use of self-help assignments between sessions, guided discovery via Socratic questioning, the setting of clear goals for therapy, and the teaching of self-help skills. Additionally, in outlining the special difficulties that the treatment of the BPD patient entails, we have explicated additional aspects of cognitive therapy that must be applied to this population: the consideration of a combination of cognitive therapy with pharmacotherapy, the need for therapists to be aware of their own dysfunctional reactions in session, the vital importance of understanding the patient's personal history so as to formulate an individualized conceptualization of each patient's problems, the use of techniques that utilize the therapeutic relationship as an agent of change, and the application of methods that *increase* the patient's affect so as to assess schemas and evoke meaningful corrective experiences in session.

As our case presentations suggest, the cognitive treatment of BPD patients is in an ongoing state of development. Many of the procedures need to be tested more rigorously. Our clinical experience tells us, however, that the approach we have outlined in this book holds great promise for the treatment of personality-disordered patients in general, and BPD patients in particular.

The cases we have reviewed are representative of our level of success in applying advanced cognitive therapy in the treatment of borderline patients. Most of the patients require long-term treatment; our data indicate a typical range of 50 to 150 sessions. Some of them, such as Gail, make painstakingly slow progress. Others, such as Walter and Edward, seem to make objective gains, only to regress at times of extreme stress. Still others, such as Evy and Helen, make clinically meaningful progress and *maintain* their therapeutic changes. We are proud indeed when we speak of our "former borderline" patients in seminars and case conferences. We continually take instruction from both our therapeutic successes and our therapeutic failures, and we have strived to communicate the distinction in our case studies.

At present, the Center for Cognitive Therapy has embarked on an ambitious program of research on the process and outcome of advanced cognitive therapy for personality disorders. This book represents one component of the training of therapists who are participating in this long-range program. Our clinical experience informs our research protocol; our research findings undoubtedly will influence our clinical procedures in turn. In this way, we continue to learn.

References

Adelman, S. A. (1985). Pills as transitional objects: A dynamic understanding of the use of medication in psychotherapy. *Psychiatry, 48*, 246–253.

Akiskal, H. (1981). Sub-affective disorders, dysthymic, cyclothymic and bipolar II disorders in the borderline realm. *Psychiatric Clinics of North America, 4*, 25–46.

American Psychiatric Association. (1980). *Diagnostic and statistical manual of mental disorders*, 3rd edition. Washington, DC: Author.

American Psychiatric Association. (1987). *Diagnostic and statistical manual of mental disorders*, 3rd edition, revised. Washington, DC: Author.

Appleton, T., Clifton, R., & Goldberg, S. (1975). The development of behavioral competence in infancy. In F. D. Horowitz (Ed.), *Review of child development research* (Vol. 4). Chicago: University of Chicago Press.

Barrera, M. E., & Maurer, D. (1981). Recognition of mother's photographed face by the three-month-old infant. *Child Development, 52*, 714–716.

Bassuk, E. L., Schoonover, S. C., & Gelenberg, A. J. (Eds.). (1983). *The practitioner's guide to psychoactive drugs*, 2nd edition. New York: Plenum Medical Book Company.

Beck, A. T. (1976). *Cognitive therapy and the emotional disorders*. New York: International Universities Press.

Beck, A. T., Emery, G., & Greenberg, R. (1985). *Anxiety disorders and phobias: A cognitive perspective*. New York: Basic Books.

Beck, A. T., Freeman, A., & Associates (1990). *Cognitive therapy of personality disorders*. New York: Guilford Press.

Beck, A. T., Rush, A. J., Shaw, B. F., & Emery, G. (1979). *Cognitive therapy of depression*. New York: Guilford Press.

Beck, A. T., Wright, F. D., Newman, C. F., & Liese, B. S. (in press). *Cognitive therapy of substance abuse disorders*. New York: Guilford Press.

Blackburn, I. M., Bishop, S., Glen, A. I. M., Whalley, L. J., & Christie, J. E. (1981). The efficacy of cognitive therapy in depression: A treatment using cognitive therapy and pharmacotherapy, each alone and in combination. *British Journal of Psychiatry, 139*, 181–189.

Brinkley, J. R., Breitman, B. D., & Friedel, R. O. (1979). Low-dose neuroleptic regimens in the treatment of borderline patients. *Archives of General Psychiatry, 36*, 319–329.

Burns, D. (1980). *Feeling good: The new mood therapy*. New York: William Morrow.

Burns, D. D., & Auerbach, A. H. (1992). Does homework compliance enhance recovery from depression? *Psychiatric Annals, 22*, 464–469.

Casey, T. R., Tryer, P. J., & Platt, S. (1985). The relationship between social functioning and psychiatric functioning in primary care. *Social Psychiatry, 20* (1), 5–9.

Cohen, L. B., & Gelber, E. R. (1975). Infant visual memory. In L. B. Cohen, & P. Salapatek (Eds.), *Infant perception: From sensation to cognition* (Vol. 1). New York: Academic Press.

Cole, J. O., Salomon, M., Gunderson, J., Sunderland, P. III, & Simmonds, P. (1984). Drug therapy in borderline patients. *Comprehensive Psychiatry, 25,* 249–254.

Courtois, C. A. (1988). *Healing the incest wound.* New York: W. W. Norton.

Cowdry, R. W., & Gardner, D. L. (1988). Pharmacotherapy of borderline personality disorder. *Archives of General Psychiatry, 45,* 111–119.

Dawson, D. F. (1988). Treatment of the borderline patient: Relationship management. *Canadian Journal of Psychiatry, 33,* 370–374.

D'Zurilla, T. J., & Goldfried, M. R. (1971). Problem solving and behavior modification. *Journal of Abnormal Psychology, 92,* 107–109.

Eber, M. (1990). Erotized transference reconsidered: Expanding the countertransference dimension. *Psychoanalytic Review, 77,* 25–39.

Edwards, D. J. A. (1990). Cognitive therapy and the restructuring of early memories through guided imagery. *Journal of Cognitive Psychotherapy: An International Quarterly, 4,* 33–50.

Elliott, C. H., Adams, R. L., & Hodge, G. K. (1992). Cognitive therapy: Possible strategies for optimizing outcome. *Psychiatric Annals, 22,* 459–463.

Ellison, J. M., & Adler, D. A. (1984). Psychopharmacologic approaches to borderline syndromes. *Comprehensive Psychiatry, 25,* 255–262.

Erikson, E. H. (1963). *Childhood and society.* New York: Norton.

Fagan, J. F. III. (1973). Infants' delayed recognition memory and forgetting. *Journal of Experimental Child Psychology, 16,* 424–450.

Fagan, J. F. III. (1977). Infant recognition memory: Studies in forgetting. *Child Development, 48,* 68–78.

Faltus, F. J. (1984). The positive effect of alprazolam in the treatment of three patients with borderline personality disorder. *American Journal of Psychiatry, 141,* 802–803.

Fantz, R. L. (1961). The origin of form perception. *Scientific American, 204,* 66–72.

Fernald, A. (1984). The perceptual and affective salience of mothers' speech to infants. In L. Feagans, C. Garvey, & R. Golinkoff (Eds.), *The origins and growth of communication.* New Brunswick, NJ: Ablex.

Fernald, A., & Simon, T. (1984). Expanded intonation contours in mothers' speech to newborns. *Developmental Psychology, 20,* 104–113.

Flavell, J. H. (1970). Concept development. In P. H. Mussen (Ed.), *Carmichael's manual of child psychology,* 3rd ed.(Vol. 1). New York: Wiley.

Flavell, J. H., Beach, D. H., & Chinsky, J. M. (1966). Spontaneous verbal rehearsal in a memory task as a function of age. *Child Development, 37,* 283–299.

Freedman, D. G. (1971). Behavioral assessment in infancy. In G. B. A. Stoelinga & J. J. van der Werff ten Bosch (Eds.), *Normal and abnormal development of brain and behavior.* Leiden: Leiden University Press.

Freeman, A. (1987). Understanding personal, cultural and family schema in psychotherapy. In A. Freeman, N. Epstein, & K. M. Simon (Eds.), *Depression in the family* (pp. 79–99). New York: Haworth Press.

Freeman, A., & Leaf, R. C. (1989). Cognitive therapy applied to personality disorders. In A. Freeman, K. M. Simon, L. E. Beutler, & H. Arkowitz (Eds.), *Comprehensive handbook of cognitive therapy.* New York: Plenum Press.

Freeman, A., Pretzer, J., Fleming, B., & Simon, K. (1989). *Clinical applications of the cognitive therapy.* New York: Plenum Press.

Gardner, D. L., & Cowdry, R. W. (1985). Alprazolam-induced dyscontrol in borderline personality disorder. *American Journal of Psychiatry, 142,* 98–100.

Gardner, D. L., & Cowdry, R. W. (1986a). Development of melancholia during carbamazepine treatment in borderline personality disorder. *Journal of Clinical Psychopharmacology, 6,* 236–239.

Gardner, D. L., & Cowdry, R. W. (1986b). Positive effects of carbamazepine on behavioral dyscontrol in borderline personality disorder. *American Journal of Psychiatry, 143,* 519–522.

Gibson, E. J., & Walk, R. D. (1960). The "visual cliff." *Scientific American, 202*, 64–71.

Goldberg, R. L. (1983). Psychodynamics of limit-setting with the borderline patient. *American Journal of Psychoanalysis, 43*, 71–75.

Goldberg, S. C., Schulz, S. C., Schulz, P. M., Resnick, R. J., Mameer, R. M., & Friedel, R. O. (1986). Borderline and schizotypal personality disorders treated with low-dose thiothixene vs. placebo. *Archives of General Psychiatry, 43*, 680–686.

Goodwin, J. M., Cheeves, K., & Connell, V. (1990). Borderline and other severe symptoms in adult survivors of incestuous abuse. *Psychiatric Annals, 20(1)*, 22–32.

Green, S. A., Goldberg, R. L., Goldstein, D. M., & Leibenluft, E. (1988). *Limit setting in clinical practice*. Washington, DC: American Psychiatric Press.

Gunderson, J. G. (1984). *Borderline personality disorder*. Washington, DC: American Psychiatric Press.

Gunderson, J. G., & Elliott, G. R. (1985). The interface between borderline personality disorder and affective disorders. *American Journal of Psychiatry, 142*, 227–228.

Gunderson, J. G., & Zanarini, M. C. (1987). Current overview of the borderline diagnosis. *The Journal of Clinical Psychiatry, 48* (8), 5–11.

Hainline, L. (1978). Developmental changes in visual scanning of face and nonface patterns by infants. *Journal of Experimental Child Psychology, 25*, 90–115.

Haith, M. M., Bergman, T., & Moore, M. J. (1977). Eye contact and face scanning in early infancy. *Science, 198*, 853–855.

Harris, G. A., & Watkins, D. (1987). *Counseling the involuntary and resistant client*. College Park, MD: American Correctional Association.

Heller, L. M. (1991). *Life at the border: Understanding and recovering from the borderline personality disorder*. West Palm Beach, Florida: Dyslimbia Press.

Hollon, S. D., & Beck, A. T. (1978). Psychotherapy and drug therapy: Comparisons and combinations. In S. L. Garfield & A. E. Bergin (Eds.), *The handbook of psychotherapy and behavior change*, 2nd ed. (pp. 437–490). New York: Wiley.

Hollon, S. D., DeRubeis, R. J., Evans, M. D., Tuason, V. B., Wiemer, M. J., & Garvey, M. (1986). *Cognitive therapy, pharmacotherapy, and combined cognitive therapy-pharmacotherapy in the treatment of depression: I. Differential outcome*. Unpublished manuscript, University of Minnesota and St. Paul–Ramsey Medical Center, Minneapolis–St. Paul.

Kazdin, A. E. (1976). Statistical analyses for single-case experimental designs. In M. Hersen & D. H. Barlow (Eds.), *Single-case experimental designs: Strategies for studying behavior change*. New York: Pergamon Press.

Kelly, G. A. (1955). *A theory of personality*. New York: Norton.

Kernberg, O. F. (1975). *Borderline conditions and pathological narcissism*. New York: Jason Aronson.

Kernberg, O. F. (1984). *Severe personality disorders*. New Haven: Yale University Press.

Koenigsberg, H. W., Kaplan, R. D., Gilmore, M. M., & Cooper, A. M. (1985). The relationship between syndrome and personality disorder in DSM-III: Experience with 2,462 patients. *American Journal of Psychiatry, 142*, 207–217.

Koerner, K., & Linehan, M. M. (1992). Integrative therapy for borderline personality disorder: Dialectical behavior therapy. In J. C. Norcross & M. R. Goldfried (Eds.), *Handbook of psychotherapy integration*. New York: Basic Books.

Kroll, J. (1986). Sexuality of the borderline patient. *Medical Aspects of Human Sexuality, 20*, 76–88.

Kroll, J. (1988). *The challenge of the borderline patient*. New York: W. W. Norton.

LaBarbera, J. D., Izard, C. E., Vietze, P., & Parisi, S. A. (1976). Four- and six-month-old infants' visual responses to joy, anger, and neutral expressions. *Child Development, 47*, 535–538.

Landau, R. J., & Goldfried, M. R. (1981). The assessment of schemata: A unifying framework for cognitive, behavioral, and traditional assessment. In P. C. Kendall & S. D. Hollon (Eds.), *Assessment strategies for cognitive-behavioral intervention*. New York: Academic Press.

Leone, N. F. (1982). Response of borderline patients to loxapine and chlorpromazine. *Journal of Clinical Psychiatry, 43*, 148–150.

Liebowitz, M. R., Quitkin, F. M., Stewart, J. W., McGrath, P. J., Harrison, W. M., Markowitz, J. S., Rabkin, J. G., Tricamo, E., Goetz, D. M., & Klein, D. (1988). Anti-depressant specificity in atypical depression. *Archives of General Psychiatry, 45,* 129–137.

Linehan, M. M. (1987). Dialectical behavior therapy: A cognitive-behavioral approach to para-suicide. *Journal of Personality Disorders, 1,* 328–333.

Links, P. S., & Steiner, M. (1988). Psychopharmacologic management of patients with borderline personality disorder. *Canadian Journal of Psychiatry, 33,* 355–359.

Links, P. S., Steiner, M., Boiago, I., & Irwin, D. (1990). Lithium therapy for borderline patients: Preliminary findings. *Journal of Personality Disorders, 4*(2), 173–181.

Masterson, J. F. (1976). *Psychotherapy of the borderline adult: A developmental approach.* New York: Brunner/Mazel.

Meichenbaum, D., & Turk, D. C. (1987). *Facilitating treatment adherence: A practitioner's guidebook.* New York: Plenum Press.

Meissner, W. W. (1988). *Treatment of the borderline spectrum.* Northvale, NJ: Jason Aronson.

Meltzoff, A. N., & Moore, M. K. (1977). Imitation of facial and manual gestures by human neonates. *Science, 198,* 75–78.

Mendelsohn, R. (1987). Resistance to countertransference. In D. S. Milman & G. D. Goldman (Eds.), *Techniques of working with resistance.* Northvale, NJ: Jason Aronson.

Millon, T. (1981) *Disorders of personality: DSM-III: Axis-II.* New York: Wiley.

Newman, C. F. (1988). Confrontation and collaboration: Congruent components in cognitive therapy. *The Cognitive Behaviorist, 10* (3), 27–30.

Newman, C. F. (1990). Therapy-threatening behaviors on the part of the cognitive-behavior therapist in the treatment of the borderline patient. *The Behavior Therapist, 13*(9), 215–216.

Newman, C. F. (1991). Cognitive therapy and the facilitation of affect: Two case illustrations. *Journal of Cognitive Psychotherapy: An International Quarterly, 5*(4), 305–316.

Newman, C. F. (in press a). Cognitive therapy of anxiety disorders. In B. B. Wolman (Ed.), *Anxiety and related disorders: A handbook.* New York: Wiley.

Newman, C. F. (in press b). The importance of between-sessions homework assignments in the cognitive therapy of depression. *Verhaltenstherapie und Psychosoziale Praxis.*

Newman, C. F., & Beck, A. T. (1990). Cognitive therapy of the affective disorders. In B. B. Wolman & G. Stricker (Eds.), *Handbook of affective disorders: Facts, theories, and treatment approaches* (pp. 343–367). New York: Wiley.

Newman, C. F., & Beck, A. T. (1992). *Cognitive therapy of rapid cycling bipolar affective disorder.* Unpublished therapy manual, Center for Cognitive Therapy, University of Pennsylvania, Philadelphia.

Newman, C. F., & Haaga, D. A. F. (in press). Cognitive skills training. In W. O'Donohue & L. Krasner (Eds.), *Handbook of skills training.* Boston: Allyn and Bacon.

Nezu, A. M., Nezu, C. M., & Perri, M. G. (1989). *Problem-solving therapy for depression: Theory, research, and clinical guidelines.* New York: Wiley.

Nielsen, G. (1983). *Borderline and acting-out adolescents: A developmental approach.* New York: Human Sciences Press.

Perse, T., & Griest, J. H. (1984). Self-destructive behavior in a patient taking trazodone. *American Journal of Psychiatry, 141,* 1646–1647.

Persons, J. B. (1989). *Cognitive therapy in practice: A case formulation approach.* New York: W. W. Norton.

Persons, J. B., Burns, D. D., & Perloff, J. M. (1988). Predictors of dropout and outcome in cognitive therapy for depression in a private practice setting. *Cognitive Therapy and Research, 12,* 557–575.

Piaget, J. (1952). *The origins of intelligence in children.* New York: International University Press.

Pretzer, J. L. (1983). *Borderline personality disorder: Too complex for cognitive therapy?* Paper presented at the 91st annual convention of the American Psychological Association, Anaheim, CA.

Primakoff, L., Epstein, N., & Covi, L. (1989). Homework compliance: An uncontrolled variable in cognitive therapy outcome research. In W. Dryden & P. Trower (Eds.), *Cognitive psychotherapy: Stasis and change* (pp. 175–187). New York: Springer.

Reus, M. D., & Markrow, S. (1984). *Alprazolam in the treatment of borderline personality disorder.* Presented at the Society of Biological Psychiatry, Los Angeles.

Rifkin, A., Quitkin, F., Carillo, C., Blumberg, A. G., & Klein, D. F. (1972). Lithium carbonate in emotionally unstable character disorder. *Archives of General Psychiatry, 27,* 519–523.

Rosen, H. (1985). *Piagetian dimensions of clinical relevance.* New York: Columbia University Press.

Rosen, H. (1989). Piagetian theory and cognitive therapy. In A. Freeman, K. M. Simon, L. E. Beutler, & H. Arkowitz (Eds.), *Comprehensive handbook of cognitive therapy* (pp. 189–212). New York: Plenum Press.

Serban, G., & Siegel, S. (1984). Response of borderline and schizotypal patients to small doses of thiothixene and haloperidol. *American Journal of Psychiatry, 141,* 1455–1458.

Shader, R. I., Jackson, A. H., & Dodes, L. M. (1974). The anti-aggressive effects of lithium in man. *Psychopharmalogia, 40,* 17–24.

Sherby, L. B. (1989). Love and hate in the treatment of borderline patients. *Contemporary Psychoanalysis, 25*(4), 574–591.

Snyder, S., & Pitts, W. M. (1986). Challenges of research with the borderline patient. *Psychopathology, 19*(3), 131–137.

Soloff, P. H. (1987). A pharmacologic approach to the borderline patient. *Psychiatric Annals, 17,* 201–205.

Soloff, P. H., George, A., Nathan, R. S., Schulz, P. M., Cornelius, J. R., Herring, J., & Perel, J. M. (1989). Amitriptyline versus haloperidol in borderlines: Final outcomes and predictors of response. *Journal of Clinical Psychopharmacology, 9*(4), 238–246.

Soloff, P. H., George, A., Nathan, R., Schulz, P. M., Ulrich, R. F., & Perel, J. M. (1986). Progress in pharmacotherapy of borderline disorders. *Archives of General Psychiatry, 43,* 691–697.

Soloff, P. H., George, A., Nathan, R. S., Schulz, P. M., & Perel, J. M. (1986). Paradoxical effects of amitriptyline in borderline patients. *American Journal of Psychiatry, 143,* 1603–1605.

Stone, M. H., Unwin, A., Beacham, B., & Swenson, C. (1988). Incest in female borderlines: Its frequency and impact. *International Journal of Family Psychiatry, 9*(3), 277–293.

Strean, H. S. (1985). *Resolving resistances in psychotherapy.* New York: Wiley.

Swenson, C. (1989). Kernberg and Linehan: Two approaches to the borderline patient. *Journal of Personality Disorders, 3*(1), 26–35.

Waldinger, R. J. (1986). Assessing borderline personality. *Medical Aspects of Human Sexuality, 20,* 76–88.

Waldinger, R. J., & Frank, A. F. (1989). Transference and the vicissitudes of medication use by borderline patients. *Psychiatry, 52*(4), 416–427.

Wright, J. H., & Schrodt, R. (1989). Combined cognitive therapy and pharmacotherapy. In A. Freeman, K. M. Simon, L. E. Beutler, & H. Arkowitz (Eds.), *Comprehensive handbook of cognitive therapy* (pp. 267–282). New York: Plenum Press.

Young, J. E. (1990). *Schema-focused cognitive therapy for personality disorders: A schema-focused approach.* Sarasota, FL: Professional Resource Exchange.

Young-Browns, G., Rosenfeld, H. M., & Horowitz, F. D. (1977). Infant discrimination of facial expressions. *Child Development, 48,* 555–562.

Zanarini, M. C., Gunderson, J. G., Marino, M. F., Schwartz, E. O., & Frankenburg, F. R. (1989). Childhood experiences of borderline patients. *Comprehensive Psychiatry, 30,* 18–25.

Name Index

Subject Index

Psychology Practitioner Guidebooks

Stress Inoculation Training
Donald Meichenbaum
ISBN: 0-205-14418-7

Management of Chronic Headaches: A Psychological Approach
Edward B. Blanchard & Fran Andrasik
ISBN: 0-205-14284-2

Clinical Utilization of Microcomputer Technology
Raymond G. Romanczyk
ISBN: 0-205-14468-3

Marital Therapy: A Behavioral-Communications Approach
Philip H. Bornstein & Marcy T. Bornstein
ISBN: 0-205-14289-3

Psychological Consultation in the Courtroom
Michael T. Nietzel & Ronald C. Dillehay
ISBN: 0-205-14426-8

Group Cognitive Therapy: A Treatment Approach for Depressed Older Adults
Elizabeth B. Yost, Larry E. Beutler, M. Anne Corbishley, & James R. Allender
ISBN: 0-205-14516-7

Dream Analysis in Psychotherapy
Lillie Weiss
ISBN: 0-205-14499-3

Understanding and Treating Attention Deficit Disorder
Edward A. Kirby & Liam K. Grimley
ISBN: 0-205-14391-1

Language and Speech Disorders in Children
Jon Eisenson
ISBN: 0-205-14315-6

Adolescent Anger Control: Cognitive-Behavioral Techniques
Eva L. Feindler & Randolph B. Ecton
ISBN: 0-205-14324-5

Pediatric Psychology: Psychological Interventions and Strategies for Pediatric Problems
Michael C. Roberts
ISBN: 0-205-14465-9

Treating Childhood and Adolescent Obesity
Daniel S. Kirschenbaum, William G. Johnson, & Peter M. Stalonas, Jr.
ISBN: 0-205-14393-8

Eating Disorders: Management of Obesity, Bulimia and Anorexia Nervosa
W. Stewart Agras
ISBN: 0-205-14262-1

Treatment of Depression: An Interpersonal Systems Approach
Ian H. Gotlib & Catherine A. Colby
ISBN: 0-205-14357-1

Psychology as a Profession: Foundations of Practice
Walter B. Pryzwansky & Robert N. Wendt
ISBN: 0-205-14459-4

Multimethod Assessment of Chronic Pain
Paul Karoly & Mark P. Jensen
ISBN: 0-205-14385-7

Hypnotherapy: A Modern Approach
William L. Golden, E. Thomas Dowd, & Fred Friedberg
ISBN: 0-205-14334-2

Behavioral Treatment for Persistent Insomnia
Patricia Lacks
ISBN: 0-205-14399-7

The Physically and Sexually Abused Child: Evaluation and Treatment
C. Eugene Walker, Barbara L. Bonner, & Keith L. Kaufman
ISBN: 0-205-14493-4

Social Skills Training Treatment for Depression
Robert E. Becker, Richard G. Heimberg, & Alan S. Bellack
ISBN: 0-205-14273-7

Teaching Child Management Skills
Richard F. Dangel & Richard A. Polster
ISBN: 0-205-14308-3

Rational-Emotive Therapy with Alcoholics and Substance Abusers
Albert Ellis, John F. McInerney, Raymond DiGiuseppe, &
Raymond J. Yeager
ISBN: 0-205-14320-2

Non-Drug Treatments for Essential Hypertension
Edward B. Blanchard, John E. Martin, & Patricia M. Dubbert
ISBN: 0-205-14286-9

Treating Obsessive-Compulsive Disorder
Samuel M. Turner & Deborah C. Beidel
ISBN: 0-205-14488-8

Self-Esteem Enhancement with Children and Adolescents
Alice W. Pope, Susan M. McHale, & W. Edward Craighead
ISBN: 0-205-14455-1

Preventing Substance Abuse. among Children and Adolescents
Jean E. Rhodes & Leonard A. Jason
ISBN: 0-205-14463-2

Clinical Practice in Adoption
Robin C. Winkler, Dirck W. Brown, Margaret van Keppel, & Amy Blanchard
ISBN: 0-205-14512-4

Behavioral Relaxation Training and Assessment
Roger Poppen
ISBN: 0-205-14457-8

Adult Obesity Therapy
Michael D. LeBow
ISBN: 0-205-14404-7

Social Skills Training for Psychiatric Patients
Robert Paul Liberman, William J. DeRisi, & Kim T. Mueser
ISBN: 0-205-14406-3

Treating Depression in Children and Adolescents
Johnny L. Matson
ISBN: 0-205-14414-4

The Practice of Brief Psychotherapy
Sol L. Garfield
ISBN: 0-205-14329-6

Reducing Delinquency: Intervention in the Community
Arnold P. Goldstein, Barry Glick, Mary Jane Irwin, Claudia Pask-McCartney, &
   Ibrahim Rubama
ISBN: 0-205-14338-5

Rational-Emotive Couples Therapy
Albert Ellis, Joyce L. Sichel, Raymond J. Yeager, Dominic J. DiMattia, & Raymond
   DiGiuseppe
ISBN: 0-205-14317-2 Paper   0-205-14433-0 Cloth

Cognitive-Behavioral Interventions with Young Offenders
Clive R. Hollin
ISBN: 0-205-14368-7 Paper   0-205-14369-5 Cloth

Gestalt Therapy: Practice and Theory, Second Edition
Margaret P. Korb, Jeffrey Gorrell, & Vernon Van De Riet
ISBN: 0-205-14395-4 Paper   0-205-14396-2 Cloth

Assessment of Eating Disorders: Obesity, Anorexia and Bulimia Nervosa
Donald A. Williamson
ISBN: 0-205-14507-8 Paper   0-205-14508-6 Cloth

Body Image Disturbance: Assessment and Treatment
J. Kevin Thompson
ISBN: 0-205-14482-9 Paper   0-205-14483-7 Cloth

Suicide Risk: Assessment and Response Guidelines
William J. Fremouw, Maria de Perczel, & Thomas E. Ellis
ISBN: 0-205-14327-X Paper   0-205-14328-8 Cloth

Treating Conduct and Oppositional Defiant Disorders in Children
Arthur M. Horne & Thomas V. Sayger
ISBN: 0-205-14371-7 Paper   0-205-14372-5 Cloth

Counseling the Bereaved
Richard A. Dershimer
ISBN: 0-205-14310-5 Paper   0-205-14311-3 Cloth

Behavioral Medicine: Concepts and Procedures
Eldon Tunks & Anthony Bellissimo
ISBN: 0-205-14484-5 Paper   0-205-14485-3 Cloth

Drug Therapy for Behavior Disorders: An Introduction
Alan Poling, Kenneth D. Gadow, & James Cleary
ISBN: 0-205-14453-5 Paper   0-205-14454-3 Cloth

The Personality Disorders: A Psychological Approach to Clinical Management
Ira Daniel Turkat
ISBN: 0-205-14486-1 Paper   0-205-14487-X Cloth

Treatment of Rape Victims: Facilitating Psychosocial Adjustment
Karen S. Calhoun & Beverly M. Atkeson
ISBN: 0-205-14296-6 Paper   0-205-14297-4 Cloth

Psychotherapy and Counseling with Minorities: A Cognitive Approach to Individual and Cultural Differences
Manuel Ramirez III
ISBN: 0-205-14461-6

Coping with Ethical Dilemmas in Psychotherapy
Martin Lakin
ISBN: 0-205-14401-2 Paper   0-205-14402-0 Cloth

Anxiety Disorders: A Rational-Emotive Perspective
Ricks Warren & George D. Zgourides
ISBN: 0-205-14497-7 Paper   0-205-14498-5 Cloth

Preventing Relapse in the Addictions: A Biopsychosocial Approach
Emil J. Chiauzzi
ISBN: 0-205-14303-2 Paper   0-205-14304-0 Cloth

Behavioral Family Intervention
Matthew R. Sanders & Mark R. Dadds
ISBN: 0-205-14599-X Paper   0-205-14600-7 Cloth

Anxiety Disorders in Youth: Cognitive-Behavioral Interventions
Philip C. Kendall
ISBN: 0-205-14589-2 Paper   0-205-14590-6 Cloth

Psychological Treatment of Cancer Patients: A Cognitive-Behavioral Approach
William L. Golden, Wayne D. Gersh & David M. Robbins
ISBN: 0-205-14551-5 Paper   0-205-14552-3 Cloth

School Consultation: Practice and Training, Second Edition
Jane Close Conoley & Collie W. Conoley
ISBN: 0-205-14561-2 Paper   0-205-14564-7 Cloth

Posttraumatic Stress Disorder: A Behavioral Approach to Assessment and Treatment
Philip A. Saigh
ISBN: 0-205-14553-1 Paper   0-205-14554-X Cloth

Cognitive Therapy of Borderline Personality Disorder
Mary Anne Layden, Cory F. Newman, Arthur Freeman, & Susan Byers Morse
ISBN: 0-205-14807-7

Social Skills for Mental Health: A Structured Learning Approach
Robert P. Sprafkin, N. Jane Gershaw, & Arnold P. Goldstein
ISBN: 0-205-14841-7

Managed Mental Health Care: A Guide for Practitioners, Employers, and Hospital Administrators
Thomas R. Giles
ISBN: 0-205-14838-7